Developing
Human
Resources

Developing
Human
Resources

Leonard Nadler

Second Edition

Library of Congress Cataloging in Publication Data

Nadler, Leonard.
 Developing human resources.

 Bibliography: p.
 Includes index.
 1. Employees, Training of. 2. Human capital.
I. Title.
HF5549.5.T7N29   1979   658.31'243   79–4147
ISBN 0-89384-044-0

DEVELOPING HUMAN RESOURCES
Second Edition

First Edition 1970

Second Edition 1979
First Printing, March 1979

ISBN 0-89384-044-0

Learning Concepts
2501 N. Lamar
Austin, Texas 78705

Jacket design by Suzanne Pustejovsky

To my wife, Zeace

Foreword

Learning Concepts is proud to welcome Leonard Nadler to its family of distinguished authors in the field of human resource development (HRD). As a publisher, I am excited by the prospect of making *Developing Human Resources* more widely available to experienced professionals and introducing it to the growing number of newcomers to the profession.

Since Dr. Nadler first published this prophetic book in 1970, he has applied and advanced his concepts through graduate classes, public workshops, and consultation to individual organizations throughout the world. The three articles in the Epilogue were chosen to illustrate some of the extensions and applications of his theory. Special thanks to the American Society for Training and Development and to Jack Epstein for their cooperation and permission to use this material.

Ray Bard
Publisher

Preface

To write of human resource development (HRD) is to try to capture the essence of a field which is rapidly emerging—twisting and turning as it does. HRD is concerned with many areas of human endeavor as well as the political and economic scene in the United States as we enter the decade of the 70's.

The past 10 years has seen an increase in our concern with people. As institutions have been changing, people have realigned themselves in new groupings. It is not possible, and not even necessary, to predict what HRD will encompass by the end of the decade. However, the central constructs will still remain. It will still be a group of activities in which the job, the individual and the organization are interacting as each develops and changes.

Some readers of this book may find fault with the use of the term "employee." It is a restrictive term and rightly so; it illustrates only one aspect of relationships between people. However, at the present, it is the relationship which is commonly shared by the largest groups of people.

Another significant relationship is that of the "citizen." This book deals only indirectly with this in terms of the discussion of nonemployee HRD (see Chapter 6). This should not signify a lesser concern with persons in their role as citizens. Rather, this is a more fluid relationship and does not contain the constraints of the employee-employer relationship. HRD on the citizen level is more akin to the broader field of adult education. In that context, it would be necessary to explore more fully some of the individual-institutional-group relationships in order to understand the implications and practices involved in HRD. It is hoped that future writers will attempt this. I have limited most of this book to the area in which I have had more experience—the employee relationship.

This book is the result of my personal confrontation with a significant change in my professional life. In 1965, I joined the faculty of The George Washington University. I had as students some of the leading "training directors" in the greater Washington area. As we explored the field in the comparative isolation of the classroom, many of us became uneasy about the words we were using and how we were using them. It did not take too long to discover that it wasn't the words—it was the concepts.

In the years intervening between then and now, I have constantly challenged my students to forget the words and look at the concepts. The result is the concepts in this book. I have had to retain some of the words, though it had been suggested that I coin some new ones. After much searching through the usual word books, I was forced to return to the use of training, education and development. As the concept is explored, discussed and researched further, newer words may emerge. For now, I am content to use the newer concepts with the older labels. If this communicates, we can then mutually explore terminology which might improve the communication of the ideas.

Although this book must stand by itself, it does reflect my interaction with many people. Most are too numerous to mention here, but some must be identified for the specific assistance they provided during its development and actual writing.

There is a group, my students, who are now numerous and therefore cannot be listed. In each class, they have challenged me on the concepts. As we neared agreement, they were able to bring their own experiences in a vast array of organizations into the classroom. This has provided some of the examples in the book. But more, it reinforced me when I paused to wonder if a clarification was really emerging or was I just adding to the confusion of an emerging field.

A much larger group is found in the American Society for Training and Development. Since joining the organization in 1954, I have been in several chapters in different parts of the United States and the world. In the past few years, I have been able to explore the HRD concept further with ASTD members in a variety of settings.

A significant contribution to my thinking was made by Forrest Belcher (Pan American Petroleum Corp.) who was president of ASTD in 1970. During his term as president-elect in 1969, we had several opportunities to discuss and test HRD. His questions and inputs were most helpful.

Others who have directly influenced the content of this book are Dr. Leonard Silvern (Education and Training Consultants), Les This (Project Associates Inc.), Dr. Shirley McCune (American Association of University Women) and Dr. Dugan Laird (United Air Lines).

I have often read professional books in which the author would single out his wife and acknowledge her contributions. I was not fully aware of how important a wife can be in a professional's life (particularly when he turns to authoring a book) until I started writing this one. I wish all authors the benefits to be derived from an intelligent, thought-provoking and critical wife who forces him to the confrontation with his own words.

Contents

section I
Function and Background

Several years ago, one of the author's students began a doctoral dissertation based on developing a glossary of terms for training. After six months of great activity, he stumbled into the author's office mumbling about the impossibility of the task. He subsequently recovered, selected another topic and successfully completed his doctoral work. Since that time, the author has not had the courage to suggest a glossary of terms as a project for a doctoral candidate.

One of the immediate problems faced in a book about training is to get agreement on the term. As will be seen in Section II, the word is seen as identifying only one of the three areas of activity concerned with releasing human potential. Therefore, in this book, the term "Human Resource Development" will be used to designate those activities which go beyond job training. It is expected that some readers will grope to find the word which, when added to HRD, would produce an acceptable acronym. For this book

1

the term will be left as HRD. It encompasses the three areas of training, education and development. The term HRD and the model suggested in this book are applicable to nonemployees as well as employees.

To clarify related terminology HRD will frequently be used in place of the words "human resource development." No special significance should be sought in the use of the letters. It is an attempt to make it easier for the reader and the author.

In Chapter 1 is a discussion of the definition of HRD, the settings in which it occurs and some of the forces which are influencing its movement.

In Chapter 2, because people are constantly being inundated by examples of "deja vu," is a brief history of HRD.

1

The Function

Defining a term is a hazardous occupation. It provides a temptation for some readers to stand off to the side and waste time in searching for faults and weaknesses. In a field which does not have an agreed upon academic base, each person is inclined to define terms based on the academic discipline in which he has been reared.

As used in this book, HRD means (1) a series of organized activities, (2) conducted within a specified time and (3) designed to produce behavioral change.

The most common activities in HRD are "training and education." Much time has been dissipated in endeavoring to either differentiate between these words or prove that they really mean the same thing. This showed HRD as essentially concerned only with training and education and caused us to miss other activities concerned with development. Or, if the reader tends to combine the words "training" and "development," there is a curious absence of the word "education." The combinations are not endless, but the wrangling is tiresome. Each does have a different meaning.

The differences are often discussed as semantic exercises, and this may have sufficed in the past. Today, the differences symbolize varying concepts of activities which all lie under the banner of HRD. The impatient reader can turn to Section II for this discussion. The present concern is with training, education and development as HRD.

As HRD has increased in significance, involved more individuals and successfully competed in obtaining a larger share of an organization's resources, the need for some distinction, if not definition, has become more acute. The definition of HRD given above requires further discussion.

A Series of Organized Experiences

HRD must be specific and organized in the sense that there are objectives, a process of learning, and provisions for evaluation. In the past, it has been common to refer to some activities as "on-the-job" training (OJT), but skepticism has arisen about the efficacy of this practice. One study indicated that "there are good reasons to believe that the informal methods that were good enough to learn yesterday's jobs will be inadequate for the jobs of tomorrow"(1).

Chance learning can take place, but is this the most effective means of developing a work force? Such a practice may have sufficed in the past, but today in the textile industry, for example, "greater emphasis is being placed on formal training rather than learning on the job"(2).

An organized experience is not meant to suggest a lock-step approach where each individual must learn the same way or at the same pace. Provision for individualized learning is gaining increasing acceptance. Group learning is being fostered where the outcomes are greater awareness and the possibility of new but individualized behaviors. Yet, both individual and group learning can be accomplished through organized means. This means some series of related activities which build, conduct, and evaluate the experience.

Various words are used, and they signify differing concepts of learning. Among the more significant ones are system, process, critical event and technology. The commonality is that they all rely on organizing the learning experience.

Conducted Within a Specified Time

When an adult is engaged in an HRD program, there is the need for specific time blocks. These should be continuous through the life of the individual with his organization, but there must be points at which the individual and the organization can stop to review the organized learning activities and assess their value to the organization and the individual.

Children have semesters, school years and grade levels. For the adult, learning takes place in different time blocks and is a process which cannot be relegated to grade levels, specifically tied to promotions or continually peppered with commencement exercises.

Yet, the adult needs reinforcement and recognition. He needs it not as a child but as an adult in our society which is an achievement-oriented society. Realistic time blocks afford the opportunity for providing recognition and reinforcing the learning as well as reemphasizing the ability of the adult to learn. Reasonably short time blocks also allow for a modular approach. It permits the adult learner to branch off into other fields and areas which are needed and appropriate, without waiting for the end of a long and possibly irrelevant sequence.

Designed to Result in Behavioral Change

The goal of HRD is change. There is no justification for the expenditure of energy and resources if there is no intent of producing change. The HRD director who is not prepared to deal with change is best advised to leave the field and find some other area of endeavor.

Behavioral change is not without its problems. Research on bringing about change is increasing, and techniques are being refined as more is learned about this complicated process. Because of great success, the queston of the right to control individuals and produce specified behavioral changes is now being raised. Ludwig von Bertalanffy challenges us to use our knowledge and skills to produce men rather than robots (3).

Criticism has been leveled against some forms of HRD as merely another experience in brainwashing. Name-calling is never helpful and obscures the more basic point of ethical obligations in using known skills in producing behavioral change.

Behavioral change in individuals is a constant and on-going process. It has been a part of life and will continue to be as long as there are feeling and reacting human beings. When using HRD, there needs to be agreement beforehand on the kinds of behavioral change being sought by both the trainee and the change agent.

Various elements of the newer technologies are designed specifically to involve the learner in his own learning. There are simulations and games to provide the learner with a confrontation and the opportunity to modify his behavior accordingly. The laboratory method is used extensively for this objective, with one difference being that the data for change comes from the behavior of the learner in the laboratory situation. The need for controls when dealing with the behavior of real live people, as contrasted with laboratory animals, is of prime concern to those responsible for HRD activities. The National Training Laboratories-Institute of Applied Behavioral Science (NTL-IABS) states in its program standards that ". . .programs should be directed to the specific purposes and needs of the client group as they are agreed upon by consultant and client. They should be designed to include only those processes and techniques appropriate to the agreed-upon purposes and needs" (4).

The Setting

Business, industry and government are the major organizational settings discussed in this book. HRD is being conducted in many other settings, but by far the greatest area of activity is within those three. The organizational setting influences the parameters for HRD, and although each organization has its differences, there are enough commonalities to include them all within this book.

Nobody knows how much money is being spent on HRD in the United States today, as conducted by business, industry and government. John Dunlop of Harvard commented, "Many corporations are already running major educational operations. G.E. spends $40,000,000 annually on educational support and training programs. In any given year, one out of every eight G.E. employees attends a training program of some kind" (5).

The cost of HRD in the federal government is an equally elusive figure. A congressional committee found that "the cost of training federal employees is estimated to have reached about $180 million per year at the end of the fiscal year 1966" (6). This estimate does not include HRD in the military but is confined to the HRD of civilian federal government employees. Obviously, the military budget for HRD is staggering, for when the military is not engaged in combat operations, its major activity is HRD.

HRD is an identifiable operation in many of our larger organizations but disappears quite rapidly as the size of the organization diminishes. Presumably, this is not because our smaller organizations do not have the need—they do not have the resources. If an organization is to conduct a meaningful HRD program, it must allocate resources to this activity. In smaller companies, the resources are usually inadequate for most purposes, and HRD in any form becomes one of the activities which are beyond their scope. One of the challenges presented today is how to assist smaller organizations in developing their human resources.

In a large multi-plant operation, HRD can be located almost anyplace in the organization. The diversity of placements is beyond belief and beyond our research capability to identify. Traditionally, HRD has been considered part of the personnel function. Within the past 10 years, there has been a slow but steady movement away from this concept and placement. It will probably accelerate as the activities which are HRD are more clearly specified, and it becomes apparent that they are not merely an extension of the personnel function.

Larger organizations will frequently have central HRD departments as well as other kinds of HRD units located within individual plants or regions. Likewise, here is found a lack of specific data which can help in reaching generalizations.

Outside of business, industry and government, there is a growing involvement in HRD. The United States is unusual in the number of volunteer organizations which are part of national life. They are nonprofit but have grown to the point where it is difficult to determine how they differ from some of our major business organizations. There are many similarities in organizational structures and problems, financial statements and governance. The manpower needs and policies are often quite similar to those of an organization of comparable size in the private sector. There will be much in this book which will apply to HRD in the setting of the volunteer agency.

Other organizations, such as labor unions, community action agencies and even professional membership organizations have the need for HRD activities. These will be referred to from time to time in this book.

A significant agency which will not be discussed is the public school system. It certainly is not because the public school system lacks the need for HRD for its employees. The model of HRD is likewise meaningful for the students. But, the field of public education provides a much different history and setting than that which will be explored in this book. Yet, it is hoped that instructors in teacher education institutions and those responsible for in-service training in the school systems will take the time to read this book and begin to build the needed HRD systems.

Need for the HRD Function

HRD is here to stay! The name may change, and currently being heard is "manpower policy," "manpower planning" and "effective utilization of manpower." In discussing manpower policy, the *Manpower Report of the President* said that such a "policy must have as its ultimate aim enabling every American to realize and utilize his full potential. This implies a concern not only for occupational training but also for education at all levels" (7). Henry David, in writing the final report for the National Manpower Council, stressed the need for investing in people and the contribution which can be made to equal opportunity (8). Both elements are important to a society which prides itself on its role in the area of world affairs. Equally important is the fulfillment of the promise inherent in a democratic society—the possibility for a good life for all. This is not preaching utopia but the reality of which a democratic society is capable.

Moving more toward the practical, there are many specific benefits which accrue to an organization which invests in its human resources. David King (9) sees systematic training (i.e., HRD) as providing assistance in areas such as:

1. shortage of labor,
2. high labor turnover,
3. expanding production,
4. diversification of products,
5. automation,
6. redundancy (lay-offs),
7. improvement of quality,
8. reduction of scrap,
9. raising the calibre of staff and
10. establishing new factories.

Some of these dimensions can be explored from the practical as well as the philosophical by looking at HRD in relation to the individual, the organization, production and society.

The Individual

Each person has a need to grow. If the opportunity is not presented within the work setting, the individual will endeavor to meet his growth needs off the job. The work situation must not only encourage and permit growth but must make specific provisions for providing individuals with opportunities to realize their potential. In Douglas McGregor's terms, the individual can grow on the job if the organization tends toward what he has called "Theory Y" (10).

Since the turn of the century, emphasis on pre-job training has been centered in our public and private school systems. Once a person entered the work force, society perceived the individual as having completed his role as a student. Today, it is realized that even an university education is inadequate and that additional HRD opportunities must be provided by employers if each person is to be permitted to grow and realize his potential contribution to himself and society.

Upward mobility in the work force is desirable and necessary, but it is impossible to correlate movement with HRD. The best that can be said at this time is that company-sponsored HRD will probably result in upward mobility, at least in the employing organization. Research is insufficient to allow any conclusions as to whether the upward mobility is the result of HRD or whether only those selected for upward mobility are provided with HRD opportunities.

The Organization

In any viable organization, internal relationships are constantly changing. In recent years, there has been movement toward planned change of organizations and organizational relationships through activities centered about the descriptive title of "organization development."

In a less planned manner, the normal factors of attrition, replacement of managers, establishment of new facilities, transfers and the other usual changes which impact on an organization require a constant program of HRD. The spate of mergers and the development of conglomerates has heightened the need for HRD to meet the needs of changing organizations.

Although the anticipated actions of the government may slow down or even halt mergers and acquisitions, it will not reduce the number of new relationships constantly developing. Warren Bennis and Philip Slater have focused on temporary societies and the need to improve our skills in dealing with new and temporary relationships (11).

Production

Processes of production have undergone massive changes in the last decade. Some of the current and accepted phrases are: engineer's degree has a halflife of 10 years; there are more scientists alive today than have existed in the entire history of mankind; a youngster entering the work force today can expect to have seven major job changes; many of the foods you eat were unknown in their present form a decade ago; and, most of the clothing you are wearing is made of recently discovered manmade fibers.

The impact of technology upon production is too apparent to require further elucidation. Changes in technology create a requisite need for behavioral changes in individuals—that is, HRD. Accompanying the rapid changes in production are the equally apparent revolutions in consumer tastes and the variety of services demanded by an affluent society. The processes of production have constantly changed, as well as the materials of production and the forms of the final products.

The reality of rapid technological change is seen in the increased need for HRD to meet the demands of today while planning for the jobs of tomorrow. There must exist the position of "planning the education and training required to equip workers for tomorrow's jobs and the facilities and programs that will accomplish these objectives most effectively" (12).

Society

There may have been a time when those concerned with HRD could function in ignorance of societal changes. The Economic Opportunity Act of 1964 provided a turning point in the recognition that jobs were the key element in our society. The act emphasized the need for economic opportunity, and the pressure has increased to relate the economic system to the social system.

HRD directors are now finding themselves in areas of activity which some of them hardly knew existed in earlier years. HRD directors are becoming deeply involved in social change, and the changes in society are having an impact upon the daily work life of the HRD staff. Today, companies are offering programs in personal budgeting, retirement planning and other topics which were formerly considered outside the realm of the usual HRD activities. The movement in that direction is gaining momentum, and the scope of the HRD activity is increasing to include more than just job-related or even economic-producing programs. The newer concepts of work and leisure are also playing their part in redesigning the job of the HRD specialist.

The Changing Work Force

If there exists interest in developing human resources, it is incumbent upon us to know the extent of that resource and how it is changing. Some of this data is difficult to obtain, and more of it is not readily understandable. More research is required, and the U.S. Department of Labor has sponsored "The Manpower Research Institutional Grant Program" since 1966.

Among its purposes is "to create centers for long-range research and training of specialists in the manpower field. . ." (13).

While waiting for the development of research and the sharing with those who need it, a picture of the changing labor force from readily available sources can still be obtained.

Age

It is surprising that the age change in the labor force should come as a shock. When those who were born 18 years ago are considered, it is not difficult to imagine that 18 years later they will have entered college, the army or the labor force. The statisticians can even help determine the numbers who will go into each pursuit. More difficult to identify are those who will be labor force dropouts and who may never even make themselves available for jobs.

By now, overcoming amazement at seeing so many young persons in the labor force should have begun. The trend can be seen in Table 1.1. The reality of it is all around. Listening to the radio, observing clothing styles, and merely being sensitive to

Table 1.1

**Labor Force Participation
of 16-34 Age Group**

Year	% Labor Force
1960	38
1965	40
1970	42
1975	45
1980	47

Source: *Manpower Report of the President.* Washington: Government Printing Office, 1970, p. 298.

the usual aspects of daily life confronts all with the reality of the numerical preponderance of youth.

As the decade of the 70's begins, the percentage of workers under 34 in the work force is 42%. This is by no means all the young people but only those actually in the work force. It is predicted that by the end of the decade the figure will have risen to 47%. It is a safe prediction that all of those will already have been born! Of course, there are variables such as wars and famine. Also, more young people may be found who prefer to remain in school rather than join the work force at an early age. However, at most, this would postpone the impact beyond 1980 but for only a few short years.

One impact of the new young members of the labor force is their ability to cope with rapidity of change. Coping with change has always been a problem and many HRD programs contain experiences to enable employees to cope with change. The startling difference is the rapidity and magnitude of change.

If any doubts still persist, you (the reader) can draw upon your own life experience to prove the point. First, make a list of the changes in the past decade. This can start at any year in which you are reading this book. Which of these changes could have been predicted 10 years earlier? Some will be fairly obvious, but it is more likely that the list will contain changes which were beyond the ken of most of us.

Now, would you care to predict the changes in the next decade? Do not use the year 2000. This has been done with a degree of embarrassment as the rapidity of change has reinforced the statement that tomorrow is already here! Therefore, just take the next 10 years and make some predictions on change. You might even write them on the inside cover of this book. Hopefully, as you continue to take it from your shelf, you will continue to look at the list. You may be quite amazed.

For the more mature (i.e., older) readers, the rapidity and magnitude of change can be expected to be more of a shock than for the younger readers. The latter have grown up and lived through this rapidity of change, and to them it is not only acceptable but natural. They perceive movement and development in much more rapid patterns than the bulk of the labor force at this time. If effective use is to be made of the newer members as they enter the labor force, it becomes necessary to direct more attention to programs for those already in the labor force. They must be exposed to more programs which raises their tolerance for change at a rapid pace.

Minority Groups

A more startling change in the labor force has been the inclusion of increasing numbers of minority group members. Still not reached is the point where there is full equality of opportunity, but certainly a long way has been traveled from the days when a Negro might only be employed as a sweeper or a woman as a telephone operator. More and more, members of the various minority groups have entered the work force in greater numbers and at higher levels. This is as it should be in a democratic society where being a member of a minority group (e.g., Negro, women, Spanish-speaking, Indian) should be no bar to any position within the organization.

The challenge being faced is that some of the minority groups have been kept out of the picture for so long that it is woefully unfair to now say to them, "You may now enter but stick to the traditional patterns of movement." This would mean that for the next generation or two they could not hope to achieve their aspirations as most of the population has been allowed to do. They cannot be told that they must take their time and wait—for time has run out. They would all be dead before they could possibly have reached any stage of equality, and they know it. Recognizing this, compensatory education programs have been introduced starting from just after infancy with programs like Headstart. This has been followed by a myriad of other programs which come and go as the appropriate activities to provide equal opportunity in the work force are being sought.

More will be said about the problem of minority group employees throughout the pages of this book. Today, this is where a good deal of the action is—and that is where the HRD activity must be. A key word in today's vocabulary is "relevant," and this must be one of the watchwords of HRD.

Skills

What of the skills being brought into the work force? They are probably inadequate, and there is little hope that they can be made more relevant. As Congressman Lloyd Meeds (Washington) noted to his colleagues, "By a unanimous vote the House and Senate passed the far-reaching Vocational Education Amendments of 1968. This bill authorized $812 million for the fiscal year beginning July 1, 1969" (14). However, as Congressman Meeds goes on to comment, the administration during the first session of the 91st Congress (1969) only requested $279.2 million. This is woefully inadequate to bring into being the essentials of a revitalized vocational education program for American youth. It will do little to give them the skills they need for the labor market of the 70's.

It is likely that skill training may have to begin at an even earlier age than is currently the practice. Walter S. Neff, in discussing the components of the work personality, has gathered some striking evidence of the need for devoting more attention to how children develop their sense of industry and the fundamentals of technology (15).

Literature Citations

1. *Formal Occupational Training of Adult Workers.* Manpower/Automation Research Monograph, no. 2 (Washington: Government Printing Office, 1964), p. 22.
2. Rose Zeisel, "Technology Transforms Textiles," *Occupational Outlook Quarterly,* December 1968, p. 19.

3. Ludwig von Bertalanffy, *Robots, Men and Minds* (New York: George Braziller, 1967).

4. *Standards for the Use of the Laboratory Method* (Washington: National Training Laboratories-Institute of Applied Behavioral Science, 1969), p. 6.

5. Eli Goldston, "New Prospects for American Business," *Daedalus*, Winter 1969, p. 101.

6. *Report Covering the Effectiveness of Implementation of the Government Employees Training Act*, 90th Congress, House Report No. 329 (Washington: Government Printing Office, 1967), p. 2.

7. *Manpower Report of the President* (Washington: Government Printing Office, 1969), p. 4.

8. Henry David, *Manpower Policies for a Democratic Society* (New York: Columbia University Press, 1965).

9. David King, *Training Within the Organization* (New York: Barnes and Noble, 1968), p. 62-66.

10. Douglas McGregor, *The Human Side of Enterprise* (New York: McGraw-Hill, 1960).

11. Warren Bennis and Philip E. Slater, *The Temporary Society* (New York: Harper and Row, 1968).

12. *Manpower Report of the President,* op. cit., p. 62.

13. *The Manpower Research Institutional Grant Program,* Manpower Administration, Department of Labor (Washington: Government Printing Office, 1969), p. 2.

14. *Congressional Record.* November 26, 1969, p. H11446.

15. Walter S. Neff, *Work and Human Behavior* (New York: Atherton Press, 1968), p. 150-164.

2

Historical Background

A satisfactory history of HRD in the United States is yet to be written. Any author or researcher attempting this task must first confront the continual problem of definitions of terms. If using the broader term of HRD is continued rather than the limited term of training, it is easy to grasp part of the picture through the history of adult education in the United States written by Malcolm Knowles (1). It is hoped that similar histories, still to be written, will help in realizing the broad scope of HRD activities so as not to become trapped by the tunnel vision dictated by the term "training." By researching and uncovering the exciting activities of HRD since the beginning of our country, the trap identified by the philosopher Santayana—who noted that he who does not learn history is condemned to repeat it—may be avoided. Harold Taylor has gone further and pointed out that those who are not familiar with their own history become disadvantaged (2). In today's world the HRD director may not consider himself in that category.

18

The absence of a meaningful history is not the result of any willful disregard. It is difficult to write a history in the absence of a clearly defined field, and HRD is still emerging. It can be generalized that no society can endure for any period of time, in any form, without some human resource development activities. They may be unsophisticated, but they must exist if the normal activities of survival are to be effective.

Historically, however, until certain steps are taken, it is not possible to identify a field. It is pointed out that "adult education" has existed for a long time, but until the work of the pioneers of the early 1920's, there was no definable field. For HRD, the pressures of the early years of World War II might be considered the era of the emergence of the field. Even then, the field was seen as "training," and it was not until 20 years later that it was broadened to "training" and "development." It is only toward the end of the 60's that some recognition of a broader concept of HRD was seen.

Looking backwards, then, a field of HRD cannot easily be found, but activities can be identified which did contribute to the development of human resources in the United States.

The Early Days

A history of the United States is usually begun with the Pilgrims or the landings at Jamestown. Yet, this is an injustice and even blind ignorance if the people who thrived here before that time are ignored.

Too little is known of that wide group of early settlers now called the American Indian. However, there is specific and indisputable evidence that a permanent settlement has existed for over 10,000 years in what is now the Ocmulgee National Monument just outside of Macon, Georgia. Aside from the types of training and education which are needed by any pre-industrial society, there is evidence that "the continued existence of the group required the education of its younger members in the skills and habits and community organization of their elders"

(3). More than 2,000 years ago they became adept at pottery making. To continue this required specific provision for training.

Of course, there is more evidence of various Indian groups living in the Southwest. The famed cliff dwellings of that area could not have been built by people without some skills in the use of handtools and even some basic knowledge of what today is called engineering and architecture (4).

There is insufficient data about the Mexican-American communities which thrived more than 100 years before the landings on the East Coast. The Spaniards, however, settled El Paso in 1598 and Sante Fe in 1609. The fortresses which were built there and the commerce which helped the cities prosper could not have been reality without some forms of training and education. It is hoped that our renewed interest in some of our minority groups will encourage the research to uncover this part of our heritage (5).

During the colonial period ending with the culmination of the American Revolution, HRD can be characterized as being of the on-the-job training (OJT) variety. Although there was the practice of apprenticeship, it frequently did not involve a systematic plan. Indentured servants were also common. The objective of the indenture sometimes was the training of the servant to assume a craftsman's role upon the completion of his term. The evidence is lacking to support these practices as contributing in any significant manner to the development of skilled persons.

HRD, in any semblance of today's use of the term, probably existed in only rare cases. The more general pattern was that of the son watching the father, the servant observing the master and the constant admonition of "do-as-I-do." There must have been some times and places where training was accomplished in a more orderly and logical fashion. So far, they have been difficult to identify. This should not lead us into assuming the absence of HRD, only the absence of the documents which might describe the activity to our satisfaction.

The Emerging Nation

As the United States entered the 19th century, there were the beginnings of the industrial revolution, the development of complicated machinery and the increasing need for some kind of more formal HRD activity. The cotton gin, for example, required some training to operate, but, once again, the data is lacking.

The early 1800's saw the development of schools concerned with mechanical arts. In today's terms, they would be called vocational or technical schools. They were not conducted by an employing organization but were extensions of the then existent school system.

Among the more notable of these institutions were Mechanics' Apprentices Library of Boston (1820); New York Mercantile Library (1820); Franklin Institute, Philadelphia (1824); Lowell Institute, Boston (1836) and Cooper Union, New York (1859).

Although identifying in-house HRD was still difficult, the necessity for some pre-job skill training had become more important. The mercantile side of the economy was expanding, but one did not "need any lengthy training or education to set up shop as a wholesaler" (6).

The Negro as a slave was an essential part of the economy of the South. Too often he is thought of only as an unskilled farmhand or a semiskilled house servant. However, the Negro was also trained as an artisan, and the old mansions of the South bore eloquent testimony to his skills (7). Add to this the fine iron work which is still to be seen in New Orleans and what happens to the picture of the dull, plodding slave who was unable to learn? Obviously, the stereotype does not fit the facts. A rewrite of American history is in progress. It is not to distort what has happened but to correct the numerous omissions of the contribution of the Negro to all areas of American life (8).

Developing Industrially

Beginning about 1860, a new feeling concerning training and vocational education can be sensed. The need for a school system designed to develop skilled mechanics was one of the factors which influenced the passage of the Morrill Land Grant Act of 1862. Agriculture had become so complicated that it could no longer be handed down from father to son. A more organized approach for this kind of HRD had become necessary. The complicated farm machinery which had been developed required trained mechanics. The agricultural and mechanical colleges founded by the Morrill Act placed higher education in the position of providing trained manpower for the growing industrial economy. These institutions also became the basis for the widespread system of higher education which is unique to the United States.

Increasing complexity of industrial production also encouraged the development of factory schools designed to produce a work force trained for a particular employer. Cloyd Steinmetz credits Hoe and Company in New York City in 1872 with having established one of the earliest factory schools (9). Similar in-plant HRD facilities for new workers began to emerge in 1888 when the Westinghouse Company established a factory school, and by 1898, Westinghouse was providing HRD for its engineers.

Factory schools were mainly concerned with preparing new workers to enter the work force. Once in the work force, apparently little was done in terms of upgrading or improving skills. One can conjecture that this may have been a result of the craft concept which was prevalent at the time. A wage-earning worker with any skill was considered a craftsman who knew his trade and did not need any additional training. To imply that training was necessary was to cast doubt on his craftsmanship.

The federal government was also involved in training its employees, though this was done with very little fanfare, and the record has almost been lost to us. In view of the current trend toward training centers, it is interesting to note that "the oldest established agency training center for Federal employees is the National Bureau of Standards Graduate School which began operations in 1908" (10).

Immigration

Toward the end of the 19th century and the beginning of the 20th century, the United States experienced an unprecedented wave of immigration. Some of the immigrants brought with them the skills they had learned in the old country, but most brought with them nothing more than a desire for a better way of life. A certain folklore has built up around them as being the least desirable. At the base of the Statue of Liberty is the oft-quoted poem by Emma Lazarus which speaks of "the wretched refuse of your teeming shore." In many minds is the picture of the dregs of humanity spilling in through Ellis Island and bringing little with them (11).

Nothing could be further from the reality of the history of that period. Oscar Handlin has given a much better picture of the immigrant in his Pulitzer Prize winning book, *The Uprooted.* He points out that it took courage and a certain amount of entrepreneurship to make the break from the old country, travel to a seaport, endure the hardship of the ocean voyage and settle in a new land where the frontier had already begun to close (12). In essence, a highly achievement-oriented work force was obtained.

The result was an increase in evening public high schools offering Americanization and English classes. During the day, training was still a matter of being taught by a fellow countryman who may have only preceded the new immigrant by a year. The "old-timer" of one year was now the training instructor.

Various pre-job training possibilities developed in response to the need. The YMCA included job training as one of the essential elements of its adult education program. Other voluntary agencies likewise sponsored vocational training. All this accrued to the benefit of the employers who now sought a trained worker rather than doing their own training. However, this was essentially limited to those organizations relying heavily on immigrant labor.

Many of the emerging companies needed a different kind of labor. They sought the college-trained engineer but frequently found that he was more educated than trained. After completion of his degree, the engineer still could not fill the job for which he had been preparing. To bridge this gap, the University of Cincinnati in 1906 introduced a plan for cooperative education (13). It is reputed to be the first organized plan whereby practical instruction in a real work situation and education in the university were mixed in an organized fashion.

There is evidence that company training schools were flourishing, for in 1913 the National Association of Corporation Schools was organized. Associations based on a particular business or industry began to emerge. Among their basic programs was the provision of HRD activities for the employees of the association's members. One of the most long-lived is the American Institute of Banking which began its programs in 1901 and still remains active today (14).

The famed General Motors Institute got its start in 1919 when Albert Sorey was offered the directorship of the School of Automotive Trades in Flint, Michigan (15). This was established to provide part time training programs for employees in Flint's growing complex of automobile plants. In 1926, it was incorporated as a nonprofit institution under the laws of the state of Michigan, and the name was changed to the General Motors Institute.

Up to 1920, the focus was still primarily on pre-job training provided by private and public schools. The passage of the Smith-Hughes Act in 1917 firmly established vocational education in the public school system. In the nonpublic area, corre- spondence schools had emerged toward the late 1890's and now began to flourish in great numbers. About 1910, private busi- ness schools became a major factor in training clerical help.

Prosperity and Depression

The period from 1920-40 features a high level of prosperity at the start, the deepest depression at the midpoint, and a slow economic comeback at the close. The extremes mitigated against organizations becoming involved in HRD. During the high level of prosperity, employers seemed little concerned about the need for providing HRD for their employees. By increasing wages and allowing for lower standards, it was pos- sible for even marginal employers to muddle through.

Interest in workers as people can be found in a variety of activities of that period. As an outgrowth of a series of earlier organizations, the American Management Association was estab- lished in 1923. The Hawthorne Studies of that period provided an impact still felt today (16).

In the period of the depression, employers had a large work force from which to draw. It was logical for the employer to seek skilled workers among the unemployed rather than to en- gage in the comparatively new activity of HRD. Governmental concern was reflected in the various public works projects which frequently had job training components. The Civilian Conservation Corps and the National Youth Administration in- volved the job training of students and young workers. The Bureau of Apprenticeship and Training was established in 1934, and although it has gone through many reorganizations and name changes, it still is a part of the HRD scene today.

As the nation emerged from the depression in the late 1930's, there were indications that HRD had begun to become a factor. Various groups began to be organized by persons in- volved in HRD and having the need to communicate with others who were likewise engaged in this new undertaking. One of the oldest such organizations is the Training Officers Conference in Washington, D. C., which was started in 1938 by government training (HRD) officers and which celebrated its 30th birthday in 1968.

The question of nomenclature once again arises. At the outset, the designation as Training Officer by the federal government was fairly general, and therefore designating the organization as the Training Officers Conference was logical. Today, most of the membership are more likely to hold the governmental title of Employee Development Officers or Employee Development Specialists. Still, the name of Training Officers Conference has remained.

The War Years

HRD emerged as a significant area of human endeavor during World War II. The sudden and immediate need to convert large numbers of our nonworking population into workers and military men heightened the role of training. Suddenly, almost everybody was either training or being trained. Sometimes the difference between being a trainee or a trainer was only a weekend—receiving a certificate of completion of the course on Friday and becoming an instructor the following Monday.

Teachers were recruited from high schools and colleges to become trainers in the armed forces and the industrial establishment. Research became a part of HRD as better ways were sought to produce the trained personnel so desperately needed. HRD moved right into the very heart of the organization. Employers could no longer rely on receiving a skilled worker or scouting the labor market until they found what they wanted. Our industrial leadership discovered that vast numbers of the population were capable of being trained and made productive in relatively short periods of time. HRD did not have to prove itself—each new worker who joined the production line was living proof of the value of an in-company training program. The Job Instruction Training (JIT) developed by "Skipper"

Allen during World War I now became the gospel whereby supervisors assumed the responsibility for training their new employees.

From this time on, HRD was established under the label of training. In subsequent periods of economic difficulty, HRD was one of the first activities to suffer, creating the paradox—in times of economic distress when there is a greater need for increased and improved performance, budgets for HRD have been reduced.

During the war period, more employees were assigned HRD responsibilities, and in 1942 several of them formed an organization which today is known as the American Society for Training and Development (ASTD) (17). From this period on, HRD emerged as a discernible aspect of organizational behavior, though still labeled as training.

The Post-War Period

With demobilization, the returning serviceman was urged to increase his knowledge and employability through the Servicemen's Readjustment Act, more commonly called the "G. I. Bill." Private schools emerged throughout the country and ultimately required closer surveillance by the Veterans Administration to weed out the less qualified and marginal facilities. Today, the G. I. Bill is still a factor, and some companies wisely advise their employees to use their G. I. benefits before seeking the benefits of company tuition refund plans.

In early 1950, the military was still concerned with HRD, and a contract was awarded to the University of Pennsylvania to study the use of films in training. From this work evolved the loop-film and the concept of the single purpose, limited-time film. Other military contracts continued to be awarded for HRD and some significant contributions resulted from the research. In the late 1960's these contracts were severely reduced as a result of the conflicts on the campus. In one case, that of the Human Resources Research Office (HumRRO) associated with The George Washington University, they produced vast amounts of research from their inception in 1951 until the termination of their relationship in 1969. The unclassified work of the project is reflected in a 287-page bibliography of their own publications (18).

One of the most significant developments of the period was the concept of the laboratory method (19). The background and theory of this approach can be read, but it must be experienced to be understood. The laboratory method has grown considerably since those early days and by the beginning of the 1970's has become a widely-used, though still highly controversial, method of bringing about behavioral change.

Human Relations for All

The early 1950's was a period of intensive supervisory training. The Hawthorne Studies of 30 years earlier were rediscovered, and the supervisor was seen as the key element in the work relationship. Although some HRD specialists still insisted on identifying needs, the general practice was that every supervisor needed human relations training. The demand increased and supervisory training even became a popular offering in public school evening programs.

Literature on HRD began to accumulate. The field was established, and though it had periods of feast and famine which paralleled the economy, very seldom was it completely abolished once it had become part of an organizational structure.

Management and executive development programs flourished. "Off-the-ranch" and "cultural island" experiences away from the work site became almost mandatory at the higher levels. Human relations became an integral part of HRD programs for managers. The November/December 1957 issue of the *Journal of the American Society of Training Directors* was entirely devoted to management development, but one writer questioned if there was not too much human relations in management training (20).

Meanwhile, B. F. Skinner was proceeding with his work (21), and some HRD specialists were actually using programmed instruction (22). By the middle of the decade, the teaching machine began to emerge though it was destined to be less of a contribution than its proponents claimed. It would be another 10 years, into the middle of the 60's, before anything would be heard of presentation devices as differentiated from programmed instruction. The term "educational technology" was still in the future though the basis for it had already been established.

On the government side, HRD for all government workers was legitimized through the Government Employees Training Act of 1958. Federal government HRD activities had been a reality much before this, as witness the Training Officers Conference (1938) and the Training Center of the Bureau of Standards (1908). Now, however, there was a law which not only permitted but encouraged HRD for all government employees.

Research in HRD has always lagged far behind the need for it. In the middle 50's occurred one of the most significant studies which has yet been produced in the training field. This study of a supervisory training program at the International Harvester Company by Edwin F. Harris and Edwin A. Fleishman is still cited and often replicated (23).

The Hectic 60's

The decade of the 60's brought vast changes in society. HRD, as an integral part of our society, has not been immune to the forces for change.

The work force has experienced a variety of significant changes. As can be seen in Table 2.1, the size of the work force in the age bracket below 34 increased from 38% of the work force in 1960 to 42% by 1970. The 35-44 age group, the cohort from which middle managers are usually drawn, dropped from 23% of the labor force to 19%. That this trend can be expected to continue is readily seen in the projections to the end of the next decade.

The educational level of our work force is rising very rapidly, and Table 2.2 indicates that at the beginning of the decade over 50% of the work force lacked a high school education, whereas by the end of the decade the figure has declined to one-third. The increased emphasis on a high school education for all can be expected to reduce that figure even further.

Table 2.1

Labor Force Participation by Age

(as percent of total labor force)

Age	1960	1965	1970	1975	1980
16-24	17	20	22	23	22
25-34	21	20	20	23	25
35-44	23	22	19	18	19
45-54	21	21	21	19	17
55-64	13	13	14	14	14
65 and over	5	4	4	4	3

Source: *Manpower Report of the President.* Washington: Government Printing Office, 1969. p. 229.

Table 2.2

Years of School Completed

(by persons 25 years and over in civilian labor force)

	1957-59	1964-66	1975
Less than 4 years high school	53.7	45.1	34.0
4 years high school or more	46.3	54.9	66.0
	100.0	100.0	100.0

Source: *Manpower Report of the President.* Washington: Government Printing Office, 1969. p. 65, Table 10.

The improved position of minority groups in the work force is becoming a matter of history. The largest single ethnic minority, the Negroes, have benefited in that "total Negro employment rose by 1.3 million between 1961 and 1968, or by about 20%; white employment increased by 15 percent" (24). Without becoming involved at this time in whether the percentage is great enough, it can be said that the work force contained more minority group members by the end of the decade than it did at the beginning.

Changes in technology have always existed. This decade has probably seen the most rapid changes ever experienced in the history of man. Explorations into outer space became a reality, and men have landed on the moon. There was no longer a question of training for jobs which do not yet exist. The bulk of the training for the astronauts showed that it was possible to prepare man for jobs which nobody had ever done before. Training was now not a reproducer of experience—it was a generator of experience.

A new social responsibility arose on the part of the people as evidenced by government programs. Beginning with the Area Redevelopment Act of 1961, the Manpower Development and Training Act of 1962 and the Economic Opportunity Act of 1964, a flood of legislation has emerged affecting training (25).

More concern was expressed over skill training than had been the case in prior years. This was reflected in the program for the 26th Annual Conference of the American Society for Training and Development which included more sessions in skill, manual and clerical training in its programs than had been the case in prior years. During the 25th Annual Conference, John Wellens of England commented on the lack of attention to operator training (26). He commented on the preoccupation with management training which he had found during the trip and within the conference.

Concern with skill training surfaced in the programs of the National Alliance of Businessmen and efforts of private companies involved in the "hard-core" experiences. A study conducted during the summer of 1969 indicated that skill training was one of the three basic elements needed in a program for new entries into the work force (27).

The federal government took another look at its own HRD programs after 10 years of the Government Employees Training Act and found little to criticize (28). This was not the picture as seen by the Henderson Committee of Congress which was highly critical of the HRD activities being provided by the government (29).

The possibilities of new roles for the government was explored by a Task Force on Occupational Training in Industry. This group suggested that there were several alternatives including:

1. Financial incentives including credits against federal income tax, levy-grant systems, direct payments, improved federal government contract procedures, vesting financial credits for training in individual workers;
2. Government Procurement Contracts;
3. Cooperative work-study programs;
4. Training servicemen for civilian jobs;
5. Technical services and promotional efforts and
6. Skill centers (30).

This Task Force also highlighted a constant problem in HRD when they cited the need for "a better understanding of how a firm arrives at its training (or nontraining) policies" (31).

A newer movement in HRD was toward change in systems as well as individuals, characterized by terms such as "organizational development" and "organizational renewal." The literature and work in this field was just beginning to gain momentum as the decade of the hectic 60's was completed.

Into the 70's

This book is being written entering the decade of the 70's. Given the sweep of prior history and the momentum which is now apparent in the field of HRD, it is unlikely that there will be any diminution. On the contrary, the 70's are being entered with increased concern for our fellow man, newer roles for our organizations and an increasing concern for training, education and development.

Literature Citations

1. Malcolm S. Knowles, *The Adult Education Movement in the United States* (New York: Holt, Rinehart and Winston, 1962).
2. Harold Taylor, *Students Without Teachers* (New York: McGraw-Hill, 1969), p. 194.

3. G. D. Pope, Jr., *Ocmulgee National Monument*, National Park Service Historical Handbook Series, No. 24 [Washington: Government Printing Office, 1956 (reprinted 1961)] , p. 12.

4. Leo Deuel, *Conquistadors Without Swords: Archeologists in the Americas* (New York: St. Martin's Press, 1967).

5. I am indebted to Armando Rodriguez of the Mexican-American Affairs Section of the U.S. Office of Education for bringing this to my attention.

6. Alfred D. Chandler, Jr., "The Role of Business in the United States: A Historical Survey," *Daedalus* (Winter, 1969), p. 26.

7. Robert C. Weaver, *Negro Labor: A National Problem* (New York: Harcourt, Brace and Co., 1946), pp. 4-5.

8. One of the many books contributing to the gap in our knowledge of the Negro is by C. Eric Lincoln, *The Negro Pilgrimage in America* (New York: Bantam Books, 1967).

9. Cloyd S. Steinmetz, "The Evolution of Training" in *Training and Development Handbook,* ed. Robert Craig and Lester Bittel (New York: McGraw-Hill, 1967), p. 5.

10. *Agency Training Centers for Federal Employees.* Fiscal year 1968, Bureau of Training, U.S. Civil Service Commission (Washington: Government Printing Office, 1968), p. 1.

11. Allen Schoener, *Portal to America: The Lower East Side 1870-1925* (New York: Holt, Rinehart and Winston, 1967). This is a collection of photographs and articles from newspapers of the time showing the life of one particular group of immigrants—the Jews—who came and settled in New York City. The multi-dimensional aspects of the immigrants may prove to be new to many readers.

12. Oscar Handlin, *The Uprooted* (New York: Grosset and Dunlap, 1951). This is a treatment of the various immigrant groups who came to the United States.

13. *The Philosophy and Operation of Cooperative Education* (Philadelphia: Drexel Institute of Technology, 1968), p. 5.

14. From the *Educational Bulletin.* New York Chapter, American Institute of Banking, 1968-1969, p. 4.

15. H. P. Rodes, "GMI's First Fifty Years," *Journal of Cooperative Education* (May 1969), pp. 6-10.

16. One source among many for these studies is F. J. Roethlisberger and J. Dickson, *Management and the Worker* (Cambridge: Harvard University Press, 1939).

17. Thomas S. Keaty, "Early Days of American Society of Training Directors," *Journal of the ASTD* (September-October 1956), pp. 2-5, 43.

18. *Bibliography of Publications*, (Alexandria, Va.: Human Resources Research Office, September 1968).

19. Leland P. Bradford, Jack R. Gibb and Kenneth D. Benne, *T-Group Theory and Laboratory Method* (New York: John Wiley and Sons, 1964).

20. John J. Hayes, "Too Much Human Relations in Management Training?", *Journal of the ASTD* (November-December, 1957), pp. 24-28.

21. B. F. Skinner, *The Technology of Teaching* (New York: Appleton-Century-Crofts, 1968).

22. Leonard Silvern was using programmed instruction in training firefighters in New York state in 1950.

23. Edwin F. Harris and Edwin A. Fleishman, "Human Relations Training and the Stability of Leadership Patterns," *Journal of Applied Psychology,* vol. 39, no. 1 (1955) pp. 20-25.

24. *Manpower Report of the President* (Washington: Government Printing Office, 1969), p. 39.

25. Leonard Nadler, "Has Federal Legislation Affected Your Training?", *Training in Business and Industry* (August, 1967), pp. 16-19. This article only discusses a few of the many acts of Congress affecting HRD. It is almost impossible to keep an up-to-date accurate list, which is one of the problems with the resources offered by the legislation.

26. Alan Cambray, "Observations on ITAC 69," *Industrial Training International* (October 1969), p. 425. His other observations on the trip are also of interest.

27. Leonard Nadler, "Support Systems for Training the Disadvantaged" (Draft report of study commissioned by *Harvard Business Review,* 1970).

28. *Investment for Tomorrow.* A Report of the Presidential Task Force on Career Advancement (Washington: Government Printing Office, 1967).

29. *Report Covering the Effectiveness of Implementation of the Government Employees Training Act,* 90th Congress, House Report No. 329. (Washington: Government Printing Office, 1967).
30. *A Government Commitment to Occupational Training in Industry* (Washington, Government Printing Office, 1968), pp. 77-104.
31. Ibid, p. 110.

section II

Activity Areas

In the four chapters in this section, the various kinds of activities which are devoted to releasing human potential will be differentiated. At present, these are subsumed under the heading of "training." As noted earlier, the designation HRD (Human Resource Development) is being used as the umbrella term for three different activity areas.

Previously, being locked into the traditional term, "training" has created more blocks and resistance than has been warranted. When talking of "trigger words," those which arouse an emotional response, the word training is high among these. It produces various kinds of negative responses among those who see it as training of animals, toilet training of children and other activities which are considered of lesser importance.

Though training people is now common, it is still somehow given a lower priority than education. Yet, it is not a matter of level but rather of clarification as to what actually is being done.

There are three different kinds of activities being conducted and only one of them is training. The relationship might be identified as follows:

Chapter	Area	Focus
3	Employee Training	Job
4	Employee Education	Individual
5	Employee Development	Organization
6	Nonemployee Development	Society

Chapters 3, 4 and 5 are concerned with the development of resources in organizations where the human resource is essentially an employee. The same model of these three areas can be applied to organizations which are concerned with human resources who are not their employees. These are membership organizations, labor unions, professional societies and community organizations. They also provide for human resource development of nonemployees—and this is discussed in Chapter 6.

Another way of showing this is indicated in Figure II.1. The three activity areas are shown as being equal and there is no hierarchical relationship implied or intended as concerns their contribution to an organization.

Figure II.1. Activity areas of HRD.

Some labels are needed which can communicate and identify the distinction among these three activities. In Figure II.2 the labels are added to the activities. In the remainder of this book, the labels will be used as indicated.

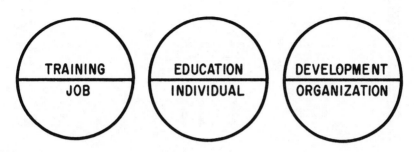

Figure II.2. Labels for HRD activities.

When placed together, the total picture is represented in Figure II.3. When the term human resource development or HRD is used, it signifies experiences in all three activity areas.

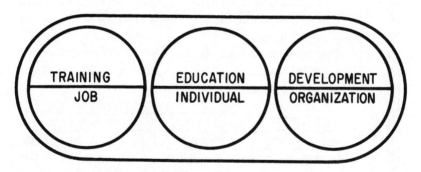

Figure II.3. The concept of human resource development.

This model applies to nonemployees (society in general) as well as to employees within any kind of organization. The distinctions will be spelled out in the chapters in this section.

3

Employee Training

As defined in Chapter 1, HRD is concerned with a series of organized activities, conducted within a specified time and designed to bring about behavioral change. This definition can now be refined to distinguish between the various kinds of activities which are encompassed.

Training is those activities which are designed to improve performance on the job the employee is presently doing or is being hired to do. It can be extended to include the necessary activities to enable the employee to move to an immediate higher level position in the organization but still within his same basic area of activity. For example, a stenographer may receive training so she can now be moved from the stenographic pool to a position as a private secretary within the organization. A manual worker could be given training to enable him to qualify to work on additional machines and, therefore, move to a higher pay scale.

New machinery and new production processes can also require additional job training. Introduction of these new elements may require performance on the job which was not formerly part of the behavior of the employee.

Purpose

The major focus of training is to enable the employee to perform better for the organization on his present job or one directly related to it.

"Training" and "education" are two terms which are usually juxtaposed, and exploring the distinction is necessary. The next chapter will discuss education more fully, but now let us look at one element—namely, goal.

The distinction is indicated in Figure 3.1. A person comes to a situation with a variety of behaviors. The purpose of training is to either introduce a new behavior or modify the existing behaviors so that a particular and specified kind of behavior results. In an educational situation, the person likewise brings a variety of behaviors, but it is now hoped that a releasing experience is provided so that he can produce more behaviors than when he entered the situation. Some of the new behaviors may be specified, whereas others are of a more general nature.

Figure 3.1. Contrasting training and education.

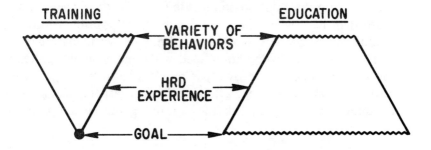

Glaser makes the distinction that training minimizes individual differences, whereas education maximizes individual differences (1).

Training can be identified in three areas: skills, attitude and knowledge. These are terms commonly used for the psychological labels—motoric, affective and cognitive.

Skills

The essence of getting the job done is to have the requisite skills to be able to perform the tasks required on the job. Among the functions of a personnel department is to identify, recruit, select and place people with job skills into the appropriate parts of the organization. Yet, skill training becomes a necessity for even in the freest of labor markets—with the supply exceeding the demand for skilled employees, there is no assurance that the new worker will be able to perform at the standard of his new organization.

Skills acquired in another organizational setting will have to be modified through training to meet the particular requirements of the employee's new organization. The same machines and even processes may be involved, but the new employee would still need some skill training on the new job so that he can utilize his skills in the patterns demanded by his new organization.

Where individuals are hired for entry-level jobs, it is necessary for the employer to provide some basic skill training. For example, in the East Pittsburgh plant of Westinghouse, it is customary for most workers to enter at the "Sweeper" level. The job title does not communicate fully, for the Sweeper does more than just sweep the floor. He is also responsible for maintaining clear and safe work areas, bringing work materials to work stations, removing completed work and generally policing the area for safety. The Sweeper requires basic training in patterns of work, safety regulations and minor aspects of material handling. This is minimal skill level training, but he can progress and move onto a machine or into some other production process. To facilitate the movement, he will receive some skill training from his supervisor.

Whenever a production line is altered, new materials utilized or other variations in production or materials introduced, it is necessary to provide additional skill training. Where possible, the training should take place before the introduction of new materials or processes. At least, it should be concurrent, particularly in situations where the production line cannot be shut down or the employee released from his work station to allow for the additional training.

New plant start-ups are of increasing concern. As manufacturing facilities have entered new geographical areas and moved toward decentralization, there has arisen an increasing need for skilled labor. One company—The Kendall Co. of Atlanta, Georgia—opened a training center in a rented building at the same time it broke ground for its new building. Comparable production facilities were set up as part of the training so that by the time the plant was operational, it had a fully trained work force performing at standards (2).

Skill training is not limited to only entry-level employees or the lower echelons of the organization. A supervisor or manager can require additional skill training in a particular production process. More commonly, new supervisory personnel can benefit from skill training related to their higher level in the organization. A manager who must produce a particular report in a specific fashion may require skill training in report writing and in meeting the requirements of the particular kind of reporting. Although attitude and knowledge are crucial to effective communications, there are some skill aspects such as writing, speaking, listening, effective use of transmission devices and the tool subjects of grammar and spelling.

Attitude

Attitude training is not as apparent but is a necessary component of many job training programs. Training related to attitudes is an essential element of an orientation program for new employees. Each organization has its own climate and an attitude which it expects will be reflected by those employed. This does not imply reacting like robots, but rather that management has expectations of the attitude of its employees. The new employee can endeavor to discover this for himself by being placed on the job and absorbing the attitudes around him. Or, more logically, he can be scheduled through an orientation program which among other things deals with attitude. This does not guarantee that the new employee will have the attitude that management wishes, but at least the new employee will know what is expected. This also gives him an option to leave the organization if he feels that the attitude expected is contradictory to his own expectations.

Attitude training assumes greater significance in those areas where there is public contact by employees. Sales persons, receptionists, telephone operators and others who are the face of the organization to its customers need training in attitudes. The job performance of these employees is a vital element in either making the organization successful or creating communication blocks with its public. Other employees who are likewise in an "exposed" position, such as social workers, policemen, firemen, guards, repairmen and delivery men, also require attitude training. In every organization there are those who deal with the "public," although the public may be varied and sometimes difficult to identify.

If an employee is assigned to a complaint department, it is obvious that he is likely to need attitude training. But, what of all the other employees who also meet the various groups served by the organization? Even the personnel department might benefit from a training program designed to improve the attitude of interviewers of new job applicants. The negative attitudes of some interviewers have contributed to the alienation of minority groups in seeking employment (3).

With the impact of minority groups entering the work force, the need for attitude training has become more apparent. Early efforts were made from 1945-50 as various states passed laws against discrimination on the job. The Civil Rights Act of 1964 and subsequent legislation has increased the need for attitude training relating to minority group employment.

Can attitudes effectively be changed in a training session? At one extreme is the technique known as "brainwashing" in which, through manipulation of the environment and by the imposition of a stress situation, an attitude is changed. At least, the visible behavior changes.

Having the ability to produce attitudinal changes also carries with it a great risk and responsibility. If attitudes can be changed, then robots might also be produced (4). Having the ability does not necessarily give anyone the right. The HRD director must approach the area of attitude training with caution, a degree of humility and an appreciation for the uniqueness of each individual.

In relation to attitude training and the job, work should be directed toward developing those attitudes which support the particular employee within his given organization. If the employee finds the direction of the attitude change distasteful, he can try to influence the direction or leave the job. When jobs are plentiful and when an employee has marketable skills, this poses no problem. Difficulty arises when the employee chooses not to move for any reason, including his investment in the company pension system.

Where a conflict exists between the attitude desired by the employer and that retained by the employee, it is doubtful if training can have much impact except to highlight the problem. Other action may become more significant than a training program.

For the citizens who have not previously been a part of the work force, attitude training is a requirement. It goes by a variety of titles such as human relations training, getting to know yourself, you and your world or you and your heritage. Generally, it is "getting the youth (i.e. new employees) to examine their own attitudes toward jobs, themselves, their community life in general" (5).

In the late 1960's, many companies became involved in hiring what were termed "hard-core disadvantaged". This was done directly by the company in conjunction with an assortment of government programs or as part of the National Alliance of Businessmen. For example, Westinghouse set up a facility in Newark, New Jersey, in 1968 designed to provide four weeks of attitude training as well as remedial education to enable the new employee to be considered for placement at its Bloomfield plant.

Companies hiring the new minority groups into their plants have also recognized the values of an attitude training program for the peer group worker—that person who works alongside the new hire. Likewise, attitude training programs for supervisors have been important in preparing the supervisor for a worker who might be different from those he had previously supervised.

As increased numbers of college graduates are entering the labor market, increased concern with preparing supervisors and management to cope with this new worker is being seen. The introduction of advanced educational technology in public school systems will produce an employee with a range of educational experiences unknown to the existing work force. Learning through educational technology can produce an employee so much different as to require continuous attitude training to effectively integrate new generations into the work force.

Knowledge

Training for knowledge is in the area of what needs to be known to do the present job. It is difficult to define the limits for sometimes a worker can be helped by having knowledge of more than just his present area of activity in order to understand the framework in which the job is being performed. For example, a salesman who is selling to customers located outside the country can benefit from training in language, the history of the particular countries in his territory, their relations with each other, the customs and traditions and even some of their music. This may seem almost too obvious. But, how about the salesman's knowledge of his own country? He will find foreigners asking questions about the United States, and if he is not prepared to respond intelligently, his entire validity may be questioned.

A mechanic who must read parts and technical manuals provided by the manufacturer may need training in English in order to perform his job at the standards set. Knowledge can become a difficult area for it is not always easy to differentiate what is needed to do the job from that kind of knowledge which would merely be helpful and not primarily within the definition of training. It is better to err on the side of providing more knowledge rather than less, but the trainer must be careful not to be misled by providing education (see the next chapter) when the objective is training.

Methodologies and Resources

The range of methodologies and resources available is too extensive and variable to warrant listing here. Therefore, this section will be devoted to indicating directions and considerations. Also, rapid advances in technology would make such a listing obsolete before the book has been published. The HRD specialist is advised to subscribe to some of the appropriate publications in the field.

General trends and practices will be discussed. These will be the practices which are currently in use. Of course, none of these can be applied without other considerations but will serve to indicate the more prevalent practices at this time.

OJT

The most common and misused term is on-the-job training (OJT). Using this term creates a problem as there is no common agreement as to what is included. Generally, it is an activity which meets the earlier definition of training in that it is organized, conducted for a specific period of time and is designed to result in behavioral change.

A study by the Manpower Administration found that most workers surveyed had just picked up the training needed to do the job. Informal approaches were the most prevalent. The study recommended that:

> Many jobs are becoming more complex as the economy undergoes technological change. There are good reasons to believe that the informal methods that were good enough to learn yesterday's jobs will be inadequate for the jobs of tomorrow. If so, we need a fundamental change in our present mixture of informal and formal occupational training, with a great deal more emphasis on the latter (6).

OJT does not have to be informal, but it appears that it frequently is. To meet the definition of training and the need of employees, it must become more formalized. Informal methods will still persist, and they must persist. There are many details which will always be conveyed from one worker to another during the various kinds of contacts that occur in the lunchroom, washroom, time clock and smoking areas. At the work site itself, the new worker can be assigned to watch but have absolutely no idea of what he is seeing. The more experienced worker may not even be aware of some of his own procedures which are necessary to the job but which have been modified by him without the knowledge of those who designed the work situation.

Supervisors, in their normal work relationships, are constantly moving between giving orders to their subordinates and providing instruction. Providing his subordinates with instruction is one of the key elements of a supervisor's job. One of the more common ways to help a supervisor perform this role is to provide him with Job Instruction Training (JIT), a program which dates back to World War I and which is experiencing an exciting revival.

Coaching is another technique used by supervisors endeavoring to improve job performance. When used appropriately, it is training. However, much as with JIT, unless it is done on an organized basis, it is unlikely that it can be considered training. This is not to downgrade the function of the supervisor as a coach, but to note that unless it is an organized activity designed to produce a specific change, it is not training.

Classroom Instruction

The most frequently used methodology is a training program in a classroom situation, somewhere on the company site. The facility may contain rooms designed for instructional purposes or conference rooms which are made available for training.

Training programs using classroom instruction are usually of fairly short duration ranging from two hours to several weeks. Unless it is entry-level training, the program will be confined to some elements of the job rather than the total job. To participate in these classes, the employee must be away from his work station. Accordingly, supervisors are reluctant to send employees to training programs with the resultant loss of productive hours. As the supervisor has relied on the personnel department to provide him with a competent employee, there may be resentment at losing the time of the worker while he is in training. However, the HRD director can help the supervisor recognize that the investment of time now can improve the effectiveness of the employee and add long-range benefits to his department. Despite any arguments for training, the supervisor is still faced with the dilemma of releasing a worker for training as against keeping him working, though at a lower level.

With the advent of newer training technologies, the polarization of the dilemma has been reduced. Aspects of job training can be accomplished in a variety of ways which do not require off-the-job learning situations. Eastman Kodak uses a set of photographs and simple one or two-line instructions right at the work bench of the assembler to reinforce existing tasks or to "train" for modifications and other minimal changes. General Electric had found it helpful to use taped instructions to help line workers adjust to changes in production. A video tape recorder (VTR) at the work site with a loop-film has also been helpful but has proven more costly and takes up needed space. The Rexall Company found that a tape recorder installed in the salesman's car could be effectively used. As the salesman reaches his next destination, he finds a cassette mailed to him by the company containing new price information, delivery dates and product information. As he goes about his business in his vehicle, he can play the tape as many times as he wishes until he has learned the information.

Another variation is to use slack time on the job for training. The New England Telephone Company has supplied training, via VTR, for its operators during slack time when they can be off the boards (7). The training is provided in the same room, right near their work stations so that if a situation should arise which needs the operators, they can easily leave the training and return to their work stations. As more technology is introduced into training situations, the work site may truly become a classroom.

The technology has produced another kind of classroom which is replete with various multimedia and especially designed facilities. In the early part of the century, company schools were common. There is now a resurgence of this kind of facility for education and development and frequently for training.

The industrial classroom, as it is sometimes called, can be located at one facility of the company, or be a traveling classroom. Retail outlets, such as food chains, have built their classrooms into specially equipped trailer trucks to bring the classroom out to their stores.

No statistic is available on the number of company schools in operation. Some of the schools are adjuncts of the regular training operation, though located in a separate facility. At the Eastman Kodak Plant in Kodak Park, Rochester, there is a Hands-On Training Center which provides four weeks of job training to enable new employees to qualify as Mechanic Helper. The new worker, usually from a minority group or not previously in the work force, is given a job and assigned to the company school for his basic job training. Upon completion of his course, after indicating minimum acceptable performance on a 95-item list, he is sent to the foreman previously designated when he was hired.

Company schools were more prevalent outside the United States for reasons which are usually of local origin. For example, in Japan, the need for company schools was a result of the intense secrecy surrounding the operations of a company, coupled with the practice of life-long employment (8). In the United States, the mobility of the work force and the resources of public and proprietary schools have mitigated the necessity for company schools. Today, the rapid changes in technology, the changed nature of the work force and the ascendance of the HRD director are factors instrumental in the development of company schools.

Public Schools

The role of the public school in providing job training is now ambiguous and debatable. For years the public school had vocational courses which were presumably designed to prepare a graduate to enter the work force. The changing demands of jobs and the relative inflexibility of the vocational schools created a gap. The schools should not be castigated for their reluctance to change. To reflect the needs of the market place, they would have had to pay high salaries to trade instructors and continually purchase the newer equipment. Few school systems have been willing to pay this price, particularly for vocational education.

In the early 60's, the movement evolved to make vocational education post-secondary; that is, after completion of the usual 12 years of schooling (9). The Manpower Development and Training Act of 1962 (MDTA) pushed schools in this direction through the provision of federal funds to supplement the local school budgets (10). The Vocational Education Amendments of 1968 emphasized the development of work-study programs to bring the job market and the schools closer together.

As the need for at least a functional level of literacy was being recognized, the field of Adult Basic Education (ABE) became more visible. There have been courses in "English" and "Citizenship" since the turn of the century when the immigrant was helped so that he could become a worker and a citizen. With the spotlight on poverty in the United States, it was discovered that there were about 25 million adults with less than an eighth grade education, according to the 1960 census. The adult public education programs increased their activity as they sought to reduce the number of illiterates and thereby increase the possibility of entering the work force.

The line between industry and education has been blurring as they begin to work more closely together to provide opportunities for all citizens to enter and be successful in the work force. One approach that has been strongly recommended is that of the Industry-Education Advisory Committee (11). The idea is far from new, but more knowledge is still needed about how to organize, develop and utilize such advisory committees which are crucial to the relationship of industry and the public schools.

Colleges and Universities

The role of institutions of higher education in preparing professionals for the work force is well known. It may not be so evident that they also provide training. Due, in part, to the snob appeal of the word "education," a great deal is heard today of "continuing education for the professions."

Actually, these are training programs. They are not designed to prepare the professional for promotion, a new job or a new career. They are experiences designed to help him stay up with the state of the art, to refresh what he learned at an earlier stage and, generally, to help him do his present job better. This is not a new role, and many times in the past, universities and colleges have provided this kind of resource (12).

Policy Considerations

When providing training, an organization must consider its policy stance and the kinds of decisions which need to be made. Within each organization, the role of the HRD director is so much different that he may vary from being high on the decision-making hierarchy to being so far down in the organization that his decision-making area is highly circumscribed and effects nobody but himself. In any case, the HRD director must bring to the attention of the decision makers the issues that they need to consider if they are sincere in providing training for their employees.

Responsibility for Training

A common question is, "In an organization, where is the responsibility for training?" DePhillips, Berliner and Cribbin note that there is general agreement that it is a line responsibility (13). At one time, there would have been little argument with this statement. It was often to be found emblazoned on the wall of the office, if not on the letterhead of the trainer. But, it avoided two questions.

First, what is meant by training? If it is used in the context stated in this book, then there is little disagreement. Job training is the responsibility of the first line supervisor. In the work situation, the immediate supervisor is the person responsible for the training of his subordinates. This means that it is the immediate supervisor, at any level of the organization, who needs to make provisions for the training. This does not require that the supervisor do the training. For reasons of availability of time, expertise in the particular task, most effective use of himself as a resource and for similar reasons, there will be times when the supervisor can be more effective by relying on an outside resource to do the training. The HRD director helps the supervisor increase his own competency as an instructor as well as advising on when outside sources may be more advantageous.

The second question is much more difficult—what is the supervisor's responsibility for education and development? Why should the supervisor use his time and his budget to provide experiences for employees which will cause them to leave his department? A supervisor is not rewarded for turnover, so why should he engage in those activities which will increase turnover for his department? Where no distinction is made among the three terms, it is likely that the line supervisor will pay some attention to training. At least he will if he recognizes how it influences the output of his own department and therefore his record with his organization. But, who asks him, "How many employees have you educated for promotion out of your unit?" How would he respond to, "What kind of development activities have you provided, even though they cannot possibly influence your production or the output of your unit?"

By the suggestion that education and development are the responsibility of the line, the supervisors are asked to use their time in activities for which the organization does not provide rewards or recognition. This conflicts with what is known about behavior in organizations. Training is the responsibility of line management. Education and development are not.

Who Is To Be Trained

The selection of trainees is more than sending employees to school or seeing who can be spared to meet a quota for a training program established by the HRD director. If training truly improves job performance, then it should be reflected in the current pay envelope of the employee as well as his future with the organization. The decision to provide training, or to withhold training, seriously affects the income of the worker.

Where there is a union, the prerogatives of the supervisor in assigning employees to training programs can be severely limited. For years, some unions have seen training as a management instrument with anti-union implications. A strong union member might be denied training opportunities whereas "company men" might be rewarded through training. Whether this is justified or not is immaterial. If the union reacts in this fashion, then the decision as to who is to be trained becomes unnecessarily complicated. Where both union and management have been involved in selecting employees for training, less friction has developed, though by no means eliminated.

Training is often an essential step in upgrading an employee. It provides him with the skills to move upward in the organization, even though he may remain in the same unit. A worker may move through training from a machine operator to a setup man. For such movement, the supervisor is the man to make the decision on training for even after the training, the employee will still be working for the same supervisor.

Budget

Much of the job training will be done by the supervisor. He may do this directly or he may assign others in his work force to do this for him. He may use an assistant supervisor or another worker who may be designated as a job coach for training purposes. In these instances, the budgetary requirements for training are minimal.

When an off-job facility is used, the question of budget becomes vital. The training may be done in a company school or an off-company facility. In these cases, a specific decision is required concerning budget. Is the training to be charged to the budget of the operating department or to the central training budget? If it is stated that training is the responsibility of the line supervisor, then there must be consistency and he should be provided with the necessary training budget.

The supervisor may not be satisfied with this arrangement, for if the personnel department has not recruited adequately prepared workers for him, then the supervisor is forced to use his own budget to compensate for what he sees as the inadequacy of that aspect of the personnel function.

Another approach to part of this problem is to have the central training unit charge for its services. This has been the practice in several large companies like Westinghouse and General Motors. The U.S. Civil Service Commission bills agencies who send participants to their inter-agency programs (14).

How Much Training

Given the definition of training used in this chapter, training should be limited to that which produces a direct return on the job. It is just as wasteful to overtrain as to undertrain the employee. An overtrained employee will become dissatisfied if the job does not allow him to use the new behaviors he has acquired through the training program. It is likely that he will then move out of the organization into another one which will provide the opportunity to use the new behaviors resulting from the training.

It is desirable to train employees for something beyond the immediate job, but the exact level should be clearly determined. The training, in this context, should not be for advancement but rather to make the employee more flexible as the needs of the job and his part of the department may change.

Training can also be done in anticipation of change. If the supervisor knows that new materials or processes are being planned, he would be wise to provide the training early enough so that the employee is ready for the change.

Evaluation

The concept of evaluating training has been, and still is, highly controversial. The techniques for effective evaluation are lacking, and the reluctance on the part of those concerned to expose themselves is also a consideration. However, more pressure is being felt to at least evaluate at the level of current competence without waiting for the more refined tools which are always just beyond the horizon.

There are different approaches to evaluation, and a readily usable distinction is offered by Donald Kirkpatrick (15) who offers the steps of reaction, learning, behavior and results.

Step 1:   Reaction.   How well did the trainees like the program?

Step 2:   Learning.   What principles, facts and techniques were learned?

Step 3:   Behavior.   What changes in job behavior resulted from the program?

Step 4:   Results.   What were the tangible results of the program in terms of reduced cost, improved quality, improved quantity, etc.?

If dealing only with training, then emphasis should be on Kirkpatrick's Step 4. The evaluation of training should be in the specific results on the job when the worker returns.

The limitation of this approach lies in the job performance before the training took place. If, prior to the training, there was not data on costs, quality and quantity, then how can change be measured? If a base line has not existed, training cannot establish data on adequate results. Training cannot be measured against a nonexistent standard. If there is concern with evaluating training, there must also be involvement in establishing the point of departure where training will produce improved job performance.

In some jobs it is possible to develop a direct cost-benefit ratio to indicate the results of the training experience. Where prior standards do not exist, it is not possible to apply cost-benefit ratios or any other meaningful quantified data. The training director should not be berated for refusing to evaluate when the criteria are not established.

In evaluating, the employee, supervisor and trainer should all be involved. Evaluation should not be used as a weapon to support the need for additional training or to deprecate the efforts of the existing program. Rather, it must be developed as a diagnostic tool to help all those concerned understand the relationship of the investment in training to the expected results.

Literature Citations

1. Robert Glaser, "Psychology and Instructional Technology," in *Training Research and Education,* ed. Robert Glaser (New York: John Wiley & Sons, 1965), p. 4.

2. "Pretraining of Production Personnel Reduces Plant Startup Losses" in *The Manager's Newsletter* issued by the American Management Association, July 1969, p. 3.

3. The effect of different styles of listening as influenced by cultural behavior is described by Edward T. Hall, "Listening Behavior: Some Cultural Differences," *Phi Delta Kappan,* March, 1969, pp. 379-380. More detail can be found in his book *The Silent Language* (Greenwich: Faweett Publications, 1959).

4. Ludwig von Bertalanffy, *Robots, Men and Minds* (New York: George Braziller, 1967).

5. *Putting the Hard-Core Unemployed Into Jobs,* Community Relations Service, Department of Justice (Washington: Government Printing Office, 1968), p. 14.

6. *Formal Occupational Training of Adult Workers,* Manpower/Automation Research Monography, no. 2, Manpower Administration, Department of Labor (Washington: Government Printing Office, 1964), p. 22.

7. "Taped TV Teachers Operators When the Lines Aren't Busy," *Training in Business and Industry*, September/October 1965, p. 35-37.
8. This was particularly true in 1965 when I wrote *Employee Training in Japan* (Los Angeles: Education and Training Consultants, 1965). It will be interesting to ascertain how the changing employment picture will affect this practice. The less than lifetime employment is described by Masaaki Imai in "Shukko, Jomukai, Ringi—The Ingredients of Executive Selection in Japan," *Personnel*, July/August 1969, pp. 20-30.
9. An excellent source for information and concepts of post-secondary vocational and technical education is Grant Venn, *Man Education and Work* (Washington: American Council on Education, 1964).
10. Various histories and background papers have appeared regarding the MDTA program. Among the more notable are Seymour Wolfbein [he served as administrator of the program for several years], *Education and Training for Full Employment* (New York: Columbia University Press, 1967).
11. Samuel W. Burt, *Industry and Vocational-Technical Education* (New York: McGraw Hill, 1967). This is a good survey of some actual practices in using advisory committees though it is written from the viewpoint of government and school administrators. It does not reflect the experiences of human resource developers in the private sector.
12. Michael H. Jessup, "An Historical Analysis of the Development of Selected Areas of University Extension Programs in the United States, 1900-1965, as Related in Professional Literature" (Ph.D. diss., The George Washington University, 1967).
13. Frank A. DePhillips, William M. Berliner and James J. Cribbin, *Management of Training Programs* (Homewood: Richard D. Irwin, 1960), p. 230.
14. The Government Employees Training Act of 1958, Section 8 (2) authorizes the Civil Service Commission to provide training on a "reimbursable basis."
15. Donald L. Kirkpatrick, "Evaluation of Training in *Training and Development Handbook*, ed. Robert Craig and Lester Bittel (New York: McGraw Hill, 1967), p. 88.

4

Employee Education

Employee human resource development is defined as those organized activities, conducted within a specified time and designed to bring about behavioral change. Employee education is defined as those HRD activities which are designed to improve the overall competence of the employee in a specified direction and beyond the job now held. In writing of future trends, Bernard J. Bienvenu suggests that the direction of effort will shift from *job* training to *worker* training (1). This is far reaching; there is still the need for job training, but there must be increased emphasis on the worker. When the worker is being prepared for a place in the organization different from what he now holds—this is employee education.

Organizations are conducting education with an avowed purpose of providing more than just training for the existing job. In a study in 1960, Oscar N. Serbein provided a list of courses in general education offered by at least 36 firms employing more than 10,000 employees each. Serbein noted that courses were designed to improve the general level of education of the employee. The courses were not expected to contribute directly to job performance (2).

Education is not merely a random approach to helping an individual develop his potential. The thrust is to develop the individual for growth within the organization as it now exists and for a clearly defined level or position within the organization. Employee education is geared to specific job placement.

Purpose

Employee education programs are designed to prepare employees to move into new positions in the existing or planned organization. The movement may be a one-step promotion which requires prior education in some new technical or non-technical areas. A broader movement is that encompassed by the term "career development."

Promotion

A primary purpose of employee education is to prepare employees for upward mobility within the organization. The short-range goal is one of preparing for movement to the immediate level position above the one the employee is now occupying. This can be in the unit where the employee is now assigned or to another unit of the organization but a step up. In some cases, lateral transfer may be involved with no increase in salary depending upon the classification structure within the organization.

Growing concern has been expressed about the need to prepare employees to become supervisors. For many years, it has been the practice to appoint individuals as supervisors and then provide the appropriate supervisory training. Through judicious use of employee education programs, it is possible to select employees with potential for supervisory positions and then provide them with the educational experiences which will enable them to fill the position. The same approach is applicable to managerial and executive levels of the organization.

Education for promotion can bring with it the challenge of an entirely new field. Although some of the employee's previous training and education may still be useful, he is being prepared for a job which is outside of his previous area of activity. The American Oil Company needed a training manager and, after careful consideration, reached out and selected a regional marketing manager to be educated for this new position. With the cooperation of the University of Chicago, they developed a one-year educational experience to develop this employee for his completely new position in the organization (3).

An advantage of providing education is that the individual receives the appropriate preparation before being placed on the job. Although there is some commitment on both sides that the new job assignment will take place, it provides the opportunity for the employee to determine if he is interested in the duties of the new position for which he is being prepared. It also provides the employer with the opportunity of gaining feedback from the educational experience as to whether the employee is indeed ready to move into the new higher level position.

Judicious use of education can mitigate and possibly avoid being trapped by the Peter Principle (4), which includes the concept that "in a hierarchy every employee tends to rise to his level of incompetence." A soundly administered educational program coupled with good personnel practices can avoid this occurrence. By educating before promotion, the employee can be helped to reach his highest level of competence and avoid being faced with a job he cannot or does not want to do. Of course, some risks must be taken if people are to be helped to realize their potential rather than be trapped into only backing a sure thing. Risks are on both sides, and education becomes a way of hedging the bet. It minimizes playing God with somebody else's life and still conserves the resources of the organization.

Essentially, the employee is being prepared through an educational experience for the duties of a job known to the organization but not yet personally experienced by the employee. When an employee is provided with an opportunity for education, there should be a clear picture in the minds of those responsible for the experience, as well as in the mind of the employee, as to the job for which he is being prepared. In a large multi-site organization, there is an added difficulty in specifying the exact position he will occupy as it may be a position in a new plant or in an existing plant in a different location.

Career Development

There are many kinds of career development activities in operation in all kinds of organizations. To understand career development, it must first be compared to the previous discussion on promotion. When an employee is being educated for promotion, it is for a one-time jump to a higher level position. It is not necessarily part of some plan for the continued growth of the employee over a longer period of time.

Impetus for career development comes from two directions. There is the need in the organization to constantly keep its positions filled, particularly at the upper echelons. The organization is aware that there will be changes in the existing work force and that through retirement, death, resignation and other reasons, the need for replacement is of constant concern. The personnel department devotes time and energy to maintaining replacement schedules for jobs at various levels within the organization. The HRD director is involved in developing the necessary educational experiences for the employees identified on the replacement schedules. The replacements are not always made from within the organization, but the organization of today endeavors to increase the possibility of internal mobility to retain its best people. Also, there is considerable cost in bringing a new person into the organization above the entry level.

As the organization plans to fill a position, it refers to the plan which stipulates the kinds of positions the employee must already have occupied and/or the educational experience required to qualify for that particular position.

Career development can include a series of one-step jumps or movement up the ladder in giant steps. The one-step approach is also called the career ladder. The Social Security Administration defines a career ladder for its employees as a sequence of two or more positions in the same classification in a given organizational entity. Each position in the ladder, except for the lowest, is clearly the successor of that at the next lower level in the sequence.

A different concept is that of branching. The employee starts on the career ladder, but provision is made for him to be able to move into another career pattern if this seems more desirable for both the individual and the organization. "Late achievers"—those individuals who do not really find the place to utilize their potential until they have been in the work force for many years—are being discovered.

The public school system has too frequently forced youngsters to make career choices while still in their early teens. Even the selection of the college and major subject is influenced more by parental forces and economic factors than what the individual really wants to do. Young people are protesting against making these decisions too early in their life. They ask for a challenge and the opportunity to be useful. This is a wonderful, exciting, healthy attitude which is demolished when the new employee is forced to decide his career too early in his work life. Yet, when career development is seen as only meeting the need of the organization, this easily occurs.

The other impetus for career development comes from the individual himself. The Forest Service of the U.S. Department of Agriculture recognized this when they recommended that "employees should be encouraged to choose specialties early in their careers because long-range training and development objectives are not really known until this choice is made" (5). They further provide for branching by the employee into other career fields at a later point of his service with them.

When developing managers, those already occupying the positions tend to look for bright young men who are like themselves. It does not really work. James V. Clark has pointed out that people grow into positions as their interests and their developing competence allow. No two generations of management personnel define these positions in quite the same way (6). This becomes even more noticeable as new entries into today's work force rebel against repeating the career patterns of the current generation of managers.

But, are career movements of managers so dissimilar? Present data indicates that there are some observable and predictable patterns in career development. The study by Eugene E. Jennings (7) has given us a basic nomenclature and model for looking at the mobile manager. It will be interesting to see if this changes in the decade of the 70's when the products of today's campus turmoil make their bid for managerial positions.

Areas of Development

Planning the HRD activities for education cannot take place until prior decisions have been made—promotion or career development, ladder or branching. Based on these purposes, the HRD director can now proceed to develop the appropriate plan.

The HRD staff contains the experts but should not attempt a development plan on an unilateral basis. Barry T. Jensen, commenting on his own experience in being developed, emphasized:

> I believe that development is a process including the company management, the education staff, the immediate supervisor, and the individual. Improvement in performance comes from changing both the individual and his environment (8).

There is the assumption that the individual already possesses the necessary skills to perform effectively in the organization where he is. If there is to be movement to a higher level position, it becomes necessary to identify the skills which the new position, at a higher level, requires. These new skills may build on those he now possesses or be a new set of completely unrelated skills which he must master if he is to move to the new position.

Where manual or technical skills are involved, they can be identified without too much difficulty. For example, if an organization were to take one of its machine operators and now plan to promote him into a technical position such as draftsman, it would require a whole new set of identifiable skills for which the individual would need an education program. As one moves up the managerial ladder, the requirement for skills becomes less significant, and more emphasis is placed on attitudes and knowledge.

Movement up the ladder of the organization usually requires less work with things and more work with people. Whether this is desirable or not is a moot point—this is the reality of higher level jobs today. One of the important skills that a manager requires is to be able to work with people, a skill commonly referred to as human relations. This is not the ability to manipulate people; rather, it is the development of the skills of listening, giving and receiving feedback and increasing self-awareness so the employee can work effectively with other people who are members of his organization. These are difficult skills to identify and achieve but nonetheless important if the employee is to be educated as part of his organization's HRD effort.

When the individual moves away from production and into the managerial ranks, attitude becomes a significant element of his educational program. If the individual has been moving up with the organization, there is a different attitude expected of him at various levels within the organization. A familiar conflict in this area arises when an individual employee is identified as having strong leadership qualities and is active in the labor union. Management identifies him as a person with potential for a supervisory position in the organization and offers him a supervisory position. By becoming a supervisor, the employee usually moves from the bargaining unit into a nonunion position, and he is no longer available for a leadership position in the union. Union members may see this as a sellout on the part of the employee, whereas management sees it as the development of an in-house resource to be more useful to the organization. In any event, the new employee will require education relating to attitudes if he is to effectively function in his new higher level job. The personnel department and the HRD department are well advised to educate the individual before he is promoted. If he rejects the objectives stated in his education program, he would not become an effective member of the supervisory team.

An employee who will be moving into a new position faces a new set of relationships with which he is unfamiliar. He needs more education in attitudes in order to function in the interpersonal world of this new environment. In a democratic society, people tend to be hesitant about the "brainwashing" aspects of education. It is a healthy caution, and the HRD director must use his expertise to develop the appropriate program concerned with attitude change without having the new supervisor become a puppet who mouths the traditional phrases which he thinks make him part of management. The education program requires opportunities for the employee to explore his own attitudes and how these impact on others.

As the employee is being prepared to enter a new area of activity, the knowledge required will be more than merely building on what he already knows. The employee is now faced with the challenge of exploring new areas of knowledge that were previously completely unknown to him or only slightly within his ken.

The employee now begins to become concerned not only with how the job is done but also why it is done and some of the implications and interactions of other fields of knowledge. It is still essential that the education program be related to the job into which the employee will move. Too much abstract knowledge, unrelated to a foreseeable goal, is wasteful and thwarts the purposes of employee education. But exposure to other fields is also a healthy growth experience when educating employees.

An employee faced with new subject areas is apt to become frustrated. His goal for the higher level job is specific and exact, but he may not have been aware of the new kinds of knowledge which he must learn to move effectively into that job. A production manager who is now moving to higher levels of management understands the reasons for management education. He might be less likely to understand why he must also study government and economics. It is important to provide additional counseling for the employee who is being challenged by various kinds of knowledge inputs for which he does not see a purpose. In some cases, it is possible to identify the exact body of knowledge which the employee needs in order to prepare him to move into the new position. However, the focus of employee education is not only on the immediate job to which he will be moving but also his total career pattern with the organization. Therefore, the employee must be helped to identify the knowledge needed beyond the next immediate step and to begin to lay the groundwork for his further development.

Methodologies and Resources

The methodologies and resources utilized in other forms of HRD are also applicable for employee education. The difference is in how they are used and emphasized. Given the purposes of employee education, there will not be OJT but a variation known as job rotation. There will be classroom instruction, but it will more likely be off-site than was the case in training.

For purposes of training, the resources required to do the job are more commonly found within the organization than is the case in education. Employee education has a much broader purpose than training, and it is desirable to give the employee an opportunity for growth over and above what exists in the organization at the present time. Also, employee education is more closely geared to the needs of the individual, as related to the organization. As individual needs have a wide range of difference, it is unlikely that the organization will have the in-house resources to meet all the needs.

Employee education programs are frequently associated with academic degrees. For many jobs, a degree is necessary as well as desirable, and there should be no hesitation about a degree being the end result of employee education. Management and HRD need have no fear of losing control over the program and the employee because a degree is involved. In this respect, a phase approach is recommended, wherein the employee, the institution and the HRD director concur on certain points in the program where all parties must agree that there is a "go" signal. Such points allow for appraisal of progress and assure that the program in which the employee is enrolled still relates to the job for which he is being prepared.

Another approach is to have the employee pursue the degree but with intermediate goals. He returns to the job at the end of each phase and before completing the degree. When carefully organized and coordinated with the academic institution, the identifiable degree can still be the end product of the academic experience. Among other practices is to offer the education program in off-duty hours, and the employee therefore invests his own time in his education. As appropriate, the organization may provide tuition refund, compensatory time, facilities, instructors or other types of support in order to relate the education to the employing organization.

Employee education does not necessarily mean a degree. There are myriads of employee education programs which are extremely helpful but which do not lead to a degree or even provide college credits. But, given the pressure for degrees in our society today, the value of this kind of program should not be ignored. The Life Office Management Association has worked, in conjunction with several institutions, to develop an associate degree, which is a two-year program leading to a de-

gree which is becoming recognized as valid for those in the field
(9).

Classroom Instruction

Business organizations do not normally have adequate classroom facilities. Although there has been a growing tendency for
organizations to allot space to classrooms, it is unlikely that
they would want to encumber this space if they realized the
resources available to them outside their walls. Samuel Burt has
commented that by using the classrooms available in the community, employers can obtain desired training facilities and reduce their own training costs (10). Of course, Burt is using
"training" in the old sense. It is more appropriate to substitute
the word "education" in his statement; then it becomes even
more significant.

The same classroom experience, no matter where it takes
place, can be used for two different objectives. It can be training for one employee but education for another, as can be seen
in a classroom experience for supervisors. For an employee who
is currently a supervisor, this aspect of the HRD program will be
training, for its purpose is to help him improve his supervisory
practices on the job he already holds. If potential supervisors
are included among the participants, the purpose for them is
one of education, as the experience is to prepare them for a
future job assignment. The potential supervisor cannot be expected to bring the same experience and insight to the HRD
experience as the supervisor who is currently on the job. This
approach to a supervisory program can be stimulating to both
learners, even though they have different purposes. The HRD
director must recognize the difference in purposes and design
the learning experience and evaluation accordingly.

Some organizations offer "general education" programs.
These are usually made available outside of regular work hours;
therefore, there is less control by the employing organization.
The employees enrolled in such programs may not have clearly

defined career development goals or be part of a specific HRD effort of the organization. The employee may be going in order to qualify himself for higher level positions when they become available. One pattern for upward mobility in an organization utilizes a post and bid system of filling above entry-level positions from the existing work force. When a position is to be filled, the personnel department posts the details, including the requirements to fill the job. The posting is not limited to bulletin boards but utilizes all the internal communication mechanisms of the organization, both formal and informal. Employees who believe they have the necessary qualifications and who are interested in the position will put in their bid for the job. To prepare for this opportunity, employees take part in education efforts on their own, though the organization is well advised to make adequate provision so that the education is appropriately directed.

Organizations are finding it desirable to make available their in-house facilities for education programs. The actual classes are conducted by qualified persons from within the organization for the benefit of others. An outside resource, in the form of a qualified instructor, can be brought in, using the organization's own physical facilities and equipment. The practice is to conduct general education programs on off-company time.

Out-of-plant employee education opportunities are much more prevalent where the employee is sent for a specific program which has been developed in conjunction with the personnel department and HRD staff. There is a mutual expectation as to what the employee will study and how this educational experience will contribute to his movement within the organization. An alternative is for the organization to make employees aware of educational opportunities available in the surrounding community, offered by the myriad institutions who are now involved in providing continuing education. The information is placed on company bulletin boards, distributed with the pay checks or listed in the company house organ. The organization is providing a service by bringing the employee and the educational resource into contact with each other. This is a less effective way of using education, as the program which the employee develops for himself may not relate to his growth needs within the organization. As a result, the employee may successfully complete the educational experience and then find that the organization does not have room for him to use the education. Frustrated in his growth, the employee seeks an organization where he can use his education. This can be reconciled by creating a stronger relationship between the educational opportunities provided for the employees and the developmental plans for the human resources of the organization.

Job Rotation

As part of education designed for career development, the employee can be given the opportunity to gain experience on the specific job or the type of job for which he is being prepared. Unfortunately, job rotation is too frequently seen as a clerical procedure for making assignments rather than utilizing it as an educational methodology. An employee should not merely be placed on another job but must be adequately prepared for the kind of experience he is going to, and the relationship of this to his total education program must be clear and specific. The kinds of experiences which he has during job rotation can affect his total experience in education. When handled poorly, it can result in unreconcilable conflict rather than growth.

Job rotation can be utilized in two patterns. But, the HRD specialist should have a clear understanding of his reasons for selecting this methodology. The employee must be involved in developing an understanding of this particular methodology and the reasons for its use at a given time.

The first pattern is a short-range rotational experience where the employee is rotated to a job for a short period of time with the purpose of having him obtain a feel for the job. He does not remain there long enough for any in-depth involvement. An example is the management intern in the federal government. The intern has a specific two-year education period which prepares him to move out of the intern classification into a middle management position. As part of his educational development, he is rotated to various departments on the average of every two months. A common complaint heard from interns is that they have not remained long enough to learn if they "are for real." They observe what is going on and may even make some minimal contributions, but they are not in the situation long enough to be able to have a success experience. They ask for the opportunity to stay longer in the situation, make some decisions and then be able to implement the decisions. A challenge for the HRD staff is to construct this job rotation for the interns so that it meets its educational goals and at the same time provides the intern with the action-experience he seeks.

The intern is a young person who has spent a considerable portion of his life as a student. He often demands a confrontation with reality. Before committing himself to more education, he wants to determine if he is indeed capable of functioning. This is an admirable desire, and too few organizations have been able to successfully meet this problem. Job rotation for interns has frequently produced frustration. As a result, the intern leaves for a position which can provide the challenge he demands.

What about more experienced employees? There is evidence that this type of dissatisfaction is less likely to arise. The experienced employee may greatly benefit from job rotation if he and the receiving group fully understand the nature and purpose of the placement. After each rotational assignment, provision should be made for those involved to assess the experience and its contribution to the educational growth of the employee.

The second pattern is the long-range job rotational assignment. This can last up to five years though there is no outside limit. It would depend upon the nature of the position for which the employee is being prepared. During this rotational assignment, the employee becomes part of the unit so that he can become involved in sufficient depth to enable him to make decisions and live with them.

In Japan, where this system is used extensively for developing upper level managers and executives, the usual period is five years. Their system is based on an employment pattern of life-long service with a given organization. In the United States where there is a higher degree of mobility, the employee may become extremely uncomfortable as he is moved from one position to another each five years. If the positions do not represent promotions, he may question whether the organization really wants him or is the rotation a way of keeping him from being promoted. The plan must be carefully developed and known to all involved.

In the United States, such rotational assignments are usually of lesser duration—two years being about the maximum. The Ford Motor Company assigns bright young men to its training staff in its various plants. The purpose is not to make them permanent members of the HRD staff. It is planned that through this experience they can gain a better picture of the organization. This is part of their education. Of course, it does mean that the HRD unit in the plant could now be staffed by individuals who themselves lack sufficient training and education to function effectively. The organization must then provide them with the training to do the job, while the job assignment is still part of their general educational development.

A difference between just a regular job assignment and a rotational job assignment for purposes of education will depend in part on the appraisal system utilized. Where the assignment is part of the employee's educational development, the emphasis must be on what he has learned. This does not ignore his output during the assignment, his relationship with fellow employees and the other elements usually involved in any performance appraisal. But, in this instance, performance is not the main purpose of the assignment, and the appraisal criteria should reflect the true purposes.

In any job rotational experience, the employee can find that the job to which he has been rotated is so stimulating that he wants to stay in this position for a longer period of time. A sound education program should provide for this contingency. The individual should be permitted to elect to stay in the job as his regular position, not as part of his educational experience, without being penalized. It should not become a stopgap—he should not be rejected by the organization. Rather, now it becomes necessary for the personnel department to reassess the career pattern for this employee and for the HRD department to develop the new educational experiences appropriate to the new goals.

Field Trips

The very title of this educational experience evokes grimaces of pain in remembrance of such activities at the primary and secondary school levels. Yet, the technique is entirely appropriate and is closely linked to job rotation. Instead of rotating to a different job, the employee "rotates" to a different physical environment. Of course, the rotation is for a short period of time.

A field trip is an organized observational experience outside of the physical plant of the learner for a stipulated set of objectives. It should not be a junket, nor should it be utilized without a clear understanding of objectives by the employee and those responsible for authorizing the trip. Part of the growth experience is that the employee must develop his faculties for observation and sharing of his experience with others.

Larger organizations have a resource which is too infrequently used. Where the organization has offices or plants at a variety of sites, organized observations of these plants is a meaningful educational experience for an employee. A variation is to bring together employees from various sites in the form of task forces and project groups. These are temporary relationships which are highly task oriented. Employees are brought together from various parts and levels of the organization to work on a given problem. It is fascinating, in a large organization, to see how little they know of what goes on in the other fellow's area of operations. A compulsion exists to go outside the organization to hunt for resources which are often sitting close at hand.

The author experienced this while working as a member of the President's Task Force on the War Against Poverty in 1964. Individuals had been brought together from many of the agencies and departments of the U.S. government. It was not uncommon, during the course of a meeting, for the agenda to be laid aside while a member of the group explained his agency to those assembled. They had woefully inadequate data concerning the work of the other government employees. Although the purpose of assignment to the Task Force was not to educate its members, many found themselves taking part in a real growth experience. There is no reason why such an opportunity cannot be provided in a meaningful way for employees in large organizations. If organized appropriately, it is a resource for employee education programs.

Field trips can also be arranged outside the company to other companies. The same kind of educational experience can be made available when HRD personnel from different companies work together to provide a mutual set of field trips. Of course, the possibility of too freely sharing company secrets must be avoided, but this does not present too great a problem for most organizations. A mutual exchange among various companies in unrelated fields could prove to be an exciting educational experience for all, including the HRD department.

Public Seminars

Increasing use is being made of an outside resource known as the public seminar. These range from one day to two weeks and are open to anybody who will pay the fee. There are no restrictions on who can attend, and the result is a heterogeneous group of participants with a variety of reasons for attendance. For HRD activities, the public seminar is mainly an educational resource.

Aspects of the seminar are considered training when they are designed to help the participant do his present job more effectively. As public seminars take a broad approach to the topic to meet the needs of a varied audience, it is likely that those attending are receiving education rather than training or, a combination of both.

Seminars are offered by a variety of organizations, individuals and groups. The seminars may involve the vast resources of an university or the contributions of a single individual. Some are conducted in hotels/motels and other public meeting places. Others are conducted by organizations who have constructed special facilities as the meeting place for their public seminars.

As noted earlier, the public seminar can be used as training, but that is probably not the most effective use of it. The seminars are much more useful as a form of education providing the employee with a greater range of growth opportunity than would be available to him in-house. The mixing of individuals from other organizations can be a stimulating experience. As with any kind of educational experience, there must be an adequate period of planning with the employee before he goes to the seminar and provision for adequate follow-up on his return. The HRD staff must closely scrutinize the program being offered. If utilized as an education technique, it is different than when it is expected to have more direct results on the job.

For educational purposes, the public seminar can have its greatest impact in exposing the employee to new ideas, concepts and experiences. It can truly be a growth experience; the employee can begin to learn the terminology and behavior that may be expected of him as he moves into new areas of operation.

A difficult problem with public seminars today is the inability to truly assess beforehand the objectives of the seminar and the capability of the sponsor. There is great fluidity in the field, and the name of the sponsoring organization does not tell who will actually conduct the experience. Attending public seminars becomes a risk experience and, as such, the HRD director should be skeptical. However, it does offer so many advantages that it should not be shunned—only used cautiously.

Colleges and Universities

Colleges and universities have been offering off-campus educational opportunities since the efforts of Prof. Benjamin Sillman in 1808. The variety and level of the offerings have shown considerable fluctuation, reflecting the needs of the clientele and the quality of the offering institution. Today, there are more opportunities of this kind available than ever before. Many of our larger institutions have specifically built conference centers for use by off-campus groups coming on campus for educational programs. Notable among these are the Continuing Education Centers sponsored by the Kellogg Foundation on many campuses and individual efforts such as the Center of Adult Education at the University of Maryland.

Colleges and universities generally provide this resource under an extension division or a general studies program. The exact designation varies from one institution to another. Many institutions are members of the National University Extension Association, and reports of their activities in this field can be found in their publication, *The Spectator.*

Program offerings from the universities vary greatly. Some of the offerings are from their regular catalog and are available off campus, in or near the work site and on the same basis as on campus. The difference may be that they do not always utilize the on-campus instructor for conducting the program. There is no absolute standard, although it is assumed that the person hired to conduct an off-campus course will meet the experience and academic requirements for teaching that same course on campus. The courses can be offered as individual units or organized so as to result in a degree program (11). If there is a degree program being offered, the HRD staff must have a clear understanding of what is involved in order to receive the appropriate degree.

The problems of working with universities were set forth in a short but extremely clear article by Ernest E. McMahon, who at the time was Dean of University Extension at Rutgers. He summarizes:

> What it all boils down to is that colleges and universities vary, and at times their policies may be hard to understand. . .Few university policies are secret; many are logical; and some may be changed (12).

Junior or community colleges are a new movement in American educational life and have been growing at a faster rate than any other part of the educational system. They are but related to a particular geographical area.

Most of these educational institutions are open to influence and will develop programs for a particular client system. It is possible for the HRD staff to work with the faculty of these educational institutions and have them provide the kind of program which will be of benefit for a specific group of employees.

Tuition Refund

As employee education relies to a great extent on out-of-house resources, the question of payment becomes important. It is more than just money, for it also relates to the kind of dependency relationship which can result. Accordingly, tuition refund is being discussed as a methodology rather than as a budget item.

The variety of tuition refund programs is great. Essentially, it is a plan whereby an employee can have his employer pay all or part of the cost of his education. It is most commonly used with programs at universities, but it has application to public seminars and other educational out-of-house experiences.

Tuition refund introduces another element into the program—that of the commitment of the parties involved. When an employer pays all or part of the cost, obviously there is commitment on the part of the organization since its resources are being used for the benefit of an individual who in turn will bring increased knowledge into the organization. On the other hand, L. W. Gruenfeld, in a study to find the effects of tuition payment on a management development program, found:

> ...Those individuals who paid part of their own tuition reported that they derived more benefit from the program. The data make it safe to assert that those individuals who were involved and committed to the program valued it more and were relatively more satisfied with it than those for whom the program was free and relatively effortless (13).

An investment of money and time will bring greater results. How much this investment should be is a matter to be negotiated between the employee and the organization. The HRD director must establish some norms that can be used as a basis for this negotiation in the interest of the employee as well as of the organization.

The development of a tuition refund policy must involve several parts of the organization. Frederick H. Black, Jr., found in his study that at least the following were involved in the tuition refund programs he surveyed: immediate supervisor, department head, personnel director, training director (i.e., HRD director), as well as an Educational Assistance Committee (14).

On a more limited geographic basis, Roger Axford and Robert Schultz conducted a study in Northern Illinois and found that an overwhelming number of companies had tuition refund programs. Of those they surveyed, 60% pay tuition after a course is completed, while 30% either prepay the costs or do not charge the employee (15). The charge is waived where the company directly contracts for the educational program from an outside source and makes it available to the employees.

Policy Considerations

In establishing policies for employee education programs, the highest levels of the organization must be involved. These programs require the disbursement of company resources with no expectation of immediate benefits accruing to the organization. The expenditures require the same high level of consideration given to any investment of company resources for future growth.

Responsibility

The responsibility for employee education cannot be in the hands of the supervisor. Although the immediate supervisor of the employee being educated must be involved, it cannot be expected that the supervisor will devote any considerable portion of his time, energy or budget to educate an employee for the purpose of having him leave his area of operation. But, the supervisor cannot and should not be ignored. The supervisor carries the man on his unit work force and must be prepared to release him for job rotation, public seminars or any of the other educational experiences which require that he leave the job. An alternative is to assign the employee to a special unit within HRD. In limited situations, such an assignment may be helpful, but in the long run, it requires additional effort to help the employee reenter the system at the conclusion of his education.

Employee education must be part of an overall plan for the most effective use of human resources. Those in HRD must work closely with the personnel department, and each unit has its unique contribution to make to releasing human potential in any organization. Both must be reflecting the decisions of management. As management makes decisions affecting organizational activities, the personnel department is responsible for seeing that an adequate work force has been recruited and selected. The HRD responsibility is to see that this work force is given the appropriate educational experiences so as to be able to

perform the functions that management has previously identified.

Who Is To Be Educated?

In implementing an employee education program, more
than just the education of employees becomes involved. When
an individual is selected to participate in such a program, a
self-fulfilling prophecy comes into play, and what arises is the
phenomenon of the "crown prince effect." When it becomes
known in the organization that a particular individual is being
educated for a promotional position, this effectively minimizes
the possibility of anybody else being considered for the position.

One way of overcoming the closed approach is to identify
several employees to be considered for the position and have
each of them receive the appropriate educational experiences.
Only one of these will be promoted at this time, but the tactic
serves to keep several employees actively engaged in growing
and competing for the position. A real problem arises when the
decision is made. Those who were not appointed may then
become less effective employees. Having a higher level of expectation by virtue of their education, they may feel pressure to
utilize their new knowledge but find they must go to another
organization in order to have this opportunity. Inability to deal
with this kind of human problem is a strong contributing factor
to the reluctance to designate a program as educational leading
to promotion to a particular position. It is much easier to continue to lump all such programs under the heading of training
and avoid the confrontation.

Yet, the personnel department and the HRD group must
identify the employees to be trained for competence on their
present job, as contrasted with those who are being educated
for advancement. Uncertainty as to purpose denies to the employee a full understanding of why he is engaged in a particular
activity. He is inhibited from making the most effective use of

this opportunity for the purpose for which it has been designed. If there is a true interest in releasing human potential, educational opportunities must be available to a broad spectrum of people in the work force without a specific designation as to who will be promoted. There are some limitations described earlier in the crown prince effect, but by opening the potential growth opportunities to a larger number of people, there would be less stigma attached to those who are not promoted at a given time.

At first glance, such an approach might seem wasteful of company resources as it provides educational experience for many individuals whereas everybody knows that only one of these will be promoted. However, how much is really known about the potential of the work force? If a series of educational experiences are provided individuals may be found within the work force whose potential for the organization far exceeds anything that had previously been identified.

Budget

Training is an expense—education is an investment. When money is spent for training employees, there should be some expectation of an immediate return as the employee should be doing the present job at a higher level of competence. When money is spent on education to prepare an individual for a future position, an immediate improvement in job performance cannot be expected as that is not the purpose of the experience.

Just as the responsibility for education cannot rest in the hands of the line supervisor, likewise the budget for educating employees must be placed closer to the point of responsibility. As the education of the employee affects many elements of the organization, the administration of these funds are best placed in the hands of a committee representing at least the HRD department, the personnel department and one or more levels of management. For an individual employee, it might also include managers from the department to which he is moving. If they are involved in responsibility for the funds for his education, they are prompted to opt for more effective utilization of the expenditures.

The budget for education can be more effectively utilized and controlled if it is administered by the HRD department. By providing educational budgets in one place, it is possible for the HRD unit to negotiate the kinds of contracts with educational resources which are of greatest benefit to the employing organization.

Evaluation

Education is difficult to evaluate. This does not mean that no evaluation can take place but that, as with all aspects of HRD, evaluation must be related to objectives. If the objective is to prepare the employee to assume a new and higher position in the company, then the evaluation must be in terms of whether the employee is adequately prepared to assume this position. It becomes almost impossible to provide a complete evaluation until the employee has been placed on the new job and there has been a performance appraisal by his new supervisor.

In view of the investment of time, money and energy, it is unwise to wait for placement and performance on the job before taking some readings. The Goodyear Tire and Rubber Company has a five-year program for educating its industrial salesmen. However, it uses a multiple-stage approach so that at each phase it is possible to evaluate the progress of the person being educated, to determine if he should continue on to the next level (16).

Not only the employee but the organization must be constantly evaluated or surveyed. A phased approach, with specifically designated check points, can verify that the position for which he is being educated still exists. It is possible that managerial decisions will change the structure of the organization, and though HRD may have organized an excellent program, the job for which the individual is being prepared no longer exists.

Also, in dealing with the potential of individuals, the various educational experiences may open new possibilities of areas of which the individual was previously not aware. There should be points at which the employee can check his progress as well as enabling the HRD director to monitor this progress against some kind of previously developed set of goals.

Rather than decry the lack of evaluation, it would be well to look at the effforts of those who are applying the current state of knowledge to evaluate at least parts of educational programs. Public seminars have not escaped scrutiny. Vera Kohn and Treadway C. Parker applied Donald Kirkpatrick's four points to evaluating public seminars conducted by the American Management Association (17). College courses are usually not evaluated in an orderly fashion, but one such attempt for a course in behavioral science was conducted by Ronald J. Burke (18). The Motorola Company provides off-duty education at its Aerospace Center in Arizona and has studies of its drop-out problem (19).

There is much that still needs to be done to develop the evaluation procedures which are appropriate to an educational program. On the long range, the criteria for evaluation is whether the employee is placed on the job for which he is now prepared. If he is not placed in that position, it may not be because of an inadequate education program, but other factors may be present. The HRD group must develop evaluative criteria so the actual reasons for lack of placement can be identified. If it is due to a defect.in the HRD program, then much remains to be done.

Even after the employee is on the job, there must be a process to identify additional areas of needed growth. It must be determined if these are training or education needs so the appropriate actions can be taken to meet these needs.

Literature Citations

1. Bernard J. Bienvenu, *New Priorities in Training* (New York: American Management Association, 1969), p. 80.

2. Oscar N. Serbein, *Educational Activities of Business* (Washington: American Council on Education, 1961), p. 75.

3. Howard A. Sulkin and Wallace G. Lonegran, "Development of a Training Manager," *Training and Development Journal,* July 1969, pp. 28-31.

4. Laurence F. Peter and Raymond Hull, *The Peter Principle* (New York: William Morrow & Co., 1969).

5. *Forest Service Training and Development Handbook,*   FSH2 6123.4 (Washington: U.S. Department of Agriculture, 1963), p. 17.

6. James V. Clark, "A Healthy Organization" *The Planning of Change,* Warren Bennis, Kenneth Benne and Robert Chin (New York: Holt, Rinehard & Winston, 1969), p. 294.

7. Eugene E. Jennings, *The Mobile Manager* (Ann Arbor: The University of Michigan, 1967).

8. Barry T. Jensen, "The Route from Little Man to Middle Man," *Training and Development Journal,* March 1969, pp. 22-25.

9. George P. Sweeney, "The Industrial College Consortium," *Training and Development Journal,* September 1969, pp. 14-18.

10. Samuel W. Burt, *Industry and Vocational-Technical Education* (New York: McGraw-Hill, 1967), p. 41.

11. A study which reflects the various patterns and directions of university extension as a resource is Michael H. Jessup, "An Historical Analysis of the Development of Selected Areas of University Extension Programs in the U.S. 1900-1965, as Related in Professional Literature" (Ed.D. diss., The George Washington University, 1967).

12. Ernest F. McMahon, "University Policies and Training Problems," *Training and Development Journal,* May 1966, p. 33.

13. L. W. Gruenfeld, "Effects of Tuition Payment and Involvement on Benefit from a Management Development Program," *Journal of Applied Psychology,* vol. 50, 1966, pp. 396-399.

14. Frederick H. Black, Jr., "Educational Assistance Programs," *Training and Development Journal,* December 1967, pp. 42-46.

15. Roger W. Axford and Robert W. Schultz, "A Yearning for Learning—While Earning!" *Training and Development Journal,* March 1969, pp. 10-13.

16. D. R. Botto, "Five Good Years Make One Salesman," *Training in Business and Industry,* May 1969, p. 37.
17. Vera Kohn and Treadway C. Parker, "Some Guidelines for Evaluating Management Development Seminars," *Training and Development Journal,* July 1969, pp. 18-23.
18. Ronald J. Burke, "A Plea for a Systematic Evaluation of Training," *Training and Development Journal,* August 1969, pp. 24-29.
19. Wilburn C. Ferguson, "Dropouts from Adult Classes in Industrial Training," *Training and Development Journal,* February 1969, pp. 44-56.

5

Employee Development

Training has as its function the improvement of performance on the job. Education is geared to moving the employee on to a predetermined different position within the organization. Employee development is concerned with preparing the employee so that he can move with the organization as it develops, changes and grows. The result could be a new job at a higher level or an expansion of the current activities of the employee into new fields which are as yet undetermined.

In both training and education, the directions of the individual and the organization are identifiable. The growth activity which is required is likewise clear. Development is concerned with the future of the organization and the individual in directions which are not as clearly definable. The goals of employee development cannot be stated in specific behavioral terminology or specific terminal behaviors. It is not possible to identify the job that will be done, under what conditions and up to what standard of proficiency. The job is in the future and will evolve as the organization moves through its life cycle. Specific behavioral objectives are acceptable in a training program and even have some applicability to an education program. They are inappropriate for the broad goals of a development program.

Purposes

Employee development activities are designed to produce a viable and flexible work force for the organization as it moves toward its future. Programs of employee development can also produce a work force which is "overtrained." It is not expected that all the growth experiences to which employees are exposed will ultimately be used. There is a risk element involved and a concept of investment which goes beyond the present needs of the organization. As with most investments, there must be spokesmen within the organization who are concerned with encouraging the risk involved in any investment. It is much easier to support training programs which have immediate benefits. One can even lend support to education programs with identifiable benefits, though several years in the future. It is much more difficult for the HRD director to encourage his organization to invest in a vague though necessary program for the development of human resources for the future.

The need for such programs is difficult to state with sufficient clarity. It is not that the general need is unclear but rather that the specifics will vary with each organization. Also, the constantly shifting patterns of work and the economy have a greater impact on development programs than on training and education. Of course, the impact on training and education is more immediate and more visible. Therefore, the organizational system can respond quickly and in a way that can be seen by all. Development programs, concerned with long-range growth, do not change as rapidly or close enough to the surface for all to see.

This chapter can only explore a few of the forces which highlight the need for an employee development program. Within five years after this is written there will probably be new forces which are beyond anyone's ability to identify at this time. But, given present trends, it can be seen that it is necessary for organizations to plan for relevant and appropriate employee development programs.

Newer Forms of Internal Organization

During World War II, using the term "task force" was extensive. Today, the use of task forces is no longer limited to military operations. The technique has won praise as an effective means of using a variety of human resources within an organization to achieve organizational objectives. A task force is created by bringing together a group of persons within an organization with little regard for their organizational placement and level. Emphasis is on the resources they can bring to the task force to achieve the stated objective. The life of a task force is of limited duration. At times, it is possible to limit the life when it is organized, but it is more usual to keep it in operation until the objectives are either met or changed. During the life of the task force, the membership may change as newer directions are identified and other human resources are needed.

The task force endeavors to minimize levels of hierarchy. In 1964, when the author was a member of the President's Task Force on the War Against Poverty, there was practically no hierarchical structure, but two layers evolved in the organization. The first consisted of those who had prime responsibility and worked directly with Sargent Shriver. The remainder of the organization functioned at a second level and frequently crossed lines from one activity to another. It was not uncommon to see those concerned with Job Corps development meeting with Community Action task force members—and both working with the placement personnel of another agency. The Task Force drew from many government agencies as well as from universities and private companies. Within the Task Force there was constant movement in and out of small groups of those concerned with only certain elements of the program. Successful work on the Task Force required a tremendous amount of flexibility on the part of its members. One had to be able to move in and out of situations as they changed. To be identified with only a particular speciality and to look only toward one's own area of expertise doomed one to isolation, failure and removal from the Task Force. Those members of the Task Force who were prepared only to contribute from their own area had a short life, and the turnover was exceedingly great. This is as it should have been, but it highlighted the inability of many individuals to work effectively in an ambiguous situation where the normal power structure is absent. It underscored the necessity for developing capable individuals who would function outside their own particular area and therefore would be in a better position to make the contribution expected from each member of the Task Force.

In the aerospace industry, one of the most dramatic activities in the 60's has been man's movement into space and his walk on the moon. The accolades to the industry have been well earned. This infant industry grew to a giant by recognizing the value of a variation of the task force known as a project group. No exact definitions are available for these words, but generally a project group brings together various techniques and experts from different parts of the organization to deal with a particular problem. It is a temporary group, and as soon as the problem has been solved or redefined, the group disappears and will probably never again come together in the same fashion. The satisfactions that usually accrue from continued membership in an organizational unit are lacking in these newer forms of organization.

How does employee development relate to these changes in organizational relationships? It increases the tolerance for ambiguity on the part of those members of the organization who are part of the development activities. Through employee development, members of the organization can be exposed to the less traditional relationships and develop the flexibility which the newer forms of organization are demanding.

The preceding paragraphs by no means cover the wide range of newer forms of organization. The reader is urged to become familiar with some of the trends, but even as they are read about, newer forms are emerging (1). These newer forms of internal organization challenge the methodologies used in the past. Earlier employee training and employee education efforts have been geared toward making the individual more productive and efficient in a known situation. Using task forces and project groups and similar temporary work relationships demands a different expectation of the individual toward his job and his relationships. Likewise, it requires a new set of allegiances. When he is on the task force, the individual is no longer reporting to his superior and may not even be located in the same physical area, as in the past. The employee is now on his own—and is now a freer person. If an organization plans to use these newer forms of internal temporary units, employee development programs must be designed to prepare employees to function successfully in these fluid and ambiguous situations.

Organization Renewal

An interesting movement of the 60's has been the concern with the health of organizations. Business leaders began to recognize that an organization can continue to function in its usual patterns, until it dies, because it has lost its viability. The course of action is not necessarily to move toward newer forms of internal organization—this is an end result which might not be appropriate for all organizations. Rather, each organization must develop within itself the mechanism for constant self-examination and renewal.

Managers have often prided themselves on maintaining the kind of organization which could respond to changes in the market place. Such behavior has been effective in the past—but today an organization must be able to anticipate change. Therefore, the organization must build within itself the mechanism and the people prepared to look for change and its implications. Past successful performance is no longer adequate. The question "What have you done lately?" must now be supplanted by "What are you doing tomorrow?"

The most dramatic examples of the need for renewal are found in organizations with multi-plant sites. The geographical distance from the center of the organization has allowed for decision making in the field, and the managers of such distant locations have usually been measured by the profit picture of their operation. Then, suddenly, the central office may find that the profit picture has taken a disastrous turn—or that the profit is still high, but the share of the market is woefully disproportionate. Then, heads roll and massive changes take place. The organization might rather have asked itself, "How did this come to pass?" It is more than the traditional means of coordination and control. The question in a broader sense is directed to the organization building within itself the route whereby it can continually be seeking areas which in the future will require renewal.

The appreciation of the need for organization renewal requires a developmental concept on the part of the management. As the organization renews and develops, so must its human resources. Employee development programs are not the only means for encouraging organization renewal, but it is doubtful if renewal plans can be successful without employee development programs.

Nature of the Work Force

Persons entering the labor force today are different in many ways from those already in the work force. New workers are more attuned to a rapidity of change which is almost horrifying to the older worker. Much has been written about the rapidity of change, and it is not necessary to repeat it in this book. For those who want some of the specifics and how they interrelate, a book is available which contains this. John McHale (2) has brought together tables and charts showing how man's speed of travel has accelerated since 7000 B.C. Obviously, the speed accomplished in the last few years almost defies the imagination of those born in the early days of this century.

The interval between discovery and application in science has sharply contracted. Photography was discovered in 1727 but took 112 years to apply. Radar was discovered in 1925 but took 15 years to apply. The solar battery was discovered in 1953 and was applied in two years!

The younger worker is more receptive to rapidity of change, for it has been part of his heritage. Some see this as the impatience of youth rather than the result of the era in which they have been born.

The younger worker comes with an activist concept of our democracy. He has been taught that a democracy is different from other forms of government in many ways and that outstanding is its ability to be responsive to its constituents. He now seeks democracy in the market place as well as the voting booth.

Recent experiences in communities and in colleges have taught the younger worker that there are times when one must become less of a discussant and more of an activist. Usually, the private sector of the economy rewards the activist, the achievement-oriented worker. However, when the goals signifying the achievement differ from those of the power structure, conflict can be the result. The labor strife of the 30's is not too far beyond the personal recall of most people. In one sense, the goals are similar to those of young people today. They want opportunities for involvement and movement. They want "a piece of the action" and to be able to move without having to repeat the traditional steps for growth in an organization.

For persons in power, and that certainly includes most readers of this book, any challenge appears to be one for gaining control. Yet, the younger member of the work force is not looking to control the work situation—he is too much of a realist for that. But, he certainly wants to influence the situation. He is not content with promises of deferred gratification. The college graduate has had four to six years of deferred gratification. The returning draftee who has completed his military service—he too has been fed on deferred gratification. The result is an earnest and healthy desire to have something happen now.

Employee development programs can meet the needs for influence and movement. A good employee development program must involve the employee and allow him to influence the kinds of experiences and activities which will be part of his program. He does not want to tell the HRD director how to organize and administer the program. He wants to be listened to—not merely treated as a formless lump of clay which will be molded into a company image.

The new employee is looking for movement within the organization, and employee development programs can provide such movement. It can answer the need for a challenge for the younger members of the work force who are not merely seeking security.

Human Potential

Releasing human potential is a necessity. People usually have more in them than expected and can be more effective than they are. The gravity pull of role expectancy and self-fulfilling prophecies have deprived many organizations of the true potential of their employees.

Employee training is necessary to get jobs done. Employee education is necessary to move people ahead in the organization and to have employees ready to assume higher level positions. Employee development is necessary if the potential of those currently working is to be released.

In the process of meeting production quotas, producing the appropriate ratio of profit and just keeping the organization going, the potential of the work force is frequently minimized.

Quotas, profit and on-going operations are essential—without these, there is no organization. But, if these become the only purposes of an organization, it is less likely to draw from the more innovative elements of the work force. The organization may have an aggressive recruiting campaign, only to find that retention is low. As individuals seek to grow on jobs, they need a legitimate and available mechanism for growth and development. If the organization does not provide it, they will either take their creativity and potential off the job or leave the job.

Practices

The practices used in employee development are not completely discernible. This is probably the largest area of the HRD picture where additional research is desperately needed. Although some of the practices of the past can be used, it is essential that newer methods and resources be explored if improved ways of developing the labor force are to be found.

Practices in employee development vary greatly and frequently are the reflection of the capability of the HRD staff responsible. The literature in this area is difficult to find, and many of the practices have not yet appeared in the professional journals. As with any emerging area, the experiences are accumulating faster than the ability to report and share them. In addition, there is a hesitancy to record experiences. Companies are still bound, like Prometheus to the rock, trying to show that a return is being received on the expenditure of the HRD dollar. One company, which must remain nameless, developed a practice of taking employees who had been with the organization for five years or more and sending them away for six months of a developmental experience completely unrelated to the position they now hold. For example, the employee who was a physicist might be sent for six months of study in the field of finance. When the HRD man related this experience, he was strongly urged to write it up for it was the kind of practice about which more people needed to know. He responded with the caution that if this practice were to appear in print, the stockholders might strongly object to spending company funds for an activity which would not bring a direct return to the organization. This is one of the largest hurdles that must be overcome in trying to put together a picture of what is happening today in the field of employee development.

An example of an employee development program can be found in the U.S. Treasury Department. In 1962, there was the realization that the computer would have an increasing impact on their operations. Accordingly, 1,500 employees were given a two-day program to familiarize them with the concept of the computer. This was truly development—it was a planned experience for a group of employees into an area which was not directly related to their job at the time. Also, there was no objective of making them computer operators. It was an employee development activity within the definition used in this book.

Where an organization does not engage in employee development, it is misleading if a scapegoat is sought in the stockholders, the public or some other large and faceless group. Identifiable individuals closer to the organization must assume the burden for lack of involvement in employee development and lack of publicity of their practices. Many of those who today have responsibility for human resource development in their organizations are still seeking the lodestone which will turn HRD into increased profits or reduced costs. These are more measurable, appeal to higher echelons and sound good in annual reports. Possibly, more development of human resource developers is needed!

The practices discussed below will differ from the previous two chapters. In addition to identifying some of the existing practices, some of the kinds of employee development activities which are thought to contribute to the purposes of this activity are suggested, but no evidence has yet been found that they are being utilized.

Organized Classes

The industrial classroom is an effective place for employee development. The HRD man should not rush into sending his people outside the company and overlook the tremendous resource which exists within the company. The difference is in the way in which the resource is used. For example, the Florida Power and Light Company developed its own "college." This was taught by employees for employees and is referred to in-house as the Training Opportunities Program (TOP). Of course, it is not training as used in this book, nor is it even employee education. There was no intent to improve either job performance or a specific growth pattern within the organization. Yet, it was amazingly popular. In 1969, the TOP offered 40 courses ranging from speed reading to advanced physics. The objective was not to improve the employees' capability on the job, though there is always the possibility that this could happen. The prime purpose was to provide employees with a developmental experience resulting in their broader use and capability. It reflects the desire of individuals for growth and in this case will probably bring future benefits to the company. Significantly, they reported that 89% of their employees had completed at least one course in TOP.

A more common organized classroom is that provided by colleges and universities. When used for employee development, counseling should be provided so the employee does not take those courses which have his training and education as their objective. The employee should be encouraged to explore new horizons and become involved in classrooms which are unrelated to anything he is now doing. Some of the more common courses might be in the liberal arts area as this usually has been one of the shortages among the work force.

Cross-job Exposure

The in-house resources for developing personnel are limitless. Too often, an employee will be identified with only one kind of work or with only one kind of activity. Stereotypes rapidly develop, and if you look around your organizations, you will find that people are classified as types. "He is a finance man" or "She is a clerical" and so on. Why is there surprise when it is discovered that the individual who prepares the company payroll spends his weekends taking art courses? If individuals are to be helped in developing, then the key is provision of opportunity for new experiences.

It is a high risk practice, but why cannot an organization transfer a salesman into a personnel position for a short period of time? This would not be directed toward making him a personnel man or even suggesting that he belong in a personnel function. It would be helpful for him to experience a different kind of stimulus in his daily work. The experience must be carefully thought out and planned, for the purpose is not job rotation. There is no objective that, as a result of this experience, the individual now will be able to do a job or know it in any significant way. Rather, it is an experience in broadening an individual so that he gets to see things he has never seen before. In larger organizations, there should be no difficulty with this kind of cross-job experience. The result can be individuals who have a much larger concept of what the organization is all about and how to accomplish its functions.

During this period of cross-job experience, the production of the employee will be lost as it would in any HRD practice. The employee should not be expected to return to his job and immediately apply what he has learned. Rather, it is opening windows on new worlds—but worlds which exist within his own organization. Of course, some of this is done with the usual orientation program. If it is a good program, a direct return in the form of reduced costs is not sought; but something called "proper attitude" and "identification with the organization." Despite inability to measure the results of orientation, it is generally agreed that such programs are a necessity.

How about reorientation? Why can not a program be provided, later in the life of the employee with the organization, when he is once again exposed to various parts of the organization which he normally would not see? Instead of just telling him about these vague parts, why not a planned opportunity for him to experience them?

Mutual Exchange Programs

There are numerous out-of-house resources which are available, and many more can be developed. A prototype for one kind of out-of-house experience—the mutual exchange program—can be found in similar activities conducted by the U.S. government since World War II. As part of the various foreign aid programs, there has been a component known as "participant training."

Through these programs, individuals have come to the United States for different lengths of time. In some cases, they came for training and education, but there were also some which fit under the classification of development. The visits to the United States were for as little as three weeks but usually were for six weeks. During this period, the participant had a series of organized visits to a variety of companies but did not spend more than one day in any company. In some cases, the visits would only be of half-day duration. It proved to be an excellent technique for one aspect of development—for expanding horizons of leaders in other countries. Of course, a good deal of the success of the program was due to the cooperation of the numerous U.S. companies who opened their doors. The author accompanied a Japanese group in the United States in 1959 as they visited several companies in the fork lift truck industry. The questions were penetrating and the answers from the hosts were amazingly complete and open.

During his work in Japan with the Agency for International Development, the author was involved in sending more than 5,000 Japanese to the United States for such developmental experiences. When the Japanese participants returned to Japan, he would usually meet with them and discuss their experiences in the United States. Although the official terminology for such developmental experiences was "observations," they were certainly much more than that. During the debriefing sessions, he was constantly amazed at the newer insights the Japanese participants had received from such a short exposure. They returned and now saw their own organizations in a new light.

There was the experience of Kazuharu Nakamura of Chubu, president of a small stove manufacturing company. He had always followed the traditional Japanese pattern of long hours and hard work for his employees. The introduction of a wage incentive plan was considered inappropriate, for wages, at that time, were not a criteria for reward in the Japanese social and industrial system (3). After visiting the United States, Mr. Nakamura returned to Japan with a new idea which he decided to implement. He established the quota of how many stoves his company needed to manufacture in a given period of time in order to return a reasonable profit on his investment. This was then broken down into daily production quotas. When the quota for the day was met, the workers were now released and had additional free time. They could spend this time with their families, at a baseball game or in various cultural pursuits which are so popular in Japan, among men as well as women. The quota for the day had to be met before the released time plan was effective. In any given day when they were not producing the quota (because of the usual idiosyncrasies of any production system), the workers might be expected to work without additional pay, within certain limits. The employer said, about three years after his return, that he had observed such a system in a small American plant. As he had visited over 20, he could not identify the exact company. By introducing this into his own company, he now had a more consistent production schedule, the workers were extremely pleased and even the quality had been improved without any special provision for this. Mr. Nakamura reported that he thought this idea, among others he had observed in the United States, had developed a feeling of independence among his workers and, at the same time, a closer relationship to the problems and ambitions of management (4).

Such growth experiences are not only available in overseas settings. There is enough cultural and individual difference within this nation's borders to make such mutual exchange programs successful. Of course, an organization with overseas branches and affiliates does have an additional resource should it engage in such activities for employee development.

Employees should not be sent on these exchange experiences with the objective of returning and immediately applying their observations. The basic purpose of this practice is to provide the employee with an opportunity for a new experience which he previously has not had and which enables him to develop a broader view of his organization and of the world at work. An exciting possibility is for a group of organizations to establish a mutual exchange program among themselves. This may exist in some places, but no evidence of it could be found. Under such a plan, a group of companies would agree to exchange employees at a variety of levels for stipulated periods of time. During the exchange, the employees would not be expected to be productive. The range of experiences would have to be carefully worked out. Of course, there is the ever present specter of the competitor "stealing" industrial secrets. (I would not want to oversimplify this problem, but it may not be a great obstacle.) The host company would not be expected to open wide its doors without any reservations, and the visitors would realize that there are certain limitations.

Such exchange programs are not a one-way developmental experience; the visitors would also be sharing. In the case of the Japanese groups, they prepared pamphlets on the history and status of their particular companies, industries and practices. These were given to their American hosts and opened up funds of information to them that would not otherwise have been available. Also, the visitors ask questions. Often, the host has a developmental experience as he seeks the answer among his own behavior and the company practices. After the visitors leave, the real developmental work might begin on some concepts triggered by the visit.

Visits need not be made by groups but could be done on an individual basis. The duration and objectives need to be mutually explored and agreed on. There are exciting possibilities in such a practice—will reports of this be found in our literature in the next five years?

Organization and Self-Renewal

John Gardner emphasizes the responsibility of the individual for his own development (5). It is likely that the key to employee development practices lies within each individual. Rather than a structure of experiences, HRD should provide each employee with the possibility of exploring his own area for renewal and development. Of course, where the expenditure of company assets is concerned, there must be some controls. But reliance on terminal behavioral outcomes inhibits the possibility of any real renewal or innovation on the part of the individual employee. The famous quote attributed to Lord Acton also has a message. He wrote, "Power tends to corrupt; absolute power corrupts absolutely." In self-renewal, specific objectives tend to limit renewal and specific terminal behaviors eliminate the possibilities of development.

A newer trend has been variously called "organization development" and "organization renewal." It is likely that other terms will be coined to identify the phenomena of an organization seeking to improve its climate and leadership for change. The rapid spread of the practice is evidenced by the organization within the American Society for Training and Development of a special Organizational Development Division. Gordon Lippitt suggests that there may even be a professional field developing in this area (6).

In any case, the practice of organization renewal is rapidly expanding. Alongside its growth is the recognition of concern with people. As this is being written, the various activities under the heading of organization renewal and/or development are steadily increasing. This trend may serve to highlight the equally important goal of employee development—of employee renewal. Hopefully, preparation will be made to allocate sufficient company resources to developing individuals as is now planned to be allocated for the renewal of the organization.

Think Tank

Increasing use has been made of the management retreat or getting them "off the ranch." It is recognized that a new environmental setting can contribute to a more effective learning possibility. Some retreats have the express purpose of solving problems within the organization and in that sense are not primarily designed for employee development. Under the guidance of a skilled leader, problems will get solved, and, in addition, the benefits of a developmental experience can be received.

The next stage, beyond the management retreat, might be the "think tank." This is an environment in which production is secondary, except the production of new ideas. Too many people relate the think tank to the various military-oriented projects, such as the Rand Corporation. On the strictly civilian side is the Center for the Study of Democratic Institutions in Santa Barbara, California. Here, a continual dialogue is maintained to clarify basic issues and widen the circles of discussion about them (7). Another kind of think tank is the Center for Advanced Study in the Behavioral Science at Stanford, California. The stimulating experience there enabled Arthur Koestler to write a book (8).

Why not have think tanks for all employees and not only for executives? These could be carefully designed centers, catering to a wide range of organizations, with the facilities and environment for creative thinking and self-renewal. The reader may immediately call to mind the myriad of conference centers springing up throughout the country. These have a good and useful purpose but are still directed toward conducting sessions. One is not free to roam alone, to spontaneously dialogue with others, to break the mealtime routines and to engage in other kinds of discovery activities in the search for self-renewal and development. The day can be foreseen when such centers will likewise proliferate, but not for many years to come. An effort in this direction was made by Frank Sherwood as he directed the U.S. Civil Service Executive Training Center at Charlottesville, Virginia. Toward the end of the first year of operation, the resounding cry in Washington was criticism for an activity which allowed participants to select their own learnings and activities. This should not be construed as a criticism of government, for there are no nongovernmental operations of this kind which are sponsored and participated in by private industry.

Policy Considerations

After having started with employee training and moving through employee education and now into employee development, it has become obvious that the move is upwards in the hierarchy of the organization. Employee development requires the commitment of the upper levels of the organization and their intense involvement and full support. This means dealing with a high risk situation, and risk taking is not as prevalent at lower levels. As employees develop, they will find within themselves latent capabilities which are not usable within their own organization. The employee must then leave and go elsewhere to meet individual growth needs and self-expectations. The process is of the swinging gate variety, for the organization can likewise expect to receive persons from outside who are now looking for a different organization which turns them on. It is more than a game of musical chairs. It is related to the goals of the individual and the stage of the various organizations. Policy making for employee development must be high enough in the organization and visible enough to all so the HRD staff is not accused of encouraging turnover.

Responsibility

It is difficult to establish the point of responsibility for employee development programs. It is related to the point of responsibility for the entire organizational growth. Both of these purposes, organizational growth and employee development, must be related. The actual operation of the program is best left in the hands of the HRD group if they are sufficiently attuned to the emerging patterns within the organization. Once again, the situation arises where seldom is a superior rewarded for devoting his time to developing individuals who then leave his particular unit. In the case of employee development, it is likely that if the individual is going to work in a project or task force, if he is going to work in any other activity outside the purview of his direct supervisor, it is unlikely that his superior will devote energies and resources to employee development. It is not necessary to remove the employee from under his present supervisor but to find ways that the organization can reward supervisors for developing employees.

It is easy to reward supervisors for training as this is directly related to the production of the unit for which he is responsible. It is more difficult to reward the supervisor for contributing to the education of his employee, and as was suggested in the previous chapter, it should not be expected that the supervisor should assume this responsibility. With employee development, behavior is sought which is generally beyond the norm found in most organizations.

Appraisal

It is important to establish a point of responsibility, for there is the necessity for appraisal even in employee development. It may be difficult to measure but not impossible. The appraisal of an employee developmental system is related to an appraisal of the organization itself. As with most measurement, it must be related to goals. This requires an adequate clarification of goals to help employees develop rather than improve specific job performance. If an organization insists on only supporting those employee development activities which it can adequately measure, it forces itself to withdraw from the arena of employee development. Such an organization may effectively conduct a training program and possibly an education program. Using the same measurement techniques, it cannot effectively have an employee development program.

The challenge being faced is to find more appropriate ways to measure employee development activities and to relate these to the organizational goals. Just as newer ways of measuring organizational patterns are being developed, more advanced ways of measuring employee development activities need to be developed. The pressure in recent years toward quantification of data and emphasis on specific behavioral outcomes are not appropriate to employee development. If refining the statistics and improving the ability to state objectives is emphasized, the entire point of employee development will probably be missed.

At the other end of the spectrum, there must be some reason for allocating organizational resources to this activity. The work being done on human resource accounting has the possibility of providing one breakthrough into a new era for employee development. The next decade should tell.

Relationship to Organizational Development

It has been suggested that organizations have life cycles and growth stages which are identifiable (9). It has not yet been possible to apply similar models to employee development. An alternative is to try to match employee development programs against the growth stages of the organization. It could help in planning programs as well as in obtaining some assessment of the desirable direction for the employee development programs.

The rapidity of change which is all around is encouraging the formation of new kinds of organizations. As the direction of an organization is identified and planned, it is important that the plans provide for appropriate kinds of personnel. Without careful planning, a dangerous time lag can develop. The leaders of the organization can decide on directions and movements and then find that they lack the appropriate personnel who are prepared to fill the new needs of the organization.

As an organization moves ahead, it must be prepared to be flexible and to react to external forces as well as to internal forces. Likewise, the human resources of the organization must also be prepared to move in appropriate directions. Any organization recognizes that not every investment will pay off. There are times when it becomes necessary for risk taking. Without risk taking, there will be little or no growth, and the organization will die. In developing its human resources, the organization must likewise be prepared for a certain amount of risk taking. It must be prepared to develop various human resources fully recognizing that not all of these resources may ultimately be utilized.

It is not suggested that organizations resort to the stockpiling which was prevalent in the early 1950's with groups such as engineers. Various organizations, utilizing the services of engineers, developed a practice of hiring more than they needed and trying to keep them on payroll until sufficient contracts had been obtained to warrant these professional employees. It resulted in a horrible waste of human resources and dissatisfaction among engineers. It is likely that any organization trying to gear up to meet market needs may have to resort to a certain amount of resource stockpiling. There should be a clear recognition that it also produces a situation in which those who are in the stockpile become bored with merely sitting and move on to other organizations, or worse, lose their motivation to fulfill themselves by their work.

The Challenge

Employee development is truly a product of the hectic 60's. It needed to be built on its counterparts of employee training and employee education. But, just as the complacency of the 50's gave way to the turbulence of the 60's, so must preparation be made to expand the limited areas of human resource development.

As this is being written in the opening days of the 70's, it is not possible to predict the issues and concerns which will prove crucial in this decade. The increasing concern with people is clear, and human resource development must move into employee development with increased concern and allocation of organizational resources.

Literature Citations

1. A fuller discussion of newer ways of organizing and other aspects of newer relationships can be found in Warren Bennis and Philip Slater, *The Temporary Society* (New York: Harper & Row, 1968).
2. See particularly Section III, "The Future of the Present," *The Future of the Future,* John McHale (New York: George Braziller, 1969).
3. Wages, fringe benefits and labor costs are discussed in Leonard Nadler, *Employee Training in Japan* (Los Angeles: Education and Training Consultants, 1965).
4. This finding, as well as others, has been reported in *Japan's Small Industry Grows Up,* second in a series of reports on American Technical Cooperation to Japanese small enterprises, 1955-1961, published jointly by the U.S. Operations Mission to Japan and the Japan Productivity Center, Tokyo, 1962.
5. John Gardner, *Self-Renewal.*
6. Gordon L. Lippitt, *Organization Renewal* (New York: Appleton-Century-Crofts, 1969), p. 291.

7. Statement of the Board of Directors quoted by Robert S. Hutchins, "The Center in the Sixties and Seventies," *The Center Magazine,* September 1969, p. 8.

8. Arthur Koestler, *The Ghost in the Machine* (New York: The Macmillian Company, 1967), p. xiii. The book itself is concerned with man's urge for self-destruction.

9. An interesting approach to this concept can be found in the short but highly provocative pamphlet by Warren H. Schmidt and Gordon L. Lippitt, *Managing the Changing Organization* (Washington: Leadership Resources Inc., 1968).

6

Nonemployee Development

Within Section II of this book, up to this point, the focus has been on employees. Now the focus shall turn to exploring HRD for nonemployees. Increasingly, organizations and agencies are becoming more involved in a variety of activities for nonemployees in the area of human resource development. Within this chapter, some of the activities in the area of HRD will be explored and discussed. But by no means will it cover all the possibilities and variations. The list of activities is virtually endless, and it is likely that the increasing social consciousness of the 60's has encouraged more activity. If the trend continues, increased activity in this area can be expected during the 70's.

The major distinction between this chapter and the preceding three chapters is that concern will now be with individuals who are not regular employees of the organization providing the HRD experience. Frequently, the person who is a nonemployee of the organization providing the HRD experience will be an employee of some other organization or those who are not employed by any organization, such as the student or the housewife. Even though neither may be planning to enter the work force in the near future, they are nonemployees benefiting from HRD programs of sponsoring organizations. Specific examples and further discussion of this point will be found later in this chapter.

Sometimes there is a partial or temporary relationship, as is found in work-study or cooperative programs. Another variation is the short-term arrangement, such as a draftee in a military situation. In general, such individuals are not expecting to have a significant or long-term work relationship with the organization. They are avowedly transient and therefore are included in the nonemployee category. Also, the organization exercises less control over such nonemployees than is usually the case with their regular work force. However, the examples cited earlier in the paragraph are neither the norm nor the bulk of the nonemployees to be discussed.

The nonemployee differs from the regular employee in two aspects. First, the nonemployee is more likely to be in a voluntary relationship from which he can withdraw. Second, there is a wider range of time possibilities with a nonemployee than with an employee.

Control over the learner can be significant. In the usual employer-employee relationship in a free society, an employee does not have to remain with an employer. He can choose to leave at any time. Actually, though he has free choice, any decision for movement is based on a variety of factors. Loss of pension plan rights, seniority, location, family relationships, transportation and age of the employee are only some of the factors which must be considered. Accordingly, the employee usually must hesitate before actively considering a change of position. Therefore, when an employee is assigned to an HRD program, he will usually comply with the management assignment with little question or hesitation.

For the nonemployee there are also constraints, but usually they are not nearly as influential as those in the life of an employee. The nonemployee may be in a completely voluntary situation in which he can withdraw at any point without the prospect of punishment by the sponsoring organization. This is common in the voluntary organizations and in some professional membership organizations where the membership does not necessarily relate to his ability to practice his profession. To withdraw from the American Medical Association can produce more negative results than withdrawing from the Adult Education Association.

There are mixed dimensions, for example, as in a school situation. A school offers HRD to its nonemployee student body. If the program is sponsored by the student's company, withdrawal from school can be seen as a rejection of the company program rather than possible dissatisfaction with the school. The voluntary behavior of the student is once again circumscribed. The student may have to remain in the school in order to receive benefits, such as those offered by the Veterans Administration or in certain programs related to welfare benefits.

Apprenticeship programs or work-study programs contain a greater degree of control but the learner still has an option to withdraw. If he exercises this option, he either eliminates or reduces the possibility of future employment with this organization and possibly others. In few cases, however, is there the same kind of almost absolute control an employer has over the HRD activities he provides for his employees.

Another distinction is in the length of the relationship. The range of nonemployee relationships can last from one day (e.g., a public seminar) to a lifetime (e.g., in a professional organization). There is usually a consistency. Public seminars have a distinct and stipulated life. Infrequently do they last more than three days. The nonemployee entering the relationship is quite aware that it is of a limited duration. A student enrolled in a four-year college curriculum knows that it will generally take him four years of a temporary relationship with the institution which is providing HRD for him. A doctoral student is not nearly so fortunate, for he does not know how long the relationship will last. However, as differing from an employee, the graduate student nonemployee has a goal, and once this has been reached, he is expected to sever his nonemployee relationship with the sponsoring institution. Even though the duration of the relationship can last for several years, both parties have entered into it with the knowledge that it is only temporary.

The HRD Concept

The same distinction will be made in this chapter as in the earlier parts of this book. Human resource development is the general designation for activities which can be described as training, education and development. Given the differences of duration and relationship, the three activities under HRD require some slight reorientation.

Training is still job oriented and provides the skills needed to be useful in an activity of a sponsoring organization. It is also the minimal skills needed to use somebody's product, or experiences related to helping the nonemployee perform his activities for an organization.

Education for nonemployees has as its purpose the general growth of the individual toward a specific goal or direction. This may be a degree or a certificate. It can be experiences which are beyond the present position of the nonemployee but which will make him more eligible for a new position at a higher level in some organization.

Development contributes to the general growth of the individual in the directions in which his organization or society is going. The experience is not directly occupational, nor is it directed toward a specific goal, except the goal of individual growth and development.

These are just general statements. In this chapter, the specifics will be spelled out with examples and further discussion. Despite this, the reader may experience some frustration, as one chapter will be insufficient to explore this vast field. Each of the following sections could warrant its own book dealing with HRD. For purposes of this book, the discussion of nonemployee HRD is limited to only the following areas: business and industry, government, voluntary and professional organizations, consulting and training organizations, schools and labor unions. The choice is made so as to include a variety of sponsoring organizations and groups yet at the same time relate these to the readers of this book. The same concepts, for a different reader group, would produce a different listing.

Business and Industry

As used in this section, the term "business and industry" basically encompasses activities in the private sector. These are profit-making companies that are organized to provide goods and/or services to a consuming public. In some cases, the public might be the ultimate consumer. In others, it may be a company that provides goods and/or services to an organization which then meets the needs of the ultimate consumer. In other words, here the concern centers around the myriad of organizations in the private sector that were the focus of the earlier parts of this book.

Customer Training

Providing training for customers is probably the most obvious and widespread practice among organizations in the private sector that provide HRD for nonemployees. There is a wide variety of such activities, and not all of them may be seen as customer training. The kinds of activities which are identified range from training the person who has bought the product to creating a market for a product where one may not have previously existed. The thrust is to enable the customer to use the equipment or product effectively.

Larger electronic firms conduct extensive customer training programs including a familiarization program when the new product is delivered. Another form of training takes place when the equipment is delivered and installed, where the customer's employees will receive training on how to operate and maintain the equipment. This is common with production machinery, computers and other large installations. The training of the customer's employees is automatic and frequently written into the purchase contract. The installation of new business machines in an office can require customer training, particularly if the customer has not previously used similar or related office machines. The telephone company conducts a series of training programs for its customers, particularly its business customers. These may be at the customer's site or within special training facilities for customers which the telephone company maintains at various points throughout the country. A common training program is a one-day activity which includes operation of equipment, telephone courtesy and procedures for taking messages.

Anyone who owns an automobile is familiar with customer training, though it may not have been seen in this light. The automobile manufacturing companies conduct mechanic training for nonemployees of private persons having dealerships. The manufacturers train the employees of their dealers so the product they produce can be serviced.

Such training is fairly common today because of a growth in the franchise operations, particularly in what is called the "fast food" area. These are the carry-out type of places which offer hamburgers as a staple, but the field is rapidly expanding to even provide gourmet foods. The franchiser, as part of his arrangement, agrees to provide nonemployee customer training. That is, the franchiser will train the employees of the franchise holder.

Although it can still be called customer training, there are some activities which are more designed to create customers for the organization. Programs are conducted involving training in order to create a market. A brokerage house may offer courses on "How to Invest" or "Your Place in the Stockmarket" as a way of encouraging new investors. Whether conducted within the brokerage house, at a community college or in a local Y, the training is designed to make the nonemployee a better investor. Of course, it is hoped that he will place his orders through the firm that has provided the instructor for the training program. For a nonemployee who takes this course with the positive intent of investing, or who is already investing, this can be called training. Where the nonemployee is merely taking the course out of interest, or because he wants more familiarity with the market, this is education. In both cases, the actual learning can be measured by the same techniques. However, a better evaluation for the nonemployee in training is to follow up as to how he uses the results of his training for guiding his investment practices. For the nonemployee who has taken it for educational purposes, the appraisal of the success of the program is in whether or not he becomes an investor.

The list of examples could easily continue. The point has been made—there are numerous activities in this area of nonemployee HRD. Unfortunately, these activities are usually not seen as HRD but as sales, public relations or some other aspect of organizational operations. As a result, the sponsoring business or industry loses the use of one of its most valuable in-house resources, its HRD operation. Also, as most HRD practitioners have limited themselves only to dealing with employees, they have overlooked an area where their services could be of more use to their own organizations.

Cooperative Programs

Cooperative programs, sometimes referred to as work-study programs, have been common in the United States particularly since the early 1900's. For years, the major focus in this area was on "distributive education" or "retail sales training." The actual practices in cooperative programs vary greatly so that any brief description would not cover the range of the field. The purpose of such programs is to provide linkage between the educational setting of the student and the real work situation for which he is being prepared. The cooperative approach is used in secondary school, in undergraduate work in college and in graduate work in universities. In the case of graduate work, a more common term is "internship."

Generally, the program works in the following manner. The learner will be enrolled in some type of educational program. As an aspect of this, he will be provided with an actual work program in an organized fashion related to his occupational goals. The host or sponsoring organization, usually in the private sector, agrees to provide a meaningful work experience. The learner works under guidance within specified terms set forth in a cooperative agreement. There is no intent that the organization providing the educational experience for the nonemployee will then hire him upon successful completion. However, an obvious benefit to the sponsoring organization is the provisions of a continual source for its manpower needs for entry-level employees.

Manpower Pool

During the 60's, many private companies entered into programs concerned with improving the manpower pool for the nation. Starting with the Plans for Progress of 1961 and continuing through the National Alliance of Businessmen in 1968, the private sector took a more active part in developing manpower resources of the nation. Although both of these programs were essentially controlled by the private sector, government funds were used to encourage more organizations to participate and to spread the burden of helping new segments of citizens to productively enter the work force. Probably the greatest movement was toward the end of the 60's with the NAB and its concentration on the "hard-core disadvantaged."

The amount of research on these programs has been sparse so far, and maybe this is just as well. More activity is needed before exposing some of these programs to the scrutiny of critical researchers. This does not mean that the programs should be above research (1). Government funds as well as private company resources are being allocated to this activity, and there should be accountability. This particular activity involves the lives of people who have too often before been given false hopes, and research is needed to determine if goals are being reached.

For the present, these programs have as their major focus not only the entry of minority group members more actively into the work force but also providing employees for specific companies. A study conducted during the summer of 1969 was started with the premise that one criteria for identifying success in such programs was to look for a turnover rate among the new hires (i.e., hard-core) which would be the same as, or lower than, that of the regular work force (2). This criteria proved misleading. Turnover was not a satisfactory criteria—rather, one had to go further and determine what happened to the new hires after they left their original employment. Did they return to the ghetto with no hope and increased antagonism toward the society which was failing them? Or, as was more often the case, did they now have an improved self-image, some job skills and the resultant mobility found among most of the work force? In the case of the Bankers Trust Company, the latter proved to be the case. The new hires now went into the hungry labor market for office employees in New York City.

This suggests that programs for the new hires may be more than just employee training and employee development programs. Organizations in the private sector are now providing training and education programs for persons who may not stay as their employees. During the period of training, they are certainly employees of the organization, for this is one of the basic components of the NAB program. However, after completing training and having a successful job experience, there is the possibility of the new hire moving out from the company which has trained him. He now becomes an indistinguishable part of the normally mobile labor force. As more experience is gained with these programs, more movement in this direction will probably be seen. The private sector, still with some assistance from the government, will provide training for persons who it does not really expect to remain with the sponsoring company. These nonemployees will be trained by Company A and then go off to work for Company B. When there are sufficient programs of this nature, there will be a more highly skilled work force. The smaller companies who cannot afford training will still be able to obtain trained workers—but they will have been purposely trained by another company. Various proposals in the 91st Congress indicated movement in this direction, though it is still probably a few years in the future.

At present, such efforts are secondary to the major activities of having companies provide jobs and training for the various groups labeled "hard-core" in society. As the 70's continue it is likely that this program will be expanded in a variety of ways, and the private sector organizations will be involved in greater depth in various kinds of nonemployee training activities.

The impression should not be left that companies engage in these activities only because of the government sponsorship. As with many government programs, this is only "seed" money with the objective of encouraging the private organizations to then continue to provide such training without government assistance. It is still too early to tell whether this will happen or not. Organizations, like Eastman Kodak, have been engaged in such training programs since 1960 without any government funds. It is a mixture of altruism and reality on the part of that company. The reality is that during most of the decade of the 60's, there was a national average unemployment rate of over 4%. Rochester, where Eastman Kodak has its major facilities, had only a 2% unemployment rate. Obviously, Eastman Kodak engaged in special and unusual activities in order to assure itself of a manpower supply. At the same time, it provided encouragement for the entire Rochester community by contributing to the development of community action agencies, such as Rochester Jobs Inc. and the Accelerated Clerical Training program sponsored by the Urban League of Rochester.

The bulk of the programs under this heading are job skill training programs. The objective of the program is to place the individual on a job, and, therefore, training was the appropriate aspect of HRD to be utilized. However, it also became necessary to provide education, particularly remedial education to raise the literacy level of these new hires to a satisfactory level. The literacy training was partly job oriented in that it enabled the individual to qualify for and hold a job. But it also provided for education above and beyond what was just merely needed on the job. This was found to be not only desirable but necessary if companies were to retain and upgrade the new hires once they had entered the work force. It was not enough merely to provide them with the training to do their present job but also to provide education so that they could have some upward mobility in the labor force. For the most part, very little has been done in the development area for these employees at this time. It is likely that as more experience is gained in these programs, the possibilities for development experiences will become more apparent and even necessary.

Government

When government is referred to, essential concern is with the federal government. During the 60's, more emphasis was placed on strengthening the local government and community in providing job training, but by the close of the decade, the successes were not overwhelming. The Nixon administration, in its early days, endeavored to press toward more funds going to the state and local levels. It was almost reminiscent of the early 60's when first the Kennedy and then the Johnson administrations espoused this approach, but there was one big difference. The Kennedy/Johnson administrations endeavored to by-pass the state and local governmental structures and provide the funds directly to local governments and the communities. The emphasis in the Nixon administration was to provide the funds essentially to the state governments.

Increasingly during the 60's, efforts are found to relate the national government to the state and local levels. A pattern of regional offices was utilized with fluctuating powers. At times, there was a great deal of decentralization with the regional offices able to make grants, as in the case of HEW. The decentralization was espoused as a way of getting the government out of Washington. In the early days of the Nixon administration, there was a regrouping of regional areas and a relocation of regional offices. At this writing, it is not possible to indicate what the long-range effect will be.

The federal government has a long history of providing training for its employees. It has an equally long history of providing HRD for nonemployees. Of course, this is not surprising, as providing HRD is one of the roles of a government in a democratic society. However, we may not always appreciate the extent to which the federal government engages in nonemployee HRD throughout the country. HRD opportunities are provided for noncitizens as well as citizens, as the United States has a major role in world-wide development. The range of programs is great, and the following discussion will give just a brief picture of the vast range of nonemployee HRD activities of the federal government.

Cooperative Extension

The Agricultural Extension Program of the Department of Agriculture is probably one of the most widespread HRD activities conducted by a federal agency. It is more commonly referred to as the Cooperative Extension Program—with the term "cooperative" included in the Smith-Lever Act of 1914 which set up the extension service. It was a matching funds program between the federal government and the states—they were cooperating; hence, the name.

The basic program is administered by a very small staff in the Department of Agriculture. They provide HRD activities for state and county employees who are involved in the program. On July 1, 1958, there were over 14,000 nonemployees to whom they provided this service.

Through a vast network of county agents who are not federal employees, the Department of Agriculture is able to reach out and help farm and rural citizens in over 3,000 counties in 50 states (3). The entire Cooperative Extension Program is a good example of a program of nonemployee HRD which then reaches out and touches other nonemployees. The basic elements of the program are in training. It is the training of farmers to do a better job and the training of other rural workers in their particular specialities. It is also the training of the farm housewife in being more effective with limited resources and opportunities.

In recent years, there has been a shift of population from the rural to urban areas. The CES has reflected this and today has "urban agents" who are directly involved with low income citizens in urban areas of the country. Various kinds of training and education programs are utilized to assist these citizens in being more effective in their personal and community activities.

There is also an educational component in programs such as 4-H or Future Farmers of America. These are programs for youth who will become farmers—it is educating them for a future role. To support these programs, there is an extensive leadership program which is a good example of a nonemployee development program. In addition to some specific leadership training, there is also the developmental phase designed to produce future leaders for the farmers of America.

Welfare

During the depression of the 30's, HRD activities were included in the federal welfare program. The intent was to make a work situation for unemployed teachers and citizens with no place to go and nothing to do when they got there. Training was offered in the hope that, with some additional job skills, the unemployed would be in a better position to take advantage of any leads that came their way. It was nonemployee training for people who hoped for the day when they could once again become employees.

In the intervening years, little was done to relate training and welfare. There were various assumptions as to why people got on welfare and some even wilder guesses as to why they stayed there. It was not until the late 50's that specific efforts were made to relate welfare to job training. In 1957, there was the Mobilization for Youth on the lower East Side of New York City. Though essentially a prototype for a community action agency, there was recognition of the need for job training to move people off welfare. In the early 60's, there were the endeavors of Raymond Hilliard in Chicago and William Braziller in the Tidewater area which includes Norfolk, Virginia. In each case, training and education were tied with welfare payments.

Since those initial endeavors, there has been increasing emphasis on the use of the welfare program as a means of providing additional job skills and remedial education to nonemployees. For example, under Title V of the Economic Opportunity Act of 1964, provision was made for welfare recipients to receive job skill education and remedial education in order to make them employable. This was a significant pioneering attempt on the part of the federal government, and despite criticism the program has continued and expanded. More and more the direction has been to include training and education as part of welfare programs. For the most part, it represents a direction in the United States of making people employable rather than merely providing them with sustenance. Of course, for certain persons in our society, particularly the aged and the handicapped, an income maintenance program is still essential. However, the focus of the federal programs is now more geared toward providing training and education for all those on welfare—nonemployees of the government.

As part of this total effort, a new area of endeavor has developed known as the Human Services area. This encompasses the wider range of new services being provided in the fields of health, education and welfare. It has required extensive training programs on the part of the federal government, either directly or through contract to private organizations. The most generally known are the Community Action Agencies originally encouraged under Title IIA of the EOA of 1964. Since that time, the concept of the CAA has become part of other federal programs, such as model cities. In addition, the federal government has contracted out training and education to various organizations and institutions, primarily nonprofit, to provide the necessary HRD experiences for those on welfare and for those in the human services area who provide services to the citizens on welfare.

Job Corps

The Job Corps program is another good example of nonemployee HRD where the government and private sector cooperated. The Job Corps, which was Title IC of the original EOA of 1964, involved private industry for the first time in a massive attempt to provide training and education to nonemployees. There had been nothing like it since the G. I. Bill days of the late 40's when some companies got into the proprietary school business to meet the training and education needs of the veterans.

There were two parts in the Job Corps. In the rural centers, employees of the Conservation, Agriculture and Interior Departments of the federal government provided training and education for nonemployees. In the urban centers, the same thing was being done by a list of companies including Westinghouse Learning, Litton Industries, Packard Bell and Federal Electric. They too provided training and education for nonemployees under contract from the federal government.

In July 1969, the Nixon administration transferred the Job Corps to the Department of Labor and evolved a new plan. The Job Corps centers were now turned over to the states, but the pattern was still for the states to subcontract to many of those same companies who had been previously involved.

Foreign Participants

With the advent of the Mutual Security Program under President Truman in the late 40's, the United States became involved in international human resource development activities. The various programs conducted in the past 25 years have usually included a component known as the "participant training program." Under this program, vast numbers of persons from other countries have been brought to the United States as part of the HRD program for developing countries. In this case, the human resources were not to be utilized in the United States, and, therefore, some might argue against including such activities in this book.

There are two significant reasons why such activities should not only be included but should be highlighted. This is truly one world, the development of human resources in any part of the world affects the balance in others. For example, the development of human resources in India provided an imbalance. More human resources were developed than could effectively be absorbed by the economy. A result has been Indians remaining in the United States on completion of their programs and becoming part of this labor force. The term "brain drain" has become quite familiar, and, for the most part, the flow has been to the United States. The participant training program of the federal government has built in procedures to avoid this, but when dealing with people and politics, it is not always possible to control either. For the most part, the participants have returned to their own countries and become a resource in developing their homelands.

A second reason for including these programs in this book is that they relate to the private sector and to the total picture of HRD. Increasingly, U.S. companies are operating abroad, enlarging their overseas operation and becoming involved in various kinds of reciprocal agreements with companies in other countries. In connection with some of these activities, U.S. companies have found themselves in the position of providing nonemployee training. These might be government officials or employees of affiliates. Sometimes, it is a foreign company which has a license to manufacture a product patented by a U.S. company. Some of this is quite close to customer training of nonemployees discussed earlier in this chapter. However, it is included here as it relates to world-wide programs of HRD. Also, the efforts of private companies operating overseas are often more beneficial to all if they are correlated with government HRD programs. Note that there is no suggestion of control by the government but rather the need to avoid duplication of efforts or working at cross-purposes in assisting a foreign country in HRD.

Confusion exists within the foreign aid programs as to which aspect of the HRD program is the objective of a particular participant program. Of course, this confusion is found throughout much of HRD activities, so no special criticism is intended at this point. But, programs have ranged through the gamut of training, education and development. There has been specific job skill training so that foreign participants could return to their countries and actually produce on the job. This has included specific skills as well as generalized skills needed to do a particular job. Education programs have also been significant. Under the participant training program, there has to be agreement as to the job to which the participant will return. In many cases, the documents which authorize the program specifically state that the participant will return to a designated job, and in many cases it will be a job higher than the one he now holds. This is truly education within the framework of HRD as used in this book.

Development type programs are common in participant training. The experiences, even the ones of shorter duration, have been designed to open up new vistas beyond their present vision or even the near future. For example, in September, 1965, AID brought over deputy province chiefs from Vietnam to study public administration in state governments which were not engaged in fighting a war. The objective was to prepare these deputy province chiefs to function after the war was over in their country. This may seem naive, in view of the duration of the war, but view it in the same terms as the plans of any organization. It was a high risk situation in that it was not known if these men would still be the deputy province chiefs in time of peace—if and when peace came to Vietnam. It was necessary to prepare them for this eventuality. Likewise, most development activities are designed for eventualities which may never come to pass.

Military

In the sense that the military branch of the government has its regular employees (i.e., career personnel), it provides HRD activities for them. In addition, there are those who are in the military only on a temporary basis. They are on the payroll of the military but are temporary employees as it is generally agreed that their stay in the military is of limited duration, and they plan to return to the work force in two or three years after induction. There are now special programs designed to meet the needs of these nonemployees.

The military is usually not seen as contributing to the labor force, except in a negative fashion. Those in the military are withdrawn from the labor force and are therefore not competing for jobs or adding to unemployment rates. These are negative factors, and the military is seldom considered as a contributor to the manpower pool for the nation's private sector. Publicity is given to the retired military officers who obtain positions with defense contractors. Less is said about programs

designed for noncareer military who are essentially nonemployees. In the late 60's, two programs evolved which are of
interest as related to HRD.

The first is Project 100,000. This is a program sponsored by
the military which is much like the hard-core disadvantaged
programs described earlier. Some young men were either deferred in the draft or denied enlistment in the armed services as
they did not meet the mental or physical requirements. Project
100,000 was designed to overcome this barrier, particularly for
those who did not meet the mental standards. Actually, the
standard is not one of mental ability but achievement. A young
man who was not sufficiently literate could not be drafted or
voluntarily join the military service.

In 1967, Secretary McNamara spoke before the Veterans of
Foreign Wars Convention and proposed a plan for a special
program for the rejectees who had not been able to meet the
mental requirements. His proposal met with enthusiasm and not
only from the VFW. He was encouraged to initiate the program
rapidly. It is referred to as Project 100,000, as this was the
target figure he announced for the program each year. These
men would be given remedial education as well as regular military training so they could adequately perform. The precedent
for this had been well established during World War II. The
program has now been operating for several years and has enabled young men to enter the military who may have wanted to
do so but who were unable to meet the mental requirements.

It may be argued that these men are now regular employees,
but to date statistics are not available which show whether or
not they remained as career employees of the military. In any
event, the program is significant for at the time the military
initially inducts them, these young men are a high risk group,
comparable to working with others who have not met the standards in this industrial and complex society. When they complete
their initial military service, they will be able to move into the
regular work force and be as mobile as any other worker in a
free society. After the term of their original enlistment, they

can choose to leave the service with no negative implications. In this sense, some of them are temporary and nonemployees within the construct of this chapter.

Another impressive activity has been Project Transition. This is a program designed to prepare the short-term military man to enter a productive role in civilian life immediately on discharge. Traditionally, since the G. I. Bill of World War II, the pattern for the serviceman was to first be discharged, then avail himself of his V.A. benefits in order to prepare himself for the job market. This presented a time lag in the entry of the discharged serviceman into the labor force. It also forced him, during a period in his adult life, to resort to a "handout" while he was receiving education. After World War II when there were millions of veterans in this status, it was a common experience. Today, a mature man receiving a stipend as a nonemployee may feel less adequate to cope with society. It signals that he is not yet a part of the regular work force and must do something to earn his way in. What a paradox—he has already served his military time and has visibly contributed to the security of his country, yet, he must now return as a nonemployee to once again find his place in the economic society.

Project Transition sought to overcome this by moving the job preparation phase back into the last part of the young man's military service. The project started, on a very limited basis, just to provide job preparation for wounded servicemen who had returned from the war in Vietnam. In a joint operation between Walter Reed Army Hospital and the General Post Office in Washington, a program was established. It proved so successful that it was rapidly expanded and became the nation-wide program known as Project Transition.

During his last six months in service, the noncareer serviceman can elect to enter the program. This prepares him, on discharge, to immediately obtain a regular skilled job in the work force. By no means has the program operated without its problems, but it has been a significant aspect of the nonemployee training education programs conducted by the military.

Voluntary and Professional Organizations

The United States has more voluntary and professional organizations and associations per person than any place in the world. Such activities have been an integral part of history, and each month that has gone by has seen newer organizations being formed and not an equivalent number being disbanded. Of course, part of this is a reflection of the population increase, but the organizations have proliferated in numbers beyond the rate of population growth. One of the hallmarks of these organizations is that they provide some kind of HRD activity for their paid staff who are employees. However, they also have HRD activities for their nonemployee leadership as well as their members. Indeed, if the organization is to survive, the need for HRD activities for its members is prime.

Leadership

Frequently, voluntary and professional organizations do not provide HRD for a significant group of nonemployees—their unpaid, voluntary leaders. It is assumed that the leaders who are highly motivated do not need the further encouragement which is one result of a well-organized HRD program.

A paradox results. The more highly developed the leadership, the more likely it is that they will serve the needs of the members and the goals of the organization. Increased membership and stronger identification can bring higher revenue and additional strength to the organization so it can reach its goals. However, as resources are limited, there is less of a tendency to use them to provide HRD for the leadership. Frequently, the leadership functions through enthusiasm and sweat and without the benefit of those HRD activities which could make their efforts more productive.

The plight of these organizations is similar to that of many service industries in the private sector. Where a nebulous item like "service" is involved, it is much more difficult to identify specific returns on expenditures for HRD than in manufacturing or other activities which lend themselves to quantification. Output rates can be measured—but can leadership be adequately assessed by counting the numbers of members on the books?

Some organizations have recognized the dilemma and engaged in significant in-depth leadership activities for their leaders. Ranking high among these is the HRD effort of the American Red Cross. HRD programs are offered at various levels for nonemployee leaders, starting in the local community and reaching to the national level. There are other examples, usually among organizations which have been in existence for a significant period of time. Those which do not provide HRD for their leadership tend to have a much shorter life. The League of Women Voters devotes a good deal of its time and energy to training its leaders in conference leadership skills, as this is one of their major functions. The Great Books Discussion Series likewise provides leadership training for the volunteers who are discussion leaders. In an organization like the American Society for Training and Development, training is provided for chapter officers and education for the newly elected officers who will be assuming new chapter responsibilities in the near future.

Much of the leadership HRD activities resemble those conducted by organizations in the private sector. The voluntary and professional organizations have recognized the need for quality programs, and budgets have been provided accordingly. Retreats for the nonemployee leadership are frequently conducted in the same off-the-ranch facilities used by some leading companies for their employee education and employee development programs. Some of the same consultants are used, and the practices have a high degree of similarity.

Membership

In most voluntary and professional organizations, training and education programs are provided as a service to the members. This is something that members expect when they pay their dues or devote their time to the organization.

There is a plethora of national conferences and massive regional meetings. The ease of transportation, coupled with improvement in facilities has contributed to the flood of national meetings conducted by the voluntary and professional organizations. Yet, too few organizations see this national conference as an HRD activity. For some organizations, it is definitely not considered HRD. The national meetings are devoted to business affairs and recreational activities. This meets the needs of the membership of that particular organization and probably should not be tampered with.

For others, the national conference is an HRD activity but is too seldom designed to meet this objective. The design is left to the logistics people rather than to consultants who can properly design this HRD activity for nonemployees. A well-designed national conference can contribute to all aspects of HRD. For the average member, sessions can be provided which help him do his present job better and even help him keep up with the state of the art. This is included in many programs such as those for medical doctors, veterinarians, engineers and school teachers.

Nonemployee education is a bit more difficult to provide but is still possible. These are sessions and experiences which help the nonemployee prepare for upward mobility. It may be from membership to leadership in his voluntary organization or to new levels in his profession. There is a certain risk element here, but it is more on the part of the nonemployee who must invest his conference time without necessarily seeing a specific return.

Nonemployee development is even more possible at national conferences, yet is too infrequently designed into the affair. These should be sessions and experiences which cause the nonemployee to reach out and stretch himself. More national conferences are becoming concerned with social issues which may not be the bread and butter of the organization but which

impact upon each citizen in the country. Controversy is encouraged. The objective is not just to stir things up but expose
the membership and the leadership to the issues of the day
which they must be prepared to confront. This may not be
comfortable, so the designers usually take the easy path of providing speakers who merely put into words the current status of
the organization or profession. Well-designed confrontation sessions are a necessity if a national conference is to be utilized to
meet the developmental needs of nonemployees.

Training and Consulting Organizations

In the 1950's, management consultants became an accepted
factor in American economic life. Since that time the use of
outside organizations and individuals has increased, and today
innumerable organizations providing the services for nonemployees are in existence. In one sense, they might be listed
under an earlier heading of "Business and Industry" as they do
provide a service. The special category is necessary as they are
designed to serve the employees of others. This is an unique
category and situation. In addition, these organizations can be
either profit or nonprofit and therefore differ from the concept
of business and industry where they are all based on the profit
motive.

The term "training and consulting" organizations is not entirely correct. They do consult, but not all of them train nonemployees. Some of them are also concerned with nonemployee
education and nonemployee development. They are deeply involved in HRD, but the archaic name of "training" has stuck.
Lately, the movement has been toward using terms like "organizational development" in the name of the firm, but it is ·diffi-
cult to identify any difference in their operations. It becomes
merely another technique as the organization endeavors to serve
its clients in the field of HRD.

For purposes of this section of the chapter, the designation
of "training and consulting" organization will still be used so as

to minimize confusion to the reader. Unfortunately, it does not reduce the confusion vis-a-vis their clients. In the absence of the differentiation among the three forms of HRD, it is almost impossible for the client to determine if he has used his resources effectively.

Until training and consulting organizations are prepared to delineate more specifically the area of HRD they are serving, this will continue to exist. Unfortunately, it does give an edge to those organizations that are training-oriented and therefore can point to specific job benefits. The other organizations allow themselves to be trapped into trying to prove there are immediate job benefits, when in essence they are providing education and development. Therefore, they could not possibly show a direct and immediate effect on the job—this was not their purpose.

Lack of clarity of purpose also impacts on the nonemployee. If his organization and the outside training and consulting organization are not clear as to their purposes, then how can the nonemployee be expected to understand the true nature of the experience with which he is being provided?

Public Seminars

Many organizations offer public seminars, though the trend seems to be easing in the early years of the 70's. These seminars, if well organized, have stated goals which are published in the brochures and stated in the materials the nonemployee receives. This is an advance over the early days when attendance was encouraged strictly on the reputation of those offering the public seminars. Having a good "stable" was important. Names of leaders increased nonemployee attendance and proved more important than a statement of objectives. People spoke of going to hear Drucker, Gellerman or Lippitt. Too rarely did they know the reason for the program—was it training, education or development? This is not to disparage the leaders in the field who made themselves available. Hearing and interacting with the leaders is much more effective than just reading their books. But, why the interaction? What was the HRD purpose for the nonemployee?

Compounding the confusion was the halo effect induced by some of the public seminars. If word got around that a particular seminar was "good," the tendency was to have several members of the organization attend. Each man might be going for a different reason, but rarely was this distinction clarified. They were all expected to take the same things from the seminar, with only the variation of individual difference. The sending company needs to ask, "Why are we sending this man?" Is it employee training, employee education or employee development? The sponsoring training and consulting organization must likewise be prepared to respond to these questions for the nonemployee it is serving.

Within the Company

Companies in the private sector spend vast sums of money bringing HRD resources into their plant sites. The variations of services do not lead to an easy distinction, but it is possible to identify the "canned" programs, the "modular" approach and the "tailor-made" program.

A canned HRD program has its advantages. It has usually been tested and the results more readily identified. The challenge to the in-house HRD man is to bring in the proper program for the appropriate audience. On an in-house basis, he can make the program available to a larger audience of homogeneous individuals. The training and consulting organization must weigh the economics of a contract against whether it has the appropriate program to meet the varying needs of the nonemployee it is being asked to serve.

The modular approach is useful in that the in-house HRD man can select those parts of the program being offered which he thinks would best suit the needs of his own organization. It also provides some flexibility so that there can be discrimination among those who need it for training, as against those who need it for other aspects of HRD. The appropriate use of educational technology has much to offer in this area.

The tailor-made program is not always the best approach to meeting HRD needs through the use of outside training and consulting organizations. It is obviously much more costly and frequently has not been as carefully researched or planned. It does provide a higher level of flexibility and the greater promise of being constructed to meet the different HRD needs within the organization.

The in-house HRD man is crucial to this and should be more than merely a procurement or contracting person. He must be able to influence the training and consulting organization, and, in turn, this outside HRD resource must be prepared to be influenced.

Schools

In this chapter only those schools which are beyond the secondary level will be considered. They offer a wide range of possibilities as they provide HRD activities for nonemployees. These are the various students who come to them on a part-time or full-time basis. The institutions to be discussed are colleges and universities, the community colleges and proprietary schools.

Colleges and Universities

The prime purpose of these institutions is to serve nonemployees. It is much like the training and consulting organization discussed earlier, in that these institutions provide all the dimensions of HRD. It is unlike the previously discussed organizations in that it serves individuals who at this time of their life are not expected to be employees in any organization. They are full-time students and are therefore in a much different category.

However, even the full-time student seeks meaningful HRD activity. If he does not get it, he is more likely to resort to overt action than the employee (4).

The assumption should not be made that all students attend college for the same purpose. Some are seeking only training. These are the students who are already employed but seek the sheepskin in order to hold on to the job which they have obtained even though they lacked adequate preparation. By far, the largest group is those who have come for education. They have a particular job in mind, and they are taking those courses or following that curriculum which will enable them to get the particular kind of job they have chosen.

A small but significant group attend for development—they are more interested in the challenges provided by the experience than in the results. These last have usually been the liberal arts students who were not preparing for any specific job. At one time, they were considered low on the interest scale of those who recruit on the college campus. This trend has significantly changed.

Private organizations are now seeking the graduate who has been developed, rather than the highly trained or educated graduate. Some organizations are using the campus as a resource to provide some education and large doses of development for their executives who have been too highly trained.

The role of the professor is rapidly coming under closer scrutiny, and this is good. (Note: The author of this book is a professor.) Traditional concepts of academic freedom have influenced not only what was taught but how. It is agreed that the subject matter should be essentially in the hands of the professor. He is the expert in that area of subject matter, or he should not be on the faculty. But, in almost all cases he knows little or nothing about the most effective way of presenting that subject matter. He has avoided any education courses and rejects any attempts at helping him improve his methodologies. As long as professors insist on extending academic freedom by allowing themselves to ignore the most effective means of providing for learning, they are guilty of denying the research and experience which can make them more effective in conveying their subject matter.

Mere transference of knowledge is no longer a legitimate objective of an institution of higher learning. The professor must review his subject matter in the concept of HRD—when is he training, educating and/or developing? He does all three but hopefully not at the same time. Also, the nature of his student body, their motives and objectives, must influence what aspect of HRD is pertinent for them at a given time and with a specific subject matter. It is a long time since professors were merely educating, if they ever were. For those in the professorial ranks concerned with HRD for nonemployees, they are offered the challenge of reviewing their curriculum and distinguishing these various aspects.

In recent years, there has been a proliferation of colleges and universities becoming engaged in offering conferences and institutes. These are available on campus, at off-campus facilities and even at plant sites. In some cases, the actual faculty of the university is involved, but more frequently it has been the extension arm of the university bringing together outside resources. In this activity, the same discussion would apply as the earlier one concerning training and consulting organizations. The universities are no different in their strengths and weaknesses, except that they seldom have a regular group providing HRD experiences for nonemployees. It is more of the network type which is also common among training and consulting organizations. That is, when a client system has given a contract for a particular HRD program, the university then endeavors to find the appropriate professionals to staff the contract. This has caused some concern among regular faculty. It is not that they resent the competition—in most cases they have been given first choice on these contracts. However, in view of their present teaching loads, they must usually decline. This then allows representatives of the university to bring together outsiders, who operate under the university banner. The nonemployees are not getting the professional resources of the university—only its contracting and recruitment abilities.

Community Colleges

Community colleges in the United States are the most rapidly growing and changing institutions above the secondary level. They have begun to move away from being junior colleges or just feeder for four-year institutions. They now see themselves as having a particular service to offer to the communities they serve, and the term "junior college" is giving way to "community college."

Among the community colleges, there are those supported by public funds and those which are private/independent two-year colleges. In a study conducted in 1968, Kenneth C. MacKay found that the institutions that responded to his questionnaire revealed "the diversity of the private ranks, the great range of institutions from large to small, city to country, and arts to technologies. . ." (5).

Being less bound by tradition and degree-granting programs, community colleges will probably become an even more significant resource for HRD nonemployee programs. Here, there exists not only the possibility of profits for the nonpublic institutions but also the possibility of performing a service.

Community colleges are also more widespread and therefore more readily available than the larger institutions. In some states like Florida, California and Virginia, there is a goal of having a sufficient number of community colleges so that no citizen is more than one-hour driving time from one of these institutions.

As the community colleges expand more vigorously into providing nonemployee HRD, they will be beset by the same problems as training and consulting organizations and colleges and universities. Expansion is so rapid that there is cause for concern that they will not address themselves to the vital issue of what resource they are providing—is a given program training, education or development?

Proprietary Schools

Within the private sector, there is a large group of educational institutions offering HRD activities. H. D. Hopkins uses the term "proprietary" schools although Harold Clark and Harold Sloan prefer the term "specialty" schools (6). There is some slight differences in the schools they are considering but not enough to warrant a different designation. The term "proprietary" is chosen because it conveys more clearly the kind of school being considered.

Proprietary schools are usually small, but in aggregate they total about 35,000 serving over 5 million students a year. They are essentially job oriented and therefore provide the training and education components of HRD. These schools do not offer degrees and have much freedom in the curriculum and faculty. For example, one study found that no state had any basic criteria for faculty in trade and technical schools (7).

These schools offer a significant resource for nonemployee HRD, particularly training, but must be used with a great degree of caution. The regulation of these schools is spotty and in most cases nonexistent. A form of internal policing is through the accrediting procedures established by the U.S. Office of Education. However, a school need not be accredited to operate, and when a school is accredited, there is still little control over its operations, curriculum or faculty. There is no single accrediting agency, but rather a number including: the Engineering Council for Professional Development, the Accrediting Commission for Business Schools, the National Association of Trade and Technical Schools, the National Home Study Council and the Commission on Accreditation of Cosmetology.

Proprietary schools are for the most part privately owned and rely upon tuition for their income. They provide HRD for nonemployees who usually come to the school for their experience. Of course, in the case of correspondence schools, the materials are sent to the nonemployee at his home or his place of work.

In the late 60's, proprietary schools came under the influence of private companies seeking to enter the education field. Some private schools were bought by large companies and merged into their conglomerate structure. Others set up special companies for education such as the Lear Siegler Education Company, which by 1969 owned over 50 schools throughout the country specializing in business subjects.

Labor Unions

In books on HRD designed for the private sector of the economy, labor unions are often ignored or castigated. At the obvious risk of antagonizing some readers, this book will include a discussion of labor unions. The role of the unions, the necessity for them or their relationships to the right-to-work laws will not be argued. They are a factor in HRD and provide HRD activities for their members and leaders. They must not be ignored if nonemployee HRD activities by significant groups in the population are to be understood.

Labor unions are always concerned with the employees of others. This is their business. However, management and labor have moved far from the early 30's when the key words were "struggle" and "fight." As Hilda Smith has commented, there is the need to understand and use a new vocabulary (8). *Shearing* must be replaced by *sharing*. It is no longer necessary to *fight* but now to *negotiate*. This is reflected in the kinds of nonemployee HRD activities offered by unions. The range includes union orientation, job skills training, and remedial and cultural activities.

Union Orientation

This area is probably the one most familiar to the nonunion person. It is the provision of training and education programs related to union membership, employment relations, politics and labor economics.

The intent, as with voluntary and professional organizations, is to create a greater identity between the nonemployee and his organization. The range of programs of this type is wide and usually directed more toward local issues than the national scene. However, during times of national elections, there are provisions for educational programs on the issues involved.

Leadership HRD programs are crucial to a union. There are training programs for stewards on how to conduct grievance hearings. Other leadership skills are also part of the nonemployee training for shop stewards. The International Association of Machinists conducts a series of basic and advanced schools. The basic schools are conducted throughout the United States, usually in conjunction with an university. The purpose is to provide a survey of the duties of local lodge officers for all members who have not previously received such training. For local lodge officers attending, it is nonemployee training. But, for general members who attend, it is nonemployee education. It is available to both. The topics covered include collective bargaining, the IAM and its goals, legislation and politics affecting labor, duties of local lodge leaders and conducting education programs in the lodge.

In late 1969, the AFL/CIO Labor Studies Center in Washington came into existence. This is a specialized center designed to provide HRD activities for national leadership for selected union members and employees. At this writing, it is still being created, but if it is as successful as its developers contend it will be, it may become an unique union-directed nonemployee HRD activity.

Job Skill Training

Too few people are aware of the job skill training programs offered by the union to its nonemployee members. Obviously, such nonemployee HRD programs are directly related to the total manpower pool development.

Apprenticeship programs of many craft unions are currently under attack for their discrimination against minority groups. This is changing, and the 70's have begun with the "Philadelphia Plan" and other programs to include minority group participants in traditional craft unions. But, the traditional apprentice programs are only one aspect of nonemployee HRD conducted by unions. The following few examples will serve to indicate the scope of such HRD activities.

Since 1959, the International Brotherhood of Electrical Workers has conducted skill improvement courses for its members. These are evening courses organized around a two-year curriculum. In 1962, the International Typographical Union opened a training center for graphic arts in Colorado Springs. The purpose is to help its members keep up with technological changes in their field.

Many unions conduct such skill training programs but not of such a vast nature. They are usually local programs. It has been difficult to find examples of union-management sponsored HRD activities, though some do exist. These are not usually publicized, as they tend to destroy the polarity which still exists in much of the labor movement and in labor-management relations.

Remedial and Cultural

Unions provide many other nonemployee HRD activities which are of note. Some of these are conducted unilaterally by the union, while some involve other organizations.

Remedial programs are particularly necessary when the union membership includes minority groups or others who are prevented from moving ahead in the labor force because of less than functional literacy. Unions have found it useful to provide various forms of nonemployee remedial education.

In Washington, through the efforts of the union and with MDTA funds, a remedial program was offered to those who plan to take apprenticeship examinations in the building trades. It is part of a trend of pre-apprenticeship programs for persons who previously would have been unable to enter the craft unions through the apprenticeship route. The programs include elements of both training and education for these nonemployees. This particular program in Washington is entitled Project Build.

At the other end of the employment scale is retirement. Unions have long fought for pension and retirement planning and now have increasing numbers of members who are eligible. In addition to programs offered by the employer, unions are also offering HRD to prepare their nonemployee members for retirement. Classes include the usual ones related to health, finance and social security benefits. There are also culturally-oriented classes to help the nonemployee member through the period of disengagement into a meaningful retirement life.

At this point, management and labor are concerned with some of the same problems, and what is urgently needed is a dialogue between those who are responsible for HRD activities in the ranks of both management and labor.

Literature Citations

1. A good deal of research has been funded by the federal government into various aspects of manpower, though not necessarily for individual programs. An annual report is issued. At the time of writing this book, the latest is *Manpower Research Projects,* sponsored by the United States Department of Labor, Manpower Administration, through June 30, 1969 (Washington: Government Printing Office, 1969).
2. Leonard Nadler, "Helping the Hard-Core Adjust to the World of Work," *Harvard Business Review,* March/April 1970, pp. 117-126.
3. Joseph L. Matthews, "The Cooperative Extension Service" in *Handbook of Adult Education,* ed. Malcolm Knowles (Washington: Adult Education Association, 1960).

4. A well-balanced discussion of the student unrest and its implications can be found in Harold Taylor, *Students Without Teachers: The Crisis in the University* (New York: McGraw-Hill, 1969).
5. Kenneth C. MacKay, "The Private College Study," Bulletin #4, *Clearinghouse on Community Service,* published by the American Association of Junior Colleges, September 1969.
6. H. D. Hopkins, "Adult Education Through Proprietary Schools" in *Handbook of Adult Education,* ed. Malcolm Knowles (Washington: Adult Education Association, 1960). Another approach is Harold Clark and Harold Sloan, *Classrooms on Main Street* (New York: Teachers College Press, 1966).
7. Elouise L. Johnson, "A Descriptive Survey of Teachers of Private Trade and Technical Schools Associated with the National Association of Trade and Technical Schools" (diss., School of Education, The George Washington University, 1967, subsequently published in a limited edition by the National Association of Trade and Technical Schools, Washington, D. C.).
8. As reported in a conversation with Hilda Smith, one of the first and most renowed labor educators in the United States, in Katherine Tift, "Labor Education in the United States, A Survey," *Labor Education Viewpoints,* Fall 1968, p. 5.

section III

Roles of the Developer

The most crucial single element in the entire pattern of human resource development is the staff available to guide and implement the HRD program. It is amazing to see organizations with a readiness and acceptance of HRD concepts that then proceed to select an individual with no background or preparation for this intricate area. Hardly a week goes by that a letter is not received from some poor soul who has just been given the HRD responsibility within his organization. He seeks book lists, a course or some other quick injection to enable him to perform the roles of the human resource developer.

Organizations which make such haphazard selections are then likely to complain that HRD has not done anything for them. They place more emphasis on the selection of a plant site or the purchase of a piece of machinery than they do on the choice of their human resource development staff. Is it any wonder that they become disenchanted?

147

Within each organization, the particular kind of human re-source developer needed and the way in which he is viewed will vary. A model of the human resource developer could probably not be built which could be used without modification by all organizations. However, it is necessary to bring together and synthesize what is known about the people who fill these roles and perform HRD functions. It is also possible to identify some of the historical trends which have created the roles and in-fluenced them.

In the emerging field of HRD, there has been hesitation in developing models. The tendency has been toward an activist approach, and any theory building or model building has re-ceived scant attention. To move ahead, however, it is necessary to engage in the model building activities which are essential in order to help explain the world.

A model is not a straight jacket nor an absolute dictum which cannot be revised. The model in this section has been revised several times since first set forth in writing in 1962. As it receives more public attention, it will probably be further modi-fied. It presents some basic points from which modifications and other models can develop.

7

Human Resource Developer

The human resource developer is that person who is involved in providing the experiences set forth in Section II. To accomplish the purposes discussed, the HRD specialist has three major roles: learning specialist, administrator and consultant. These three are set forth, with their subroles, in Figure 7.1. An individual, functioning in human resource development, must be aware of these three major roles even though he may not function in all of them. Development of human resources has now reached the level of complexity where various kinds of specialists are needed and where some roles become more important than others.

For those concerned with the totality of human resource development, it is essential that they provide for all three roles within the organization and clear delineation as to who is performing each of the roles. At any one time, it is highly unlikely that a particular individual will be filling all three roles. It is impossible to establish absolute criteria for when the HRD specialist should be more active in one role than in another. The variables will be identified and discussed in this chapter.

At the outset, it should be recognized that the size of the organization is *not* one of these variables. Attempts have been made to set up a ratio between the number of employees and the number of HRD staff. Such quantification ignores the variability of the contribution that HRD can make to each organization. The nature of the work force involved, geographical location, and product or service are all significant variables in determining the size of the HRD staff. A more significant figure might be the expenditure per employee for HRD activities. Here there is a lack of terminology and agreement on HRD costs. Therefore, it becomes almost impossible to determine what is actually being spent to make some comparisons (1).

No matter how many variables, there must be an examination of the individuals—the HRD staff. Within the organization there must be the capability for functioning in all three major roles or at least recognizing the need for having such capability within the organization. For given roles, or subroles, the human resource developer might decide to use out-of-house resources. Such a choice is not a reflection on the individual HRD specialist or his staff. It is rather a recognition of the complexity of the field today and the desire to make the most effective use of what resources are available. No matter what the decision, the availability of the three roles is necessary for all organizations.

Segments pictured in Figure 7.1 are of equal size. This is for convenience and does not represent reality. The relative size of each of these components varies with the organization and the individuals involved in HRD. The model is helpful in providing a framework so that each organization can examine itself and take a closer look at its human resource development activities.

Role concepts discussed in this section were used as the basis for sessions during the annual ASTD conference in 1968 and again in 1969. Exploration of role concepts was also used at a workshop at the Adult Education Galaxy Conference in Washington in December, 1969. The same workshop experience has

LEARNING SPECIALIST
Instructor
Curriculum Builder
Methods and Materials Developer

ADMINISTRATOR
Developer: Personnel
Supervisor: On-Going Programs
Maintainer: Community Relations
Arranger: Facilities, Finance

CONSULTANT
Advocate
Expert
Stimulator
Change Agent

Figure 7.1. Roles of the human resource developer.

been used with a variety of other organizations and individuals and has received helpful feedback. Participants in this experience have reported that they found the model helpful in examining their own roles in their organizations in human resource development. Some of the participants in the workshops have added that the model was helpful for performance appraisal of human resource development staff, as well as goal-setting for further development in relation to organization development.

The worksheet (see Figure 7.2) has proven helpful in another area. Participants in the workshop have taken it back to their supervisors and managers and discussed it with them. It helps orient non-HRD managers to the possibilities of HRD within their organization and their own departments. It has not yet been possible to collect sufficient data on the use of this worksheet to report it. Hopefully, this will be done in the future.

The form of the worksheet shown in Figure 7.2 was modified, varying with the particular group and the purpose of the workshop (2). After a brief discussion of the variety of roles, which will be found in Chapters 8-10, the participants are asked to individually look at their roles and mark Column 1 accordingly. After they have developed the role model of their own job, they discuss it with others in their work group. Then, they are ready for the all important question of change. In essence, what are the forces for change which will impact upon the roles of the HRD specialist? This can be approached in the broad generalities of the world, the closer aspect of the nation, or the direct implications of change in the very organization of the individual.

In Column ›2 of the worksheet, the participant notes the changes which he thinks will affect some of the individual roles. From this, he can move to Column 3 and develop a new profile of his roles as he expects them to be. The perceptions involved here are important and can be the basis for much exploration with his supervisor as well as other professional colleagues.

The new profile helps the HRD specialist identify his own needs in Column 4 and then begin the search for resources. The process should not end with this but can be repeated individually or with others.

Basis for this exploration is the model of the roles used in this book. Therefore, the historical development of the roles, some factors affecting the roles and placement of the HRD staff in the organization will be examined.

Historical Development of Roles

How did the roles emerge? Although limited by the absence of a definitive study of HRD as it has emerged in the United

Roles	Column 1 Present Job*	Column 2 Forces for Change	Column 3 Future Job†	Column 4 Developmental Needs	Column 5 Resources
Learning Specialist					
1. Instructor	1 2 3 4 5		- 0 +		
2. Curriculum Builder	1 2 3 4 5		- 0 +		
3. Methods and Materials Dev.	1 2 3 4 5		- 0 +		
Administrator					
4. Developer: Personnel	1 2 3 4 5		- 0 +		
5. Maintainer: Community Relations	1 2 3 4 5		- 0 +		
6. Supervisor: On-Going Programs	1 2 3 4 5		- 0 +		
7. Arranger: Facilities, Finance	1 2 3 4 5		- 0 +		
Consultant					
8. Advocate	1 2 3 4 5		- 0 +		
9. Expert	1 2 3 4 5		- 0 +		
10. Stimulator	1 2 3 4 5		- 0 +		
11. Change Agent	1 2 3 4 5		- 0 +		

*1 indicates *a great deal;* 2, *quite a bit;* 3, *some;* 4, *very little;* 5, *none.*
† - indicates *less;* 0, *the same;* +, *more.*

Figure 7.2. Worksheet of HRD roles.

States, there are some trends which are reported in Chapter 2 of this book.

Looking at history should not be a trap. It is not necessary for each organization to reproduce the footsteps of those who trod the HRD turf before them. The existing history reflects the forces in the nation at that time and the nature of economic, social and political development. The history must also be related to the development of organizations at different points in history. It is not necessary for an organization today to replicate this pattern. Indeed, to do so would be wasteful. But, knowing how the roles emerged is helpful to allow an organization to benefit from the experience of others.

Prior to World War II, the role was fragmented and difficult to identify in many organizations. There were, of course, various kinds of human resource development activities and operations, but it is not possible to find a continuous line. After World War II, the scene is much clearer, and, therefore, it is possible to identify the roles as they emerged through this historical period of time. In essence, it is a matter of covering the last 30 years of human resource development and identifying the kinds of people who have been involved.

Note should be made of the various attempts to identify the "training director" and other people involved in human resource development. Unfortunately, there is a lack of comparability as the studies have often involved much different populations. Even where the studies used ASTD members as the respondents, there is no comparability. The membership of this organization has not only grown but also changed within its history. If these changes could be analyzed, they would be most helpful, but it is doubtful if such a project is feasible.

Another limitation is that not all those engaged in human resource development are ASTD members. In 1969, the membership of this organization was over 9,000, which certainly identified it as the leading organization in the field. Yet, it has been estimated that well over 30,000 persons are filling positions in the field of human resource development.

Various projects are underway to identify more clearly the personnel in the field and the kinds of things they do. As the development of human resources becomes more significant, it is likely that the quantity and quality of research concerning the human resource developer will increase.

Learning Specialist

It is generally agreed that the major impetus of human resource development in the United States was prompted by the massive need for workers and soldiers during World War II. Teachers of various kinds were recruited out of the public schools and college classrooms. They were transplanted into business, industry, government and the armed forces. They were brought in as instructors to teach classes. Guidance was provided from the federal government in the form of curricula, audio-visual aids and training guides. The Office of War Information sponsored the now famous Training Within Industry program with the "J" series (3). The resurgence of the Job Instruction Training units provides visible testimony to the worth of the material developed during those days.

Essentially, the human resource developer at that time was a learning specialist concerned mainly with instruction. The pressing need was to have people prepared to do a particular job at a particular time. In the context of human resource development, the major focus was on training.

Two approaches were used to evaluate the training. The first, and most obvious, was the actual performance on the job. With the given shortage of human resources at the time, little was done with the results of the evaluation. Emphasis was placed on production and meeting the tight schedules imposed by the war. Little data remains from any evaluative studies conducted during that period.

A more direct method was to evaluate in terms of the output of the HRD function. How many people were being "produced" who could fill vacant spots within the organization?

This was a good and valuable method and should not be depreciated. However, after the termination of the war and well into the 50's, the tendency to assess the contribution of a training program in terms of "the number of heads produced" was still being found. It would not be surprising to find organizations, even today, who still evaluate their training programs in terms of the number of people trained, the number of hours spent in training and like quantifiable measures. The statistical approach is gleefully employed, for it allows for computer print-outs and walls lined with multicolored comparative charts.

The war alone should not be blamed for this phenomenon. Even the ubiquitous computer is not to blame. The tendency for the headcount predates the war and the computer. Many teachers recruited by industry during the war years had previously worked under the Smith-Hughes Act of 1917 and subsequent legislation. Under this approach, the states could recover funds from the federal government for some costs related to vocational education. This required detailed records on registration, attendance and various other statistical reports. The vocational teacher, particularly of adults, was rewarded for numbers. Is it strange that the vocational educators took this behavior into their new situation? Once again, reports became a basis for rewards—this time the headcount went to management.

The vocational teacher is not to be blamed. What other criteria was available to him? At that time, there was little to offer any human resource developer as guidance for evaluation of his program. The school teacher turned human resource developer searched for ways to accommodate to the new organizational relationships and used his previous successful behavior as the starting point.

The difficulty is that too many developers are still using the headcount today. Some of them cannot even rationalize by pointing to their prior teaching records, as they do not come from a teaching background. Others are not old enough to have been among the group who went from the schools to the production line during World War II. Still, many organizations exist that persist in using headcounts.

As the other HRD roles are impacting upon the learning specialist role, additional approaches to evaluation are being introduced. Management by objectives has been applied to human resource development and is helpful. With the delineation of roles, the learning specialist is more concerned with developing criteria for evaluating the learning experience. Other roles relate to the linkage of learning into the work situation and evaluation on the job.

Administrator

After the war, many organizations found themselves with a surprising number of people involved in HRD activities. Most of these people were essentially learning specialists concerned with instruction. But, this was the time of the human relations thrust, and during the 50's, the number of people involved in HRD increased. Some programs were related to training, but a greater concern with education and development activities was evolving.

As the human resource development operations grew larger and more complex, it became evident that there was the need for an individual who could perform the necessary administrative functions. Some learning specialists moved into this evolving role, though bemoaning the loss of contact with the student in the classroom. The experience of these learning specialists was much like that of a sales manager who has a successful career and is receiving ego satisfaction from dealing directly with customers. Now, the growing organization demands managers, and the effective salesman is moved into the administrative role. How many good salesmen have been lost by making them poor managers? How many good learning specialists have been lost by making them administrators?

Still, this is not a problem unique to human resource development. This is a common phenomenon in many areas where entry-level jobs require competencies much different from those which offer promotional possibilities.

Some learning specialists reluctantly became administrators, and the lack of enthusiasm was so apparent that management began seeking its administrators in other parts of the organization. It was not, and still is not, uncommon to find administrators of HRD activities whose sole credentials are that they are administrators and therefore can administer anything. It is not necessary that the administrator of human resource development come through the ranks as a learning specialist. But, he must know the field of education and the factors involved in creating a favorable climate for learning.

There is no need to polarize and insist that the administrator should have been a learning specialist. It is not proposed that one must have had direct experience in order to help another in a learning situation. To illustrate, working with a group of nurses in a hospital in supervisory training, the author could usually tell when the material was getting close to the gut level. Inevitably, there would be a pause after a point of confrontation. Then, one of the leaders in the group would pierce the silence with—"How many hours have you spent in a ward?" Having been at the receiving end of this question, he would certainly not be prepared to pose a similar one to those who are, or would be, administrators of human resource development activities. However, he does believe that the administrator of this function must bring to the situation more than just administrative skills which have been sufficient in other situations.

In-House Consultant

The early 50's saw the emergence of the management consultant. He would come into the organization from the outside and after carefully examining selected aspects, he would make his report and move on. He could be epitomized by the phrase attributed to Abraham Lincoln—he was prone to give "horseback opinions." This refers to the period of history when justice was administered by circuit judges who traveled from town to town on horseback. They would come into a town, hear the case while still occupying the saddle, render a decision and then trot on to the next town.

This is not meant to cast aspersion on the recommendations of the management consultants. Yet, to this day, consultants are usually not viewed with enthusiasm. They are tolerated with a high degree of suspicion as to their competency and motives. It has been said that a consultant is very much like the bottom half of a double boiler—he is all steamed up but does not know what is cooking on top.

Despite this, as the 60's progressed, consulting on human resource development became significant. When Gordon Lippitt with others organized Leadership Resources Inc. in 1960, it was an unique organization. It was almost alone in its challenge to apply behavioral sciences to the market place through consulting and training. By the middle of the 60's, there were many more organizations in the field, and by the end of the decade it was big business, with many larger corporations offering their services in the market place. For example, on October 1, 1969, the Training and Development Department of Westinghouse Electric Company was transferred from its place in the corporate structure into the Westinghouse Learning Corporation. The experience and services of this highly qualified HRD staff was now available to anybody who wanted to contract with Westinghouse Learning.

As it became apparent that training for job skills was not enough, a movement progressed toward positively providing education and development. Those who still persist in ignoring the distinction between education and training are probably having difficulty in their organizations, particularly relating objectives and the results of training. Even more difficult is the understanding of the need for some in-house consulting as part of the human resource development activity.

Toward the close of the 60's, a new cluster of activities called "organization development" evolved. In 1968, ASTD recognized this trend and organized a special division. At that time, there was only one other activity—sales—which had been accorded this recognition within the society. The trend was further underscored by persons who had formerly used the title of "Director of Training." Some of them now changed their titles to "Director of Organization Development."

The actual work of an organization developer is still evolving. Differences of opinion exist regarding what an individual does in this role, though there is some agreement that he serves as an in-house consultant. The role is still too new and varied to allow one to utilize the benefits of historical hindsight, as was done in the discussion of the two earlier roles.

A distinction can be made regarding this new role which has implications for the way the role can be fulfilled. The learning specialist role is essentially concerned with the individual learner and rightly so. The emphasis in recent years has been on providing greater opportunities for individual learning and providing for individual differences.

However, Malcolm Knowles raises the point that the movement of adult educators (who are one kind of human resource developer) may be "away from the definition of his constituency in terms of individuals towards its definition in terms of social systems" (4). The emerging role of the human resource developer as an in-house consultant is a major aspect of this new definition.

Factors Affecting the Roles

Possibility of a human resource developer functioning in one or more of these roles is affected by three factors—the person, the organization and the problem. Within each of these factors are almost innumerable variables, and only a few of them will be discussed here. Through even a brief discussion at this time, the human resource developer and his organization can be made more aware of some of the constraints. They can then apply their energy to reducing these, rather than the often heard, "Training is not a profession, anybody can do it, no special skills are needed by people in this field, and what difference does it make?"

By accepting the constraints and even adding some which are not pertinent, the human resource developer is depriving his organization and its employees of the benefits inherent in sound HRD activities. The degree to which a human resource developer is prepared to discuss these constraints within his organization is likely a direct reflection of his own self-image and perception of the significance of human resource development.

The Person

Despite the fact that the person responsible for human resource development is probably the single most crucial factor affecting the role, there is still lacking sufficient understanding of who or what this person is. Various attempts have been made to identify him and to draw a composite picture. No one picture emerges, but what does become apparent is that the persons responsible for HRD usually come to the position with a variety of backgrounds and skills, with little of the background having been planned in anticipation of an HRD assignment.

The engineer, the personnel director, the controller—all have some commonality of academic backgrounds which prepare them for the position. The human resource developer is more like the executive who comes to his high post from a variety of backgrounds. The difference is that the executive is not expected to perform in a specialized area but as a generalist. The human resource developer may need some of the abilities of the generalist but requires something more to accomplish his functions as a specialist.

It is unlikely that the human resource developer has had an organized program leading toward this position. There are many reasons, but basically there is a lack of agreement on the body of knowledge needed by the human resource developer. This applies to most, but not all, of his roles. As a result, there is no agreement on the academic experiences which would be appropriate. For several years during the early 60's, the ASTD had a Pro-D (Professional Development) Committee headed by Norman Alhiser of the University of Wisconsin. The author was privileged to be a member of that committee—but the honor did not extend to any productive output. The committee just could not get a handle on even an approach, much less a core of knowledge.

Lack of agreement has never seemed to hamper universities. Gerald Whitlock brought together some data related to the various kinds of offerings for persons in this field (5). An analysis of his work is hampered by lack of definitions, but it does provide a glimpse of the range of possibilities. He reports a study in 1962 of 200 members of ASTD to which he received a 54% response, or 135 individuals. Within this group, there were 21 different job titles. Even here, where 35 respondents labeled themselves as "Training Director," it is not even possible to say that their job elements were comparable.

The academic preparation of HRD personnel is also equally unclear. If the reader prefers, at this point he can substitute the term "trainer," but it will do nothing to clarify the situation. Whitlock reported that course work in "Organization and Operation of a Training Program" was available in 10 different institutions of higher education. Within the 10, he found that six of them located these programs in the education department. However, when he gathered data on courses in "The Principles and Methods of Training," he found a much wider scatter. Similar courses were being offered in various departments, schools and colleges of the same university.

Course titles and even departments provide insufficient indication of course content. No mechanism exists at present to gather this kind of information, though occasional attempts are made. This statement is based on the requests received by the author from graduate students in other institutions who are doing some kind of work related to this field. To date, there has been no feedback, nor is there any indication in the literature that there has been any careful look at course offerings and course content.

In 1970, ASTD endeavored to respond to this need for some clarification. Forrest Belcher, 1970 national president of ASTD, set up a task force on "Curriculum in Higher Education." Task force chairman is Malcolm Knowles of Boston University and the author is a member.

Another indicator of the confusion is the kind of ads which appear in the *Training and Development Journal,* the official ASTD publication. Given the limitations imposed by space and ad writers, there are still some trends which might be helpful. Table 7.1 compares the data reported by Gerald Whitlock on a study of the ads from 1956-62 (6). Another study was performed by the author for the period of January 1968 through September 1969. Of course, given the ways ads are written, there may be some differences in perception of just what is meant by particular words like "related field."

Without overstating the statistical significance, a review of Table 7.1 can provide some trend lines. More employers are now specifically asking for degrees. The nature of the degree has not significantly changed, although personnel management and marketing seem to have slipped, at least at the bachelor's level. At the master's level, the decline in those asking for business administration is certainly worthy of note. Likewise, fewer are asking for the M.A. in psychology. Even if psychology is increased by the addition of the field of behavioral science, this category is still far lower in the more recent listing. Of note is the increase of employers asking for the M.A. in education. Likewise, the increase of those asking for the Ph.D. and the Ed.D.

Generally, the demand is probably similar to the general labor market where degrees are being sought now more than ever before. The shifts in specialized areas may be the result of factors other than increased awareness on the part of the employers. But, if the employers are seeking persons for HRD activities who have the M.A. in education, that is a movement worthy of further exploration. What are the institutions of higher education doing to meet this need?

Table 7.1

Degrees Requested in Position-Open Ads
(in percentage)

Area	1956-62*	1968-69+
Degree requirement not specified	32.0	29.0
Bachelor's Degree		
No major specified	23.0	27.0
Education	7.0	6.0
Business Administration	3.0	4.0
Psychology	3.0	4.0
Personnel Management	3.0	1.5
Marketing	2.0	0.7
Other (three different)	0.0	2.0
Master's Degree		
No major specified	8.0	8.0
Business Administration	10.0	3.1
Psychology	7.0	4.5
Education	0.0	5.0
Personnel Management	0.0	1.0
Behavioral Science	0.0	1.0
Other (two different)	0.0	1.0
Doctorate		
Ph.D.	1.0	2.0
Ed.D.	0.5	0.7
Totals**	99.5	100.5

*Gerald H. Whitlock, "Trainer Education and Training," in *Training and Development Handbook,* ed. Robert L. Craig and Lester R. Bittel (New York: McGraw-Hill, 1967), p. 534.

+Based upon ads appearing in the *Training and Development Journal,* January 1968 through September 1969.

**Variation in total due to rounding. Also, 126 ads were reviewed but 156 choices are represented as some employers listed more than one field.

Since 1962 and the advent of the Manpower Development and Training Act, there has been increased interest in HRD. The Manpower Administration, as of 1970, was preparing to fund 10 universities in programs to prepare manpower development personnel. Unfortunately, they are using the term more in the sense of the field of economics and related to manpower planning, rather than manpower development.

Is it any wonder, then, that the human resource developer has come to his position from a wide variety of academic backgrounds? In addition, his previous positions have likely not been in the field, and, therefore, another variable is introduced.

Whitlock reported only four institutions offering graduate degrees in the field—Purdue, Illinois, Cornell and George Washington. In the early 70's, there is a discernible movement in the direction of additional graduate offerings in this field. Many members of the Commission of Professors of Adult Education of the Adult Education Association have indicated an interest in including preparation for professional HRD positions in their graduate offerings. However, none has yet announced a specific program for human resource developers in the sense it is being used in this book (7).

In the absence of a mechanism for gathering information about such course offerings, it can only be assumed that there has probably been some movement in the field, but nobody is sure what direction it has taken. There is no group which has assumed leadership in the academic fields related to human resource development. Obviously, then, the academic background of the human resource developer, as well as his previous job experience, can be expected to have a significance as to how he sees his roles and the variety of functions related to them.

An additional factor is the self-image of the human resource developer. If he sees himself as being in a transient position from which he will move in a short period of time, he is less likely to devote his energies to building on-going programs and organizational mechanisms to support these programs. He may even deprecate his position. He does not want to be labeled as a "trainer" and, therefore, may merely perform whatever functions appear to have been associated with the job title in the past, rather than attempting any kinds of creative behavior as he fills the position of the human resource developer in his organization.

Too frequently, the person filling the role reports that he is doing well, despite his lack of special qualifications for the job. Therefore, anybody can do the job of the human resource developer. This type of self-image does little to attract individuals to HRD positions. He may be significantly depriving his organization of effectively using human resource development in its organizational pattern.

The personal objectives of the human resource developer also affects his perception of his roles. If he is interested in moving ahead in the organization, he may play down his activities as a human resource developer and try to highlight his abilities as an administrator. In terms of the individual, if he sees himself as part of the personnel department function, he is likely to urge human resource development to engage in those activities which are directly related to the personnel function. This is admirable, but it is only one part of the total organization to which the human resource developer should be relating. However, as he sees himself as part of personnel, he may hesitate to engage in other areas of activity which go beyond the traditional personnel functions, as he could be seen as empire building, and it might thwart his chances of promotion back into the personnel line.

Up to now, some wonderful people have been responsible for the HRD activities, and they have many accomplishments to which they can point. As the field develops further, the "grandfather clause" concept will have to be recognized. The practitioner with many years of experience cannot be expected to now go back to an organized curriculum in the field. Of course, in the program at The George Washington University, quite a few "old-timers" with better than 15 years in the field have come in for a graduate degree. However, at present, this is not typical.

The challenge and confrontation will come from the younger HRD specialist who brings to the situation some organized academic training. The current practitioner with no academic background will be hard-pressed to retain his leadership. It is hoped that he will not cope with the problem by continually denying the efficacy of academic preparation for human resource developers.

The Organization

Organizations have perceptions of individuals and positions. These have been built up over a period of time and frequently are difficult to change. An individual coming in to fill an established position in the organization, which previously was held by another person, will find himself confronted with being cast in the image of his predecessor. He may even find that in the early days he is still being called by his predecessor's name. Many in the organization will still react to the human resource department as, "Well, that was Mr. Smith's department." Also, the new resource developer finds himself confronted with the statement, "But that department never did that before."

The personality of his predecessor as well as his previous achievements—or lack of achievements—will be part of the cloak he must wear until he establishes his own personality and identification through a series of positive activities. Of course, this is not peculiar to the human resource developer. This occurs when there is any change of leadership in a segment of the organization. The difficulty is that there is a greater understanding and agreement about what a controller does, the functions of a purchasing director or a personnel director. There is much less understanding and agreement on what a human resource developer does, and therefore the organization is more likely to judge on the performance of its human resource developer in the past, rather than on human resource developers in general.

But the problem of prior perceptions is not limited only to new persons coming into the organization or into a position for the first time. Where a person has been functioning in an existing HRD department, but only as an instructor, he can likewise be trapped. He may now recognize the need for being involved in the broader spectrum of human resource development. He endeavors to operate across all three roles. He finds that the organization still views his operations in the earlier and more traditional pattern. Thus, the organization may still evaluate his performance in terms of prior criteria, and, therefore, he is still limited to the headcount or a cost-benefit ratio or some other quantifiable measure.

The particular stage of development of the organization can also be a serious factor affecting how it sees the contributions of its HRD activity. When faced with a labor shortage, the organization might be willing to engage in various kinds of HRD activities, which prior to this time would have been vetoed. An organization suddenly confronted with a reorganization or the realization that most of its executives are approaching retirement is much closer to being ready to look at itself. If there has been an effective HRD program, the organization will now reap the benefits of the work of many prior years. The particular life stage has a distinct effect on how ready the organization is to see its HRD function as an in-house resource.

The Problem

The discussion under the previous subheadings have indicated that the HRD director may not be utilized by the organization because of his own lack of skills as well as the perceptions of the organization. Even where these factors are supportive, there is still a constraint in the HRD director which is imposed by the nature of the problem to be solved by his activity.

Not every problem can be solved by HRD programs. Obviously, if a new step in the production cycle requires a worker with three hands, no amount of HRD activity will meet this need. Other alternatives are available, such as redesigning the job or introducing new equipment. The HRD director may not be aware that such alternatives exist and need not feel inadequate because he lacks this knowledge. He must recognize his own limitations as well as those of the HRD operation. His contribution, however, may still be available and helpful. The HRD specialist could, in his role as in-house consultant, assist others in identifying some of the alternative solutions to this problem. Where absolute technical knowledge is a prerequisite to solving the problem, the HRD specialist must recognize his diminished role.

Time is also a constraint in developing human resources. If it is a problem which needs immediate solution, then the development of human resources over the next year may have little to contribute. It may be a desirable alternative and generate more interest in the long-range planning for HRD. But, it may not meet the immediate situation, and therefore the organization would be wise to seek other alternatives.

Placement in the Organization

A continuing argument is the placement of the human resource development function within the organization. In most places, it has historically been placed under the personnel function and still remains there today. There are those who suggest that the placement is immaterial, that the important element is to get the job done. This avoids the basic issue—which job is to get done? If it is merely to support the personnel function, then to pursue this further is indeed a waste of time. If the development of human resources has become something different from the traditional personnel function, then the placement within the organization needs to be reexamined.

Operational placement is crucial in terms of who the HRD director reports to within the organization. It is not possible to correlate influence directly to position in the organization, but there is an implied relationship to which many respond.

Despite newer forms of organization, much work is still accomplished in traditional ways using forms which served in the past. To relate to a variety of units within the organization requires some form of staff position or placement within the organization which legitimizes cutting across the organizational structure. Usually, the higher the placement within the organization, the more likely the acceptance by all those concerned of any behavior which does not follow organizational lines. Human resource development affects all areas of the organization and therefore must be in the main stream and not off to the side. It must be in a position to respond to on-going operations as well as being in a position to be involved in the new directions toward which the organization is moving.

There is a symbolic inference by placement within any organization. Titles, physical location of offices and other non-verbal signs are determinants of how a function is seen by others in the same organization. The perception of organizational placement, as different from the actual organization placement, can facilitate the work of a particular unit or seriously impede it. The specific placement cannot be stated because within the culture of each organization, there are different implications as to placement and titles (8). Rather, it is suggested that this needs be explored for each organization and appropriate placement made.

Titles

It may be argued that titles are irrelevant and the importance is in the contribution the person makes to the organization. If this is so, then this criteria should be applied to all parts of the organization. Why are there special seminars by the American Management Association for the "Assistant to the President?" Why is so much time spent in identifying appropriate titles at all levels of the organization? Why are there attempts to find ways to enhance the position of the janitor by calling him a "Maintenance Engineer" and the person in charge of washrooms a "Sanitary Engineer?" There is a dignity which flows with a title which combines the self-image of the holder and the perception of the organization.

Titles are important and are constantly changing to more adequately represent the kind of work that is being done. If titles are not important, then why in the late 60's was there a movement on the part of many leaders in human resource development to change their titles? The movement was from "Training Director" to "Organization Development Director." Obviously, titles are important and cannot be shoved aside as mere name-calling or exercises in semantics.

It is not being urged that the title "Human Resource Developer" or anything akin to it is the only one that should be used. Within each organization, the title must be clarified—but to burden human resource developers with titles like "Personnel Management Specialist" as is done in some federal government organizations contributes to an unnecessary confusion.

The Personnel Department

It is easy to trace the placement of HRD in the federal government because of Presidential Executive Order 7196 in 1938 which placed training under personnel. In the past 10 years, attempts have been made within some of the agencies to remove this function from the personnel office. It has been successfully accomplished in some government organizations, but by no means is it general.

The position of the federal government was shown in their study entitled *The Federal Personnel Man* (9). The HRD personnel (Employee Development Officers in Federal and Civil Service terms) were subsumed under the personnel series.

In an attempt to clarify the situation, Leonard Ackerman conducted a study using the same population but separating the EDO's out of the total study. His data highlights the differences in the background and activities of the personnel man as compared to HRD specialists (10).

Within the private sector, it is more difficult to pinpoint the forces which determine the HRD placement. Any study on such placement is almost impossible for there is no constancy which allows for comparisons. Indeed, it is probably not even desirable—and may not even be necessary. The latter is true only if the personnel people will allow HRD freedom to be placed in another part of the organization.

When HRD remains under personnel, recruitment of suitable individuals can be hampered. HRD specialists are faced with a block. To move ahead, they must leave HRD and become personnel specialists. The competencies for a personnel specialist are not the same as those for the human resource developer.

Literature Citations

1. Advances in the concept of human resource accounting may contribute to concepts of evaluation. The literature is growing. Two good articles are R. Lee Brumet, William C. Pyle and Eric G. Flamholtz, "Human Resource Accounting in Industry," *Personnel Administration,* July/August 1969, pp. 34-46. Also see James E. Barrett, "The Case for Evaluation of Training Expenses," *Business Horizons,* April 1969, pp. 67-72.
2. The workshop was developed by Forrest Belcher (Pan American Petroleum Corp.), Dugan Laird (United Air Lines), Benjamin Tregoe (Kepner-Tregoe and Associates) and the author. The first use of this particular model was during the ASTD Conference in Miami in May, 1969.
3. The first work in this field was done in 1917, not in 1940. See Charles A. Allen, *The Instructor, The Man and the Job* (New York: Lippincott, 1919).
4. An actual experience is discussed by Malcolm Knowles, "How Andragogy Works in Leadership Training in the Girl Scouts," *Adult Leadership,* October 1968, pp. 161-162, 190-194.
5. Gerald Whitlock, "Trainer Education and Training," in *Training and Development Handbook,* ed. Robert L. Craig and Lester R. Bittel (New York: McGraw-Hill, 1967), pp. 527-555.

6. Ibid., p. 533.
7. The author has been trying to get institutions of higher education involved for some years. For example, see Leonard Nadler, "Training Directors and Professional Educations Institutions," *Adult Leadership,* February 1965, pp. 248-250, 266-268.
8. The effect of culture on all aspects of HRD has been too frequently overlooked. I describe some of this in Leonard Nadler, "The Organization as a Micro-Culture," *Personnel Journal,* December 1969, pp. 949-956.
9. *The Federal Personnel Man.* (Washington: U.S. Civil Service Commission, 1966).
10. Leonard Ackerman, "A Study of Selected Employee Development Specialists in the Federal Government: Their Background and Perceptions of Their Role and Organizational Location" (Ed.D. diss., The George Washington University, 1967).

8

Learning Specialist

Each role has its contribution to make to the effective development of human resources within an organization. The focus of this chapter is on the HRD person as he functions as a learning specialist. Primary concern will be with the person who is on the HRD staff as a regular full-time employee. There will not be an in-depth discussion of those who serve in this role as temporary or part-time employees.

Within the learning specialist role there are three subroles: (1) instructor, (2) curriculum builder and (3) methods and materials developer. As the three subroles are discussed, it will be seen that there is a high degree of interaction among them. For discussion purposes, emphasis will be on the three subroles as being separate. In some organizations, there will be three different people, or groups of people, in the subroles. It is not uncommon, however, to find situations where one employee is filling the entire spectrum of activities associated with the learning specialist.

The subroles are interrelated. An HRD specialist can serve as an instructor but also be responsible for the curriculum building, as well as developing his own methods and materials. Situations also exist where the HRD specialist builds curriculum, but the actual instruction is done by other personnel. This is common in OJT activities where the instruction will be performed by foremen or other line personnel.

The term "learning experience" will be used frequently throughout this chapter. It is not limited to classroom experiences but signifies other kinds of situations which are designed to bring about new learnings and new behaviors. Some of these experiences do not require the presence of a live instructor. Despite limited use of educational technology today, it is still possible to create learning situations which do not revolve around a person as a stimulus.

The time and place of the actual learning experience varies greatly. In continuous production operations, the timing of the learning experience is much different than for a group functioning in the 9:00 a.m. to 5:00 p.m. format. The place may be in-plant or at some isolated learning environment. The techniques involved can range from formal presentations to very informal and unstructured learning situations.

Instructor

Functions of the instructor have significantly changed over the years. In its simplest form, the instructor can be perceived as the traditional teacher. Indeed, in some situations this is entirely appropriate. But, even in the classroom, teaching has changed. Limitation on the flexibility of the individual in this subrole is reflected in the often quoted phrase, "We teach as we have been taught." Instructors, particularly those who lack additional professional preparation, have a tendency to develop within their own minds a role model of some teacher they had in the past who "turned them on." The impression of this teacher, dimmed and altered by the passage of time, influences today's teacher as he stands in front of a class. If sufficiently introspective, today's teacher may even be able to see mannerisms, gestures and phrases which are much like the master teacher he had in the past. Without sufficient professional preparation augmented by in-service opportunities, the instructor is doomed to emulate a teacher out of his past.

It is not an impossible situation. Today's teacher is not irrevocably trapped by his own past. It is possible for today's teachers to be creative, finding newer ways of managing learning experiences and utilizing the expanding resource of technology. However, this will not happen by accident, threat or hope. There must be carefully planned experiences to help the instructor appreciate the new relationships and develop appropriate expertness.

The teacher, particularly of adults, is no longer a lecturer. He is not a person imparting knowledge, but, rather, he performs a number of different functions which relate to the role of instructor. As can be seen, the term "instructor" is inadequate, but in the absence of any agreed upon terminology, it will have to suffice for the present.

Educational Change Agent

It is more common today to think of the instructor as an educational change agent. That is, he is working within an educational setting to help bring about change. As with any good change agent, he is as concerned with the process of change as with the goal. He concentrates on helping people to change rather than dragging or pushing them to a preconceived goal— even if it is the goal of the learner. To use the terms of the transactional psychologist, the educational change agent is endeavoring to create a situation which is built on actualizing the learner rather than manipulating him (1). This is not easy to do, as too often the site of the learning experience is approached as a battlefield rather than as a learning laboratory. It is instructor versus the learner with instructor having the worst of it, for he is the one who must take the initiative, entertain and even please the learner. Evaluations are too frequently built on the halo effect, asking questions like—How well did the instructor perform? Did the learner like the instructor?

In his role as an educational change agent, the instructor creates a learning environment and provides for the possibility of learning. The expertise of the instructor is not so much in his ability to speak clearly as in his ability to communicate. Frequently, a person is found functioning as an instructor, or aspiring to be an instructor, who concentrates on stage presence. His assumption is that having the proper fund of jokes and an effective manner of delivery constitutes a helpful learning environment. Or, there is the itinerant preacher type who plans his learning based on exhortations and appeals to the emotions of the learner. There is also the logical thinker type who relies on being able to organize and present his material so that nobody could reach any other conclusion than that which he has determined.

All these types, and there are others, rely basically on one-way communication in which the instructor tells the students what they must learn. Such instructors have probably heard about involving the learner in his own learning. But, they usually apply this by having him fill out worksheets or responding to questions. Such instructors usually know little about the concepts of process and the ways in which the learner cannot only be involved in but also influence his own learning.

Attitude is always a difficult concept but even more so when it is related to a learning situation. The enthusiasm, or lack of it, which the instructor brings to the situation is an important part of the learning environment (2). The instructor does not only look to the learner to change. As an educational change agent, the instructor recognizes that he can also be changed by the learning experience which he is directing.

The Learner

Of prime importance in the learning experience is the learner himself. The more the instructor is able to understand the learner, the more helpful and creative is the possibility within the learning experience. Too little time is spent in getting to know the learner, and therefore an instructor is perplexed because the material that is successful with one group is woefully useless with another. The following discussion will only briefly identify some of the aspects of the adult learner which the instructor must consider as he develops and conducts the learning experience (3).

First, there is the psychological aspect, concerned essentially with three elements—self-direction, intent to apply and experience. The adult learner has a need to be able to exercise some direction within the learning experience. Here, a distinction must be made between influence and control.

The control of the learning situation need not be in the hands of any single individual—neither the learner nor the instructor. However, both must be in a position to influence the learning situation. Of course, the instructor has certain responsibilities imposed upon him by virtue of his role as an instructor. He cannot allow himself to be permissive to the point of sitting back and having the learners take over completely, unless this is specifically the nature of the learning experience (e.g., some aspects of laboratory learning, particularly those referred to as sensitivity training). The adult learner, by virtue of being an adult in society, strives to be self-directing whether it be in the learning situation or the work situation. The effective instructor provides the opportunity for the learner to influence the learning experience.

The adult learner is also influenced by his need for applying the new learnings to his real life situation. When applied to HRD, this is most crucial when related to training. The linkage between the learning situation and the actual job situation must be specific and definite to meet the need of the learner to apply it to his life within an almost immediate time frame. When looking at education, there is still the intent to apply, but it is in a much longer time frame though the intent to apply is still present. Development makes some people uncomfortable because, though there is the intent to apply, it contains a higher future orientation, and not everybody is able to cope with this. Future orientation makes both the learner and the organization uneasy unless there is recognition that the future orientation is a realistic part of the program.

Experience is a dichotomous element. On one hand, some theories of psychology point out that one learns by association. Experience provides a broad associative base which provides the adult learner with the possibility of learning more. Yet, experience may have imprinted negative impressions upon the learner, such as his inability to learn or the demeaning aspects of some less effective learning situations he has known. The instructor, in a learning situation with adults, cannot approach the learner as if he was a clean slate. The adult learner has been written on, dropped and battered. He brings to the situation the memory of previous learning situations. The effective instructor recognizes and capitalizes on previous experiences. He builds on these so that learning can be enhanced rather than impeded.

On the physiological side, the adult learner is older than the child. This is obvious yet is too frequently ignored. Ample research now shows that he loses acuity in sight and hearing (4). This does not mean that the adult is blind or deaf but that it becomes more difficult for him to use these senses under certain conditions. Also, his response time is slower, which has given rise to the folk tales about "old dogs can't learn new tricks" or "older people are not as intelligent as younger people." Available research (5) indicates that the older learner can still learn effectively but that he learns differently than the younger learner.

The effect of culture and other sociological factors needs to be understood by the instructor and the learner (6). One carries with him much cultural baggage which affects how he learns and what he is ready to learn.

The author worked in Japan at a time when the case study method was being introduced as part of the emerging trend in management training. The Japanese he observed, managers from some of the larger companies, were almost ritualistic in their approach to the case and the methodology. Inevitably, the power structure of the companies represented could be seen in the progression of responses from the learners. The man with the highest status would always speak first. As a Westerner, the author could not always predict who had the highest status. It was a subtle mixture of the company, the age of the man and his university which were among the factors. But, the group knew and behaved accordingly. From evidence today, the use of the case method, the managerial grid and other techniques have impacted to the point where the sessions in Japan reflect the changing culture there. They are more outgoing and less tradition bound. However, the amenities are still observed in ways which are confusing to the non-Japanese.

It is always easier to see the cultural differences when crossing national borders. It is more difficult to identify the cultural differences as they exist within the same organization. Within each organization are smaller units, and each develop their own microcultural behavior. Culture is defined as the habits and customs that people develop to cope with change. As organizations move through their regular existence, and particularly as they respond to change, new microcultural behavior develops. An instructor must be aware of this, for to conflict with the culture of the organization can bring about a disaster in the learning situation. James Belasco and Harrison Trice have referred to these factors as the "Ceremonial Aspects of Training" (7). These are as vital and significant as the subject matter or the methodology. The cultural effects are reflected when using a site away from the work place in order to produce a "cultural island." That is, enabling the learners to experience new behaviors which are not tied to their usual cultural behavior back on the job.

Have you ever noticed how learners sit in a learning situation, particularly if they are returning to the same room several times? Unless something is done, they will go back to exactly the same seats. A "territorial imperative" can be at work (8).

There is still no research to substantiate how this influences learning behavior. The adult learner may situate himself in a particular seat and then challenge the instructor to move him—the challenge is psychological as well as physiological. The learner is inwardly chanting, "They shall not pass," and this can refer to ideas as well as people.

With the influence of culture on clothing, it is sometimes specified in a learning situation that casual clothing will be the order of the day. Is this merely to make the learner more comfortable, or is this an attempt to communicate something beyond the apparel? Is the learner being asked to assume a new cultural pattern within the learning situation? An outward manifestation—the observable cultural behavior—is in the clothes worn to the learning situation. Some encounter groups, those of the nude variety, are likewise endeavoring to deal with the role of clothing in culture but in a way which may find less acceptance among many and even possibly block some kinds of learning.

An aspect which reflects social psychology is the concept of the developmental tasks of an individual—more commonly referred to as the life cycle (9). There are many variations of this, and one model is shown in Table 8.1. Given where the adult learner is on the life cycle, he is more or less prepared to devote energies to different kinds of learning experiences.

The learner who is concerned with community may be less likely to successfully complete a program which has as an end result the necessity for moving to a new community. For example, an employee who is young and has promise is selected. He is told that his next opportunity is at a different plant location far removed from the present community with which he may have a high level of identification. As part of the process to prepare him for the new position, he will be involved in an HRD program.

During the course of the program, the reports indicate that this man just will not be able to successfully complete the program. Without any other data, this man's career with the com-

Table 8.1

Life Cycle of Adults

---

1. Job preparation
2. Job—enter the labor market
3. Marriage
4. Family
5. Community
6. Leisure time—more options
   on how time is spent
7. Disengagement—preparation
   for retirement
8. Retirement—not withdrawal,
   but a new career

---

pany can be irreconcilably damaged. The reports now indicate—this man cannot learn. Yet, it may be that he is resisting
the move to a new location, not the learning. The result can be
the loss of a good employee.

For each individual, the life cycle and its interpretation will
vary. Yet, it does provide an approach to understanding some of
the behavior which does not seem congruent in the learning
situation.

Methodology

Once again, there is a lack of agreement on terminology.
The varying backgrounds of individuals engaged in HRD, the
confusion as to its boundaries and the lack of a recognized body
of knowledge all contribute to this confusion. Attempts have
been made among various kinds of adult educators to bring
some order out of this confusion. Coolie Verner has contributed
by recommending:

Method: the organization of the learning experience
            (i.e., class meeting, get more)
Technique: the process for facilitating learning (i.e., role-
            play, group discussion, panel, etc.)
Device: the mechanical instruments to augment the
            methods and techniques (i.e., audio-visuals,
            physical arrangements) (10).

The general use of these terms would be helpful. However, it is not certain that there is enough agreement among the readers to use them is this discrete fashion. Rather than become embroiled at this point and miss the essence of what the instructor does, the term "methodology" will be used to encompass all three. This is not to understate the problem; it must be confronted at some point. However, it is not one of the more crucial just now, and there are others which must command more time and attention. Of course, the admonition of Coolie Verner, who suggests that attention be given to these terms if research in this area is to be meaningful and useful, should be recognized.

Methodologies available to the instructor are many and varied. Despite all protestations about how little the learner gets from the one-way communication of a lecture, it is still frequently used. One of the many challenges presented is how to get instructors to use the wide variety of methodologies available to them.

Not everybody is convinced of the need for a variety of methodologies. Robert Dubin and Thomas C. Taveggia are convinced that there are no differences in effectiveness between one teaching method and another (11). However, their point of view is not generally shared, and the exponents of one form of method over another can be expected to continue.

There are many factors involved in selecting methodology, and the instructor is usually only one element in the selection process. More research is needed on this point, but some observations can be made.

A learning specialist is limited in the selection of methodologies by many factors. Not the least of these is his own limited knowledge and experience. No one learning specialist can possibly be completely familiar with the vast reservoir of methodologies available now and the flood of those constantly being developed. However, the learning specialist should know where to turn in order to increase his familiarity. For example, the exhibits presented in conjunction with the annual ASTD conference and the various expositions for HRD personnel are a constant source of information and amazement.

What of other factors? Within an organization, there are some traditional ways in which certain tasks have always been learned. There is a tradition as to the kinds of experiences an executive should have before he is considered ready for promotion. It is difficult for the instructor to wander too far from these established patterns. Instead, it may be necessary to function within one of the other roles of HRD (e.g., consultant) to prepare the organization for different ways of learning. Underlying the selection of methodologies is also the self-image of the instructor. Does he feel more comfortable in a highly controlled learning situation or one which is highly task oriented? Is he more comfortable in an unstructured and process-oriented learning situation? Within this continuum, there is a wide range of possibilities. The selection of the appropriate methodology may be more related to the expertise and comfort of the instructor than appropriateness for the learner.

The instructor may be bound by the successes and failures in the past within his own organization. If the case method has proven effective for instructing managers in the past, the instructor may be hard-pressed if he wishes to introduce other methodologies. The logic usually runs something like: We have used the case method in the past, and we have good managers now; therefore, the use of the case method is the way we should be developing our managers. Also, there are the usual examples of an executive having gone to a particular experience and coming back either very imbued with its value or overwhelmed by its invasion of privacy. The experience for this executive will influence the possibility of the instructor either introducing or rejecting the experience.

Multimedia

Through the years, instructional aids and materials come and go. Some have remained to be helpful, but all have left their mark. Among them are role-playing, brainstorming, case method, sensitivity training and programmed instruction. Each has made its contribution but not without the trauma that appears to accompany the introduction of any new methodology. As each one was introduced, it gathered around it exponents who claimed that this was *the* method for learning. Unfortunately, the pressure of commercialism today augurs for this tendency not only to continue but to increase.

There is some hope in the tendency to use the term "multimedia." This connotes the possibility that no one form of media is the most important but that a learning experience can be enhanced by a variety of media. As used here, media is closer to Coolie Verner's devices than to methods or techniques. It is the delivery system which assists in learning but, which, of and by itself is not sufficient for total learning. Media will not be discussed in any depth in this book as the field changes too rapidly. Any listing of media or multimedia at this point would be made inadequate by the time lag imposed between preparation of this manuscipt and the publication of this book. Certainly, after any book has been in the HRD library for two years, the section on media would be ancient history and unusuable.

Given the present sensory age, the use of media becomes not only helpful but essential. If adult learning situations are to compete for the time and attention of the adult, they must do so in the realm of adult experience. People are becoming much more visual, and the requirements for producing visual learning are important. The same problem is being faced today which confronted the public schools prior to World War II when the

16mm film was introduced. Films had essentially been a form of entertainment, and now they were being brought into the classroom. This did not mean that learning could not be entertaining, but entertainment is not designed to change behavior. If behavioral change is indeed the objective of HRD activities, then the use of media must be directed toward this rather than being a time filler or just making the learner happy.

When using media, the instructor must constantly ask himself, "Who is in charge here?" The media, no matter how good or how well planned, should not be controlling the instructor. Rather, no matter how elaborate the media, the instructor must retain his control over the learning situation and decide the appropriateness of the media at that particular point in the learning situation.

Take, for example, the film *The Eye of the Beholder*. This training film was produced in the early 50's and is still widely used. It was far ahead of its time when it was first issued, and, unfortunately, in the hands of some current practitioners, it still remains under-utilized. The film is designed so it can be turned off at midpoint. The manual for discussion which comes with the film specifically states, "Run the film to the midpoint.... Turn off the projector and turn on the room lights as this seems to be a good point at which to stop and discuss" (12). Still, too frequently it is used in its entirety without the midpoint stop.

Another attempt, in 1967, to develop audience involvement was a series of films made for ETV, as well as for company use, entitled *Looking Into Leadership* (13). Because the author was part of the series, he knows the effort which was necessary to design a film which provided for audience involvement during the course of the film. Unfortunately, the series was never adequately utilized to allow for sufficient feedback on the practicability of this approach.

Video tape as well as some new film series are now including specific provision for audience involvement. It is still difficult to get some instructors to turn off the projector before the film is completed, but we are moving in that direction. When instructors have increased mastery over the physical factors of media, they are more likely to use this approach more frequently and more meaningfully.

Evaluation

A valid learning experience should have evaluation built into it. There are many reasons for evaluation, and it takes many forms. Here the main concern is with evaluation of the learning experience while it is being conducted and upon its completion. It is not an evaluation of whether or how the learner will actually use the experience on his job. The responsibility for evaluating the results of training on the job or behavior within the organization goes far beyond the purview of the instructor. In evaluating the actual learning experience, the instructor must relate to objectives. Where the HRD activity has specifically been training, the objectives can usually be specified using the approach of Robert Mager (14). In education and development activities, the objectives are more difficult to specify, and the instructor might find more help in the work of Benjamin Bloom and others (15). Admittedly, Bloom's work is more difficult to use than Mager's, but this does not release the instructor from his responsibility to use the best measures available in stating objectives. A clear statement of objectives must precede any meaningful evaluation.

Also, the particular aspect of HRD involved will influence the kind of evaluation. Usually, training is centered on one component and, therefore, is easier to evaluate. Education and development usually contain a series of related learning experiences and are more complicated. This makes evaluation more difficult but does not lessen the need for it nor the value to be gained from effective evaluation.

The learner should be involved in the evaluation process. He might even be involved in designing the evaluation. The extent to which the learner is involved will once again reflect the concept the instructor has of the learner. Is he to be trusted? This relates back to the battlefield concept which has often been so apparent in grade school and not entirely absent from the university level. If the goal is truly to learn, then the learner should be vitally involved. He can contribute to identifying what has been learned and where learning has fallen short of its goals. If the learner has been involved in his own learning, he should also be involved in his own evaluation.

Before the evaluation is conducted, the instructor should have a clear idea of what he intends to do with the results. This affects his whole instructional process. Too frequently, the evaluation (test) is given during the last session of the learning experience. The learners may receive a grade, certificate or some other indication that they made it. But, they do not know what they made! Which questions did they get right? What was wrong? Where are the soft spots in their learning? For that matter, which answers did they get right but for the wrong reasons? Unless the feedback is planned beforehand, it will not take place. In the situation described in this paragraph, it is relatively easy to shift the test to the session before the last. This allows for feedback while the learning group is still intact, and access to the instructor is a reality.

Other forms of evaluation should likewise include provision for feedback. As part of the evaluation process, the instructor should be able to answer—What will be done with the results of the evaluation? Who should receive these results and in what forms? How are these results intended to influence future learning situations of a similar kind? Feedback is an essential element in the evaluation system and, in itself, is part of the learning for all concerned.

Curriculum Builder

The term "builder" has been specifically chosen when referring to curriculum. It is meant to convey a continual process which produces observable output. Curriculum is the content to be learned and the organization of the sequence in which the learning should take place. It is usually composed of a series of learning units which are organized into a logical sequence.

The actual sequence of the learning may be modified by the instructor at the time the learning experience occurs. It is incumbent upon the instructor to know enough about how the curriculum was built and the concept underlying the particular curriculum so that he can vary, as needed, without destroying the basic conceptualization. The curriculum builder will be influenced by his own conception of the importance of the curriculum to the learning situation. He will also be influenced by his own philosophy of the adult learner and the psychological theories to which he subscribes. There are no absolutes though there are some general guidelines. Gordon Lippitt and Leslie This, in a two-part article in the *Training and Development Journal* in April and May 1966, listed six theories of learning: (1) behaviorist, (2) Gestalt, (3) Freudian, (4) functionalist, (5) mathematical models and (6) current learning theories (i.e., postulate system, social learning theory) (16). It is not necessary for a curriculum builder to subscribe to any one of these schools. He should know that they exist and the implications they have for his work as a curriculum builder.

Involving Others

The effective curriculum builder does not sit in a little office cutting and pasting as he puts together a curriculum from various sources. Rather, he must be out where the action is—actually communicating with those who are related to the learning situation. In HRD, this includes more than the learner and the instructor. There is the person to whom the learner has a responsibility, as well as the learner's own peer group.

One criticism being leveled at the HRD programs for "disadvantaged" today is that too few learners are involved in the curriculum building process. The disadvantaged cannot build the curriculum by themselves—they obviously cannot know the subject matter they must learn to be more effective in the economy. However, too infrequently is the learner involved. Rather, a curriculum is developed which is a smorgasbord. Hopefully, the learner will ingest the appropriate parts of it and become an effective employee. The disadvantaged may be unemployed and even illiterate, but he is not ignorant nor ineffective. To stay alive, he has developed a high level of adaptability and the faculty for learning what it takes to survive. As more of the disadvantaged join the labor force and move up from entry-level positions, more will be involved in building curriculum.

Curriculum content should always be available to be influenced by those who are concerned with the learning. Robert Mager and Cecil Clark reviewed various studies concerned with learner control of the instruction and/or curriculum. In general, they observed that learners frequently came to the situation already knowning some of what they were going to be taught. Also, learners who have control of the curriculum tend to learn faster (17).

Actual curriculum building is not limited to an analysis of job behavior, the job description or a task analysis. In building a learning experience for individuals, rather than for a machine, the various parts of the learner's system must be involved. This is necessary to support the new behaviors produced in the learning experience. Any curriculum builder needs the competencies of dealing with individuals and groups and having the patience to build the curriculum with reference to the contributions of these various individuals and groups. After working with them the curriculum builder now has the responsibility of selecting the appropriate content. Then the curriculum builder can begin to identify the sequence of the learning experiences which will enable the learner to learn the content.

Once again, the effect of the curriculum builder's own philosophy of adult learning and his familiarity with the various schools of psychology will influence the way in which he builds the curriculum for implementation.

Outlines and Guides

The observable output of the curriculum builder will be specific in the forms of guides, outlines, syllabi and other kinds of teaching materials which indicate how the curriculum is to be implemented. On the mechanical side, one of the classic books on preparing such guides is *How to Prepare Training Manuals* by Lynn A. Emerson (18). Though this book was published in 1952, it is still helpful to the curriculum builder who may be expected to produce an actual manual. Since its publication, this field has benefited from improved methods of reproduction, and, therefore, it is possible to produce curriculum guides in other forms. However, the curriculum should be specifically and clearly stated so that all involved, including the learner, can refer back to it and know what was intended to be accomplished.

Even though the curriculum is published, it should still be amenable to change. The instructor cannot be locked into the curriculum as if it were a legal document requiring elaborate procedures for modification. The curriculum builder must build in flexibility so the curriculum can be modified throughout the learning process.

During the learning experience, there should be the opportunity for both the instructor and the learner to make modifications. In many cases, the curriculum should contain alternatives. It must respond to the ways in which learning takes place in particular situations and the possibilities of variation with the development of the group and the passage of time.

Evaluation

The curriculum should indicate specifically the kinds of evaluation which are required at various points. The evaluation should be directed not only to the change brought about in the learner but also to what changes need to be brought about in the curriculum. A result of each learning situation should be to reappraise the effectiveness of the curriculum and the extent to which it needs to be altered before its next use.

The curriculum can actually contain the test material to be used or the kinds of experiences which will provide evaluation data. Where this is done, the data collection instruments or exercises must be included as part of the curriculum process. The curriculum builder, if he is not fully competent in test construction, may either use some standardized tests or call upon outside resources for assistance.

In using the traditional pretest and post-test, the curriculum builder must be cautious about the obvious data he collects. Harold E. Crawford reports an experience of the Honeywell Company in using an off-the-shelf program in effective listening, which was widely marketed. He decided to reverse the procedure of the pretest and the post-test. He gave the post-test first, conducted the program and then gave the pretest. Crawford found that the pretest was harder and therefore had to produce lower scores than the post-test no matter what went on in the training program (19). More HRD persons are needed with the courage to be critical of evaluation, particularly that provided in packaged programs.

Just as the curriculum builder involved the learner, the learner's boss and the learner's peers in developing the curriculum, he should likewise involve them in the evaluation procedure. The data should be fed back to them. These three groups should likewise be involved in the process of redesigning the curriculum.

At times, other groups should also be involved. In retail training, the customer can make significant inputs to the curriculum. He knows what the sales person should be doing to him and for him. If the customer does not know, then it may indicate the need for customer training. Consumers have their opinions but are too infrequently asked for them. Even in a production operation, there is still a "customer." He is the employee who receives the output of the person being trained. As a receiver of this output he may have much to offer to the curriculum builder.

Methods and Materials Developer

Once again, it is not the purpose of this section to become involved in the distinction among methods, techniques and devices. Rather, this section deals with the development of methodologies and their relation to the curriculum. Methodologies should be explored after the curriculum has been built. The injunction of the architect that "function determines form" has application here. Until the function (curriculum) has been developed and clarified, there should be little exploration of form (i.e., role-playing, programmed instruction, et cetera). Assuming that the essential curriculum has been built, it is now possible to commence the work on methods and materials. Sometimes, the same specialist who has built the curriculum will also be developing the methods and materials. However, as the range of methods increases and the scope of materials becomes more involved with electronics and technology, it cannot be expected that the curriculum builder will also have the capability for developing the methods and materials.

The curriculum builder should be aware of the range of possibilities though he need not have the skills for developing them. At a very elemental level, it is much like the curriculum builder who, within his curriculum, cites the need for certain points to be made and suggests the use of a transparency. He may not be able to actually make the transparency and may have no artistic ability to do this. On the other hand, the methods and materials builder to whom he turns should be more than a draftsman or artist. He too must know something of the psychological and learning implications of the different kinds of materials being employed, as well as keeping abreast of the rapid changes being made in the various forms of educational technology.

Educational Technology

What is educational technology? A definition cannot be attempted without recognizing that it could not possibly receive general acceptance. P. Kenneth Komoski, who has been involved for many years, has urged that there be a clarification of the messy speech which surrounds this specialization (20).

As used here, educational technology represents the application of the concepts of technology to the field of learning. This has basically resulted in improved presentation devices for learning. It is the development of effective delivery systems for learning after the curriculum has been built. Educational technology is designed to assist the instructor and even assume some of his functions. It does not replace the instructor but frees him for other activities which require the man-man interface rather than the man-machine interface.

The educational technologist as a specialist has only been around since the 60's. The advent of the teaching machines in the early part of the 60's was the first major input by the educational technologist. It is unfortunate that today too many educational technologists are still limiting themselves to only the teaching machine or some of its offspring. The polarization of man versus machine is an artificial one and, unfortunately, tends to obscure the question of what is to be learned and how. Until the subject matter is developed from the objectives and the nature of the learner taken into account, no commitment should be made as to the particular form of the learning experience.

Various kinds of educational technology are readily available to the methods and materials developer who works in concert with the curriculum builder and the instructor. One of the problems in the past has been the tendency of the educational technologist to move in his own direction without remaining fully aware of the curriculum builder or the instructor. The implications and the statements that technology would replace the instructor were inappropriate, and still surviving is the heat they generated. To threaten the instructor with being replaced by technology and then expect him to use that technology is to indicate a willful ignorance of human behavior. The educational technologists have become less vocal on this score and now are talking about role-plays and simulation which require a live instructor.

Conflict still exists between behavioral technology and behavioral science, and much needs to be done to bring the two together to jointly contribute to learning situations. Some educational technologists continue throwing epithets of "Luddites," "machine wreckers" and "reactionaries" at the instructor and curriculum builder. Is it any wonder that there is resistance to accepting the legitimate contributions that the technologists can make?

When the instructor and curriculum builder have only a limited background in instructional technologies and the various psychological theories of learning, there is a tendency to become overwhelmed by the glamour of the devices offered by the educational technologist. Many are the devices (hardware) with their unblinking blind eyes staring accusingly at their purchasers because of the lack of adequate material (software).

Make or Buy

The methods and materials developer must decide whether he should develop resources in-house or move out of house, particularly for his materials. There is no easy answer to this. There are a variety of public seminars being conducted to assist developers in arriving at these make-buy decisions. At this point, there will be no in-depth discussion on this as there are too many variables which must be considered. The nature of the market offerings change so rapidly that it is impossible to make any specific judgment. It is necessary, however, to look at some considerations.

The make-buy decision is influenced by the kinds of organizations in the field and the resources they provide. For example, there are those who specialize in providing off-the-shelf material. That is, the materials that they have carefully and professionally developed which are now packaged or boxed. Some of these materials must be used exactly as designed, such as programmed instruction. Others contain within them the flexibility to modify for the particular learners and conditions. This is more the situation with films and other projected learning aids.

There was a time when the manufacturers of video tape suggested that their equipment would give the HRD staff the resource for creating in-house films. It was only later, after purchasing some of the more expensive equipment, that it became clear that producing a film was more complicated than running a video tape.

Internal budget procedures may influence the make-buy decision. The methods and materials developer may find that in his organization he can have adequate budget for purchasing some of the raw materials with which he can work. However, to purchase a finished off-the-shelf product may be more difficult. The internal budgeting procedures may be directing the decisions regarding learning materials.

A too apparent trap is the cost-use ratio applied to materials. After making the purchase, the HRD unit is pressed to report how often it has been used—what is the cost per student? This encourages using the material as frequently as possible so as to be able to report a good ratio. The learning implications of the material may be less important for they do not lend themselves to statistical reporting.

As more private companies are entering the education field, the make-buy decision will become more difficult. Though the range of materials available will increase, so will the sales pressure. There is nothing unethical implied here. It is the usual concept of caveat emptor—let the buyer beware. This injunction should likewise apply to methods and the use of outside consulting and training firms who bring to the situation a particular method. In the absence of any certification procedures, and there is very little pressure in this direction, the HRD person concerned with methods will have to evolve his own criteria.

Evaluate

Just as the instructional process and the curriculum are to be evaluated, so will methods and materials. This is difficult and underscores a problem with methods and materials. They are not discrete elements but are related to the instructor and curriculum. A good film may be reflected in the evaluation by data which say that the instructor did a good job. This may be a result even though the instructor had nothing to do with the production of the film and possibly even little to do with its selection.

Evaluation of methods and materials is more appropriately obtained by feedback from the instructor rather than the learner. The instructor and curriculum builder should be directly involved in evaluating methods and materials. The learner should not be ignored, but he is less able to contribute to this particular area of evaluation. In any event, the methods and materials should be subjected to evaluation and the appropriate feedback so that they can continue to be improved and made more relevant to the learning situation.

Staffing

Given the parameters discussed above, what kind of individuals should be sought for these HRD positions? At this time, it is highly unlikely that this can be too readily answered. For the most part, there are too few institutions of higher learning which prepare the necessary individuals.

An instructor might come from a teacher-training institution. This could be supplemented by actual experience. In the case of vocational instructors, the experience should be in the field which he is teaching. This will be discussed further when the world of the HRD administrator is explored.

The armed services for many years have concentrated on producing good instructors. There was the recognition that in HRD operations involving large numbers of learners, the subrole of the instructor could be separated from the other subroles of the learning specialist. This enabled the military to concentrate on meeting their need for instructors by using persons with little or no professional preparation. This instructor relies heavily on professionally produced curricula and materials.

The curriculum builder is much more difficult to find. There are too few HRD specialists concerned with developing curriculum. It is the least visible part of the learning specialist role and is not nearly as glamorous as the instructor who is highly visible or the methods and materials developer whose physical imprint upon the learning situation is obvious. The curriculum builder functions behind the scenes but in concert with other parts of the organization. This may be a less rewarding job for those in HRD who have high ego needs. As a result, too often the curriculum has been put together by individuals who do not have the necessary background to function effectively in this area.

Today, the methods and materials developer is becoming the easiest position to staff. Special programs at universities have evolved which are designed to meet the needs of methods and materials developers. Leading in the field are programs such as the audio-visual offerings at Indiana University. On the educational technology side is the program offered at Catholic University, Washington, D. C. This latter program emphasizes the Skinnerian approach with heavy emphasis on devices. Where the methods and materials developer brings a single psychological orientation to the situation, he will find it difficult to work with the instructors and curriculum builders who may have identified with other psychological schools. The HRD director in building his staff must recognize the limitation and opportunities provided by selecting individuals with various psychological and educational identifications.

It is not always necessary to have at least three different individuals staffing the subroles of the learning specialist. It is more common to find that the staff includes learning specialists who serve in more than one subrole. It is not unusual to find learning specialists who are expected to meet the requirements of all three subroles.

The concept of HRD within the organization influences the staffing and operation of these three subroles of the learning specialist. In a large organization where the three subroles all carry status, there may be little difficulty in getting people to identify within these roles. However, where the HRD function is small, it is unlikely that any of these subroles will carry with it sufficient prestige and salary to attract the kinds of individuals who can also function as administrators or in-house consultants.

The concept of the "new careers" program (21) has implications for aspects of the materials developer role. It is possible the sub-professionals can perform some of this function at a more than adequate level when guidance is supplied by appropriate curriculum builders and instructors. With leadership from competent administrators, this is already being done among organizations who have designated "training assistants" or "training aides." These are usually individuals without a college degree who are able to perform the methods and materials developer role at a fairly high level. They might not be able to serve as the educational technologist, but they can perform some of the other functions particularly in the area of materials construction.

For each organization, the concepts for staffing these roles is a matter of concern. It is not only that these roles be performed, but how they relate to the total HRD function and to the objectives of HRD within the organization. Ultimately, the effective performance of these roles is dependent upon the administrative leadership provided within HRD.

Literature Citations

1. One model of this concept can be found in Everett L. Shostrom, *Man, the Manipulator: The Inner Journey from Manipulation to Actualization* (New York: Bantam Books, 1968).
2. A discussion of the attitude of the instructor as well as the learner can be found in Robert Mager, *Developing Attitude Toward Learning* (Palo Alton: Fearon Publishers, 1968).
3. Although it is quite a few years old, the reader will still find a high degree of relevancy in J. R. Kidd, *How Adults Learn* (New York: Association Press, 1959).

4. A report of the some of the research, though without sources, is contained in a short but helpful article by Gary Dickinson, "Facts on Sight and Hearing in Training Adults," *Training in Business and Industry,* October 1969, pp. 56-57.

5. A compilation of some of this research can be found in Jane C. Zahn, "Differences Between Adults and Youths Affecting Learning," *Adult Education,* Winter 1967, pp. 67-77.

6. Robert W. Burns, *Sociological Backgrounds of Adult Education* (Originally published by the Center for the Study of Liberal Education for Adults in 1964; the Center has now been disbanded and its publications are available from the University of Syracuse).

7. The study is reported in James Belasco and Harrison M. Trice, "Unanticipated Returns of Training," *Training and Development Journal,* July 1969, pp. 12-17.

8. Robert Ardrey, *The Territorial Imperative* (New York: Atheneum, 1966). He basically reports on research and observations with animals. Although he makes the leap into human behavior, I am not convinced the data can be so easily transferred. However, it is a place to start as we look further into human behavior related to territory and prerogatives.

9. Some aspects of the life cycle as well as research related to adult learning can be found in Raymond G. Kuhlen, ed. *Psychological Backgrounds of Adult Education* (Originally published by the Center for the Study of Liberal Education for Adults in 1963; the Center has now been disbanded and its publications are available from the University of Syracuse).

10. Coolie Verner, "Definition of Terms" in *Adult Education: Outlines of an Emerging Field of University Study,* Gales Jensen, A. A. Liveright and Wilbur Hallenbeck (Washington: Adult Education Association, 1964), pp. 35-37.

11. Robert Dubin and Thomas C. Taveggia, *The Teaching-Learning Paradox* (Published in 1968 by the Center for the Advanced Study of Educational Administration, University of Oregon). A report of this was also carried under the heading of " 'The Little Black Box' of Teaching and Learning," *Trans-Action,* October 1969, p. 10.

12. The film is available from Stuart Reynolds Productions, 9465 Wilshire Boulevard, Beverly Hills, California.

13. The series of eight films was developed by Warren Schmidt, Gordon Lippitt, Leslie This and Leonard Nadler. Information on the series is available from Educational Systems and Design Co., Westport, Connecticut.

14. Robert F. Mager, *Preparing Instructional Objectives* (Palo Alto: Fearon Publishers, 1962).

15. The two books which are helpful in this area are Benjamin Bloom, ed., *Taxonomy of Educational Objectives, Handbook I: Cognitive Domain* (New York: David McKay, 1956). Also, David R. Krathwhol, Benjamin Bloom and Bertram B. Masia, *Taxonomy of Educational Objectives, Handbook II: Affective Domain* (New York: David McKay, 1964).

16. Leslie This and Gordon Lippitt, "Learning Theories and Training," *Training and Development Journal,* Part I: April 1966, pp. 2-11 and Part II: May 1966, pp. 10-17.

17. Several studies related to this are reported by Robert F. Mager and Cecil Clark, "Exploration in Student-controlled Instruction" in *Current Research on Instruction,* ed. Richard C. Anderson, et al. (Englewood Cliffs: Prentice-Hall, 1969), p. 56.

18. Although it may no longer be in print, the book referred to is Lynn A. Emerson, *How to Prepare Training Manuals: A Guide in the Preparation of Written Instructional Materials* (New York: The State Education Department, 1952).

19. Harold E. Crawford, "A Note of Caution on Listening Training," *Training and Development Journal,* pp. 23-28.

20. P. Kenneth Komoski, "The Continuing Confusion about Technology and Education," *Educational Technology,* November 1969, pp. 70-74.

21. The New Careers program is an exciting concept which should involve persons engaged in HRD. Information can be obtained from Frank Riessman, Director, New Careers Development Center, 239 Greene Street, Room 23B, New York University, New York, New York, 10003.

9

Administrator

When moving into the role of the HRD specialist as an administrator, the practitioner in the field faces a variety of conflicts. Many individuals become involved in HRD because of a high degree of concern with people. There is a desire to become involved in those activities which are people centered and people oriented. Although an administrator must be concerned with people, he functions much differently than the HRD person serving as a learning specialist.

The difference in roles has contributed to management's practice of assigning administrators to the HRD function who have come from outside operations. In simplistic terms, the learning specialist is expected to have a high concern with people but less of an interest in the kind of duties expected of an administrator. Obviously, they are different jobs. Too often the mistake is made of taking a good specialist and forcing him to be a poor administrator. The fields of health, education and engineering have all experienced this problem. Yet, advancement is in the

202

administrative line. Therefore, the HRD person who wishes to move ahead in the field—who seeks advancement in his own or other organizations—must explore his own needs as they relate to the subroles of HRD. The learning specialist can become an administrator but should do so out of choice rather than frustration.

There are many ways to look at administration. In studies done by Robert Livingston and Daniel Davies, they identified four major areas in which all administrators function (1). When this is used as a model, the subroles of the HRD administrator are (1) developer of personnel, (2) maintainer of community relations, (3) supervisor of on-going programs and (4) arranger of facilities and finances.

Although these four areas apply to any administrator, there is particular significance as applied to the HRD administrator. As will be seen in the discussion, just being a competent administrator is insufficient. The administrator of human resource development activities must have a sound understanding of the learning process and of the educational elements involved. He is an administrator but an administrator of an educational function, usually in a nonschool agency. Once again, it should be pointed out that this does not imply that he must have served as a learning specialist before becoming an administrator of HRD. However, he needs a sufficient background in education so that he can make the most effective use of his opportunities as an administrator of a function based on learning (i.e., education).

Developer of Personnel

To avoid confusion, the distinction must be made at the outset that in this section concern will be with the personnel working in HRD or directly related to it. A major purpose of all HRD activities is the development of all personnel. In that context, HRD is concerned with the entire organization or group served by HRD. In the discussion of this subrole, focus will be on the HRD personnel who should be developed as a task of the HRD administrator.

Regular Staff

There is no magic formula as to the size of the regular staff. The importance lies in which of the various subroles need to be performed by regular in-house personnel assigned to HRD. As can be seen by the overview in Chapter 7, there are 11 subroles which have been identified at this time. It is not unlikely that additional subroles will evolve as concern with people increases, and additional attention is devoted to human resource development. At this time, even the staffing of the 11 identified subroles is not an easy matter. Frequently, the various subroles are combined, and one individual is expected to fill more than one subrole. For example, there may be only one person administering the HRD function and therefore serving in the four subroles discussed in this chapter. He will be expected to do all of the administrative aspects of HRD. In addition, he may also at times function as a learning specialist.

The source of the regular staff influences their identification with the HRD function. Where the HRD staff consider this job assignment as an essential stage of their professional life, are adequately prepared and are very much involved, then it is certainly much different than where the HRD personnel merely see this assignment as a stepping stone to a higher or different position. The administrator is challenged to organize his HRD operation in such a manner that professional growth and development is encouraged and recognized within the HRD function. Reward systems have to be structured so there is sufficient reason for the employee to remain within this function rather than to seek his rewards in another part of the organization or a different organization.

This does not mean that when an individual is wholly within HRD, mobility within his organization is absolutely stopped.

This should not be the case in any part of the organization and certainly not in HRD. But, there should be a sufficiently lengthy relationship so that new HRD people are not in the constant state of "rediscovering the wheel." HRD has progressed to the point where certain levels of preparation are essential if the organization is to realize a significant return on its investment in HRD activities.

Temporary and Part Time

In addition to the regular staff, it is common, and sometimes essential, to provide for temporary and part-time personnel. These can come from in-house sources or out-of-house resources.

On the in-house side, frequent use is made of line personnel who are assigned to the HRD function either on a temporary or part-time basis. As a temporary employee, it may be for a period of several months, or even as long as a year. On part time, it can be an assignment of merely a certain number of hours a day in order to take part in a particular program. Those who are assigned to HRD for a phase of their career should not be considered as temporary but as regular members of the staff.

An example of temporary assignment is in the Hands On Training Center of Eastman Kodak Company at Kodak Park in Rochester. In this facility, a line foreman is assigned as an instructor for six months. This is a specific temporary assignment with no intention that the foreman will remain on the staff of the Center. After the six-month temporary assignment, he will return to his regular job as a line foreman.

A part-time training assignment can be illustrated by one of the author's experiences when he was a Training Supervisor with the Department of Civil Service in New York State in 1955. The department was responsible for supervisory training in the mental institutions throughout the state. The pattern that evolved was to use actual supervisors to conduct the supervisory training program (2). Selected supervisors were given a one-week Conference Leadership Program which prepared them to conduct the supervisory training conference with materials developed and supplied by the central training unit. The supervisors then returned to their own institutions and conducted the sessions. Their assignment was for two hours a week for 15 weeks. Of course, there was some provision for preparation for the session. However, aside from the limited time spent as a training conference leader, the supervisor remained on his job carrying out the regular duties of his position.

Out-of-house people are usually not considered part of the responsibility of the HRD administrator and therein lies one problem. If the HRD administrator has brought in an outside individual, either on a temporary or part-time basis, the administrator also has the responsibility to see that the person so involved is adequately briefed and performs to the standard expected for the particular assignment. The most common part-time personnel are the learning specialists (i.e., speakers or instructors) brought in from the outside to conduct a portion of an HRD activity. It may be a particular individual or several individuals through one of the numerous training and consulting organizations which dot the HRD landscape.

The administrator cannot be expected to devote an inordinate amount of time to the temporary/part-time learning specialist. After all, the resource has been brought in because of expertise, and the organization is paying a fee for professional services. Still, unless the administrator is purchasing a "canned" program, there is the need for linkage with the organization. It might be as minimal as a luncheon with the person before the program begins. There may be the necessity for a plant tour or some other kind of orientation if the outside learning specialist is to relate to the needs of the organization.

The learning specialist role is not the only one where out-of-house personnel, temporary or part-time, are utilized. It is probably the most frequent and certainly the most visible. Yet, the concept remains the same no matter which subrole is being filled. The administrator must do more than just sign the purchase requisition or the contract. He must be able to effectively communicate with this resource person so that a knowledge of current practices in HRD is essential for the administrator.

Temporary persons from outside are not too common. The more frequent practice is that of part time. Of course, the personnel purist might insist that a learning specialist-instructor who conducts a three-day program is a temporary rather than part-time resource. The personnel practices in the individual organization will usually determine the classification for the services to be performed, particularly where the outside resource is paid as an employee (as in some government agencies) rather than as a private contractor.

A long-term temporary relationship is also possible. Because of the academic year and sabbaticals, this is often found among members of the academic community. The *Federal Trainer* reported that:

> University professors make valuable summer hires. Research and staff studies are often their cup of tea. CSC's New York Regional Training Center hired a sociology instructor...to look at Federal practices in training minimally-skilled workers and their supervisors. The professor plans to publish his research, which meanwhile benefits CSC. In this case the research findings on the bureaucratic barriers to effective training are being circulated among Commission staff who plan and conduct such training. The refreshing insights of an astute outsider can be as valuable as his work contribution itself (3).

Whether in-house or out-of-house, the temporary and part-time persons associated with HRD need appropriate support from the HRD administrator. It should be more than tolerating the presence of a temporary or part-time outsider—it should be the recognition of the opportunity provided by having additional new personnel working within the HRD function.

Professional Growth

The administrator of HRD must see that his staff not only provides HRD opportunities to the organization but that they avail themselves of opportunities for their own growth and development. Frequently, HRD operations have worked effectively in providing opportunities for non-HRD personnel. The brochures and other materials indicating the extent of the opportunities are indeed impressive, but when asked to identify how some of these opportunities can be made available to HRD staff, the silence is deafening. For example, ASTD has over 9,000 members but fewer than 1,000 of them attend the annual conference. Assuming that the annual conference meets a need in the professional growth area, and this is a fair assumption, why are not more HRD personnel attending? No study has been done in this area, but numerous informal conversations disclose responses such as, "I am not high enough in my organization to go to meetings like that," or, "We have never asked for that in our budget."

Lack of participation in professional growth activities is related to the concept of the administrator who believes that no special kind of preparation is needed for a person to be assigned to HRD activities. The administrator will probably have extended this thinking to himself and thereby justify his own lack of participation in professional growth experiences. Inevitably, the self-fulfilling prophecy takes effect, and the decision is reached that professional growth opportunities need not be provided for anybody involved in the HRD function. When an administrator has reached this point, it is indeed unfortunate for all concerned. He is depriving his organization of the many values to be gained by having a professionally alert and up-to-date HRD staff.

At a minimal level, the HRD administrator should make adequate provision for his staff to have access to the latest books, periodicals and journals on aspects of HRD. There are numerous public seminars available which are directed specifically toward HRD personnel. Professional organizations exist in the HRD field, and among the leaders is the American Society for Training and Development. The HRD administrator should encourage his staff to be active in the professional organization, regularly read the *Training and Development Journal* and attend the national conference as well as the local and regional institutes and workshops. Indeed, the HRD administrator should be setting the example of professional behavior for his staff by himself being active in the affairs of the organization and influencing its directions of growth.

For other HRD subroles, there are organizations which are likewise designed to contribute to professional growth. As the field continues to grow and change, formation of additional organizations can be expected. The problem now is the proliferation of organizations concerned with human resource development. At present, the methods and materials developer might be encouraged to also join the National Society for Programmed Instruction or the Department of Audio-Visual Instruction of NEA.

The self-image of the HRD administrator is obviously reflected in the professional growth opportunities he provides for his staff and for himself. As with many other kinds of professional personnel, if the HRD administrator cannot provide adequate growth opportunities, he may find his good people moving on to other jobs in other organizations where positive opportunities for professional growth and development are available. It is unfortunate when the very function it is organized to provide is not extended to the HRD staff.

Supervisor of On-Going Programs

The HRD activity is a continuing and on-going process. Almost every organization engages in some form of HRD, though not all organizations make specific provision for it. They tend to favor the British system of "sitting by Nellie." In the

U.S. this is called OJT, but more often it is merely an unstructured observation program rather than a real contribution to learning for an individual.

Within a particular organization, the nature of the HRD activities is the result of many factors which are special and peculiar to that organization and to its employees. The wide range of possible programs in HRD requires an equally wide repetoire of supervisory styles by the HRD administrator. The size of the HRD staff, the extent of its function and the HRD concepts in the organization will all impact on the kinds of leadership the HRD administrator must provide when functioning in this subrole.

Assigns Personnel

The size of the HRD staff affects the assignment of personnel. Where it is a small group, there is very little to assign in the way of personnel. However, even a small staff may be involved in large and meaningful programs. By bringing in outside resources, the HRD administrator can provide learning experiences far in excess of what might be expected when only measured by staff size.

Assigning personnel is more than just a matter of scheduling who is available, at what time, to go to which place. Where there is a multi-site operation, the HRD man may be expected to spend a good deal of his time in the field. Some individuals thrive on this kind of assignment, whereas for others it is tantamount to being sent into exile. At present, the HRD operation has many areas of insecurity, not the least of which is the area discussed many times before—the lack of identification with a professional group or a recognized discipline. In addition to this ambiguity, being sent "on the road" for considerable periods of time can contribute to inducing anxiety in the staff.

In a large organization, a practice can evolve whereby certain HRD staff members become identified with particular departments or operations. At times, this can be helpful. The higher the level of trust, the more likely that the HRD person can contribute to the success of those he is serving. Of course, this must be measured against the problem of over-identification and becoming too involved in the workings of a particular department. The same hesitations must apply when HRD personnel are assigned to a particular geographical area.

To date, little has been done to investigate the most effective way to assign personnel when the variables are multi-plant, geography or specializations such as clerical or engineering. Much more needs to be learned about how to use the HRD staff effectively, particularly in larger organizations.

Where the HRD function is staffed with more than a single person, delegation is useful if not necessary. This is true of any supervisor, and it would be well for the HRD supervisor to carefully study some of the material contained in his own programs. In an organization of any size, it is impossible for the supervisor to do all that is necessary. He must learn how to delegate and to whom to delegate. He may have certain areas in which he feels more comfortable and more productive which he prefers to reserve for himself. This is not unlike the usual problem of any technical person who becomes a supervisor. The HRD person who has been functioning as a learning specialist and now becomes an HRD administrator must be prepared to leave the classroom and the satisfaction he has been receiving from the direct relationship with the students in the learning experience. This does not mean that he will no longer provide any leadership in the classroom, but he must be prepared to assign this to others so he can devote more of his time to the requirements of his administrative role.

Records

Record keeping is one of the banes in the life of any personnel involved in the learning process. The public school teacher is plagued with all kinds of scholastic and nonscholastic reports, forms, tallies and lists. In recent years, the Teacher Aide has emerged to enable the classroom teacher to be relieved of some of the record keeping (4).

Where company assets are involved, record keeping becomes a prime aspect of any administrator's functions. The supervisor must provide for those records which are necessary for the purpose of reporting to various levels of management. It serves, for example, to report achievements and progress within his own function. This need not be limited only to the headcount which has been discussed earlier, even though this is easily the most convenient report—readily quantifiable and reproducible on colored charts and graphs. There are other kinds of reports which are helpful to management, and the HRD supervisor must identify the kinds of records which must be maintained to provide the necessary information to all those concerned.

A narrative report at the end of some programs can be helpful. In a training program for supervisors, there is usually generated a certain amount of "if only they would" type of information. The supervisors, as they go through the program, vow that their job could be easier, more meaningful and more productive, if only management (or some other *they*) would also do. . .(one can fill this in quite easily during any supervisory program). To ignore this as name-calling, scapegoating, flight or any other manifestation of trying to shift responsibility is to be unfair to many good supervisors. They want to do their job, or at least this assumption should be made unless proven otherwise. The training program can serve as a nonthreatening line of communication upwards through end-of-program narrative reports.

A technique used by the author is the "they" sheet. During a training program, each time a confrontation is met with pointing the verbal finger at some other group, the trainee who made the statement puts it on a sheet of newsprint conveniently placed on the wall of the training room. Near the end of the program, whether one day or several, time is taken to review the "they" sheet. It has usually been found that most of the items are no longer meaningful or relevant. However, if some notations still remain and the group concensus supports it, a note will go from the out-of-house resource person to the HRD administrator. He is encouraged to include this material in reports which he makes to management. It is amazing the number of times the HRD administrator and his management have responded with—"We never knew that. . ." Of course, if there was not the need for this kind of communication, there might not have been the necessity for a training program.

One practice is to keep a record for each employee. If this is done, there must be a high degree of cooperation with the personnel department or other parts of the organization where individual personnel files are maintained. Particularly, having gone further into the computerization of personnel data, it is likely that the HRD information can be included within the data bank already developed. This can provide not only the statistical data needed for certain kinds of reports but also provide a history of development of individual employees during their time on the company payroll.

As a supervisor, one record which must be maintained is that of appraisal of personnel. The HRD supervisor is responsible for performance appraisal of HRD staff, just as any other supervisor in his organization. Not only should the HRD supervisor be highly competent in completing such an appraisal but also in maintaining appropriate records. This assures that the appraisal is not just a once-a-year operation but the basis for a continuing approach to the growth of individuals.

Evaluation

The constant cries for evaluation are deafening. One gets the feeling that there is no evaluation of HRD—that it is all a matter of hurrying, though the direction is unknown. Actually, a great deal of evaluation is constantly being conducted as part of HRD activities. Efforts should be concerned with making them more meaningful and sharing them with other members of the organization.

Evaluation is essentially the process of finding out what has happened. In pure learning terms, it is the activity designed to determine if the objectives of the learning have been met. This implies that learning starts with objectives, and this is not always the case.

This book is not designed as a primer on evaluation, so the discussion will be on the role of the administrator in evaluation rather than the process itself. To say that the administrator encourages evaluation is to sidestep the basic issues. The administrator cannot encourage a process which he knows little about or which makes him insecure. If the administrator is to provide leadership to his staff in the evaluation process, he must know what it is, how it is done and how it can be used. He must also be aware of its limitations. Once again if he does not know education and the behavioral sciences, it is doubtful if the administrator of human resource development can provide the leadership the position demands.

Evaluation should be part of every on-going program which relates to HRD. There are some sophisticated techniques available, and these may require the services of an outside specialist in order to develop the appropriate ones for the particular situation. There are some which are more readily available for use by the learning specialist. Standardized tests may be appropriate if they relate directly to the objectives of the learning situation.

More than outcomes must be evaluated. Each part of the learning process should be subject to evaluation. Equally important is that the results of the evaluation should be shared. In a recent learning experience, members of the client system developed a workshop learning experience for themselves through the use of a steering committee. This was supplemented by an evaluation group of several of the participants (they were all instructors in a company school) who designed and administered an evaluation instrument. At the next planning meeting, it was discovered that despite all previous plans, no adequate provision had been made for distributing the results of the evaluation to all the participants. Even the members of the steering committee and one member of the evaluation group had not seen the report on the evaluation. Further probing disclosed that it had not been the pattern in the past to share the results of evaluation. The evaluation files were most complete, but they were not to be shared. Organizational behavior had to be changed before the results could adequately be shared with all concerned.

Research

Research differs from evaluation but is still a responsibility of the HRD supervisor. Research is a systematic experience designed to identify facts or principles concerning a particular topic. It does not start out with objectives, though it will usually have carefully stated hypotheses or statements of purpose.

Research can range from determining the effectiveness of a particular instructional methodology to identifying the change in organizational behavior as a result of a particular kind of human resource development. It should be capable of replication both for testing of validity and for use by other persons.

The HRD supervisor should encourage research and provide for the results of research being made constantly available to his staff. Conducting research requires certain highly developed skills which may not always be present on the HRD staff. In such situations, the HRD supervisor may once again turn to an outside resource. As graduate programs in HRD continue to increase, there will be larger numbers of graduate students seeking appropriate dissertation topics. Also, there will be more professors involved in the field, and they, too, will be available to at least design, if not conduct, the desired research.

A good deal of research is being generated today by government programs, principally those under the Manpower Administration (5). The HRD administrator may want to become involved in research by obtaining funds available from the federal government for that purpose. However, if he prefers not to have the federal government involved, he can seek out other sources of research funds. As yet, they are not easy to identify and even more difficult to obtain. If he can encourage his own organization to support research, this is highly desirable. It is also exceedingly difficult as he may not be able to show a direct return to his organization for the expense. Within HRD, research is a highly desirable activity but does not of itself generate a profit or reduce cost. Therefore, it is more difficult to justify the allocation of resources to research in the absence of being able to promise any direct return for it.

Develop Policy

The HRD supervisor is responsible for developing policy concerning the development of human resources in his organization. The process of developing policies should be consistent with the usual procedures within his organization for policy formulation and declaration. There are times when the policy formulation may arise from his role as an in-house consultant, but there are some policies which relate more to his administrative role.

Does the company provide tuition refund for out-of-house HRD activities? If so, is there a policy? Having the practice of tuition refund does not automatically assure that there is a policy. The absence of policy encourages the use of tuition refund as a system for granting favors rather than a system for developing human resources. A policy must be developed and be available to all so they share in the benefits.

The distinction between training, education and development should also be reflected in policy statements. In a larger organization where there are HRD personnel at various levels and places within the organization, policy is necessary so that the relationships between the various HRD personnel are supportive rather than combative. Also, employees within the organization should benefit, based on corporate policy rather than only on the individual perception of the HRD man in their part of the organization. There is literally no end to the kinds of areas in HRD which require policy statements. However, policy should not be a constraint but rather a mandate for providing growth opportunities throughout the organization.

Maintainer of Community Relations

The term "community" as used here refers to groupings of individuals to whom the HRD administrator relates. These groupings will have a commonality but are not restricted to a particular geographical area. The community may be outside the organization as well as inside. It signifies various groups to whom the HRD administrator must relate and maintain lines of communication as well as some degree of personal relationship.

Within Management

The necessity for maintaining relationships with various groups within management is an essential part of the functions of the HRD administrator. It is partly from this practice that the newer roles of the HRD person as an in-house consultant has emerged. (Details on this newer role will be found in the next chapter.)

As he serves as an administrator maintaining relationships with management, the HRD person has been asked to respond to more and more questions concerning overall policy and the direction in which the organization is going. Unless there is a greater on-going relationship between the HRD administrator and management, the HRD administrator is not able to serve his organization at the various stages of its organizational life.

The stockholder might be considered as part of management for purposes of HRD. The HRD administrator has a role in maintaining relations with stockholders. The HRD staff contains persons who are proficient in communications and organizing and conducting large meetings. It is only logical that the organization call upon the expertise of the HRD group for stockholder meetings. That this is not frequently done is probably the result of the narrow definition of HRD found in too many organizations. It is considered appropriate only for employees and maybe for customers. Beyond that, the resources of the HRD group are not effectively utilized. There is no reason why the stockholder cannot benefit from the resources available on the HRD staff. For the HRD administrator, it might encourage the stockholders and management to more fully recognize the resource they have in-house.

Those To Be Served

HRD cannot be conducted sitting behind a desk, sending out memos and writing reports. The HRD administrator must be sure that his curriculum builder is working directly with those who should be involved in building the curriculum such as the learner, his supervisor and his peer group. Other aspects of the HRD function likewise should be accomplished with the direct involvement of those members of the organizational community who will be served by the HRD activity.

In addition, HRD has a responsibility for making growth opportunities available to all members of the organization. Some organizations publish catalogs and listings of HRD activities which are available to various ranges of employees. These consist of anything from a one-page flier to a one-inch thick catalog.

An important and constant question is who should be trained, educated and/or developed. There is no simple answer to this; it requires that the HRD personnel maintain relationships with the various communities within the organization and develop the mechanisms to encourage response to the opportunities offered. The HRD function must not only be highly visible but also readily accessible. There should be a continuing relationship rather than merely at those times when there is "registration" or other activities which are strictly of a periodic nature. The HRD staff should be in constant contact with the various communities it serves. The HRD administrator must create opportunities for continuing relationships.

With Outside Sources

The world of the HRD administrator cannot be circumscribed by his own organization. There are outside communities with whom he maintains relationships. One of these are other organizations who are in the same kind of business or same activity. Industry associations and similar groupings provide a mechanism for building such relationships. Within the framework of aerospace, for example, there are communities with whom he can establish relationships so as to be in contact with his counterparts in similar or related organizations.

More and more HRD is involved with the government. As broader concepts of manpower planning are developing, the HRD administrator will be maintaining relationships with at least his local governmental unit. The budget for the local school system, allocations for transportation and similar local expenditures relate to the concept and practice of HRD. Many government programs depend upon the states creating an agency or organization. The HRD administrator must maintain a relationship with these groups at the state and local levels. For example, the Office of State Technical Services of the U.S. Department of Commerce provides a variety of HRD services. Through workshops, seminars, short courses and various other forms of extension activities, they convey the latest scientific and technical knowledge to scientists, engineers, technicians and managers in industry, business and commerce. These services are not made available directly to companies. The process is to provide this resource through a state agency. Unless the HRD administrator has maintained a relationship with the state agency, he will not know of their availability, and they will now know of his needs (6).

At the federal level, the flood of legislation affecting HRD is steadily increasing. There is no indication that this trend will lessen. Rather, all signs point to an increasing role for the federal government in the development of human resources. The exact role is still vague, and there are varying points of view as to just what it should be (7). No matter what the direction, it is obvious that the HRD administrator must maintain relationships with the federal government so that he can influence the legislation as well as being aware of the resources available to his organization.

A march on Washington by the HRD people is not suggested but at least an awareness is required that what happens in Washington can impact strongly upon the internal HRD operations. In the first session of the 91st Congress (1969), more than 30 bills were introduced which directly related to HRD (8). How many HRD administrators knew of these bills? How many communicated with their congressmen? So far, there have been no significant legislative moves, but if any one of those 30 bills had passed, there could be massive changes in HRD in this country.

The need to relate to schools may seem almost too obvious, yet the linkage here is woefully inadequate. Maintaining relationships through advisory committees has been reviewed by Samuel Burt (9). The emerging junior/community colleges have selected community services as a prime target. This includes helping the areas they serve meet their manpower needs. HRD administrators should see them not only as a casual resource but also maintain a continuing relationship so that the junior college is aware of some of the directions of HRD. This will prove valuable as the junior colleges do not have the flexibility of a private consulting organization. They must rely on budgets which are authorized a year in advance. The private community colleges do have a bit more flexibility, but even they have limitations on their ability to respond rapidly. To the degree the HRD administrator can maintain a relationship with them, he can assist in their growth and influence them as they move toward building a community resource.

For scientists and engineers, maintaining relationships with colleges and universities is an absolute necessity. Unless there is a continually maintained relationship, a serious gap can develop between the preparation provided by the university and the offerings available to organizations as they send their employees to the universities. The whole field of continuing professional education indicates the need for establishing and maintaining very close relationships between HRD and the academic community.

Although apprenticeship programs have been declining in the United States, there are indications of renewed interest. Where apprenticeship programs are utilized, the maintenance of relationships with the school system is required by law.

Geographical Community

Most organizations function within geographical limits. The raw materials they use may come from afar, and their finished product may be shipped even further. But, during the manufacturing process, there is a physical plant which occupies space in a particular geographical community.

The advent of the NAB program has underscored the relationship to community affairs. Organizations are now designating company officers as "Directors of Urban Affairs." Although the HRD administrator should not be the director of urban affairs, he must maintain relationships with his geographical community so that HRD can respond to the needs of the geographical community as well as the organization. Of course, where the organization is a Community Action Agency, a voluntary agency or involved in some other area of community development, the linkage is automatic. For the organization in the private sector, it has been less obvious in the past, though this is now changing.

HRD facilities and equipment might well be an additional resource for the community as it strives to solve some of its problems. The HRD staff, who are learning specialists, can enhance the public image of their organization by making their expertise available to the community through organized company channels. This has been done in some of the programs for minority groups and hard-core. It can be done in other situations. Some companies will make provision for employees to serve as faculty at local high schools or colleges for limited periods of time. The HRD instructor could contribute to understanding how learning takes place and the myriad of methodologies available to the instructor. Although the curriculum may be decided by other groups, as it should be, the methods and materials developer could be the guide into the wide world of educational technology and multimedia.

Opportunities in the geographical community are plentiful. One must be careful not to allow these activities to consume too much of the resources of the HRD operation.

Arranger of Facilities and Finances

HRD personnel are essentially creative individuals. They are concerned with providing for growth of individuals and organizations. As Ralph E. Boynton has pointed out, they are apt to consider financial planning and controlling as a waste of time. But, the HRD administrator cannot avoid his responsibility for financial administration (10). Without adequate finance and facilities, it is not possible for the program to meet its goals. All aspects of HRD are influenced by the financial picture and resources available. This does not mean making a bookkeeper or booking agent of the HRD administrator. These functions can be delegated to other personnel either within or related to the HRD function. But, the administrator must assume the responsibility for seeing that these functions are performed as they relate to the development of human resources in his organization.

Equipment and Materials

The use of equipment and materials in HRD is constantly growing. The introduction of educational technology has moved HRD from its early stages of merely having a 16mm projector or an overhead projector. Today, there are still HRD operations which have no equipment and no provisions for obtaining equipment.

As used here, equipment signifies items which are used in instruction but are not themselves expendable or intended to be used up. This includes projection equipment, audio-visual devices, chairs, carrells, (11), charts, et cetera. Materials are the expendables used in the learning process; it is expected that they will be used and must be replaced. Materials include chalk, magic markers, worksheets, books which the student will retain and other items to be used during learning.

If the philosophy of the HRD administrator is that equipment is unnecessary, then the absence of equipment is understandable. His philosophical base may be questioned, but his lack of equipment cannot be questioned. If he believes in supplementing the human instructor with instructional equipment, then the administrator must take the steps that are required in his organization to obtain the equipment which he thinks would support the learning process.

The HRD administrator will be faced with the same kind of decision that confronts many administrators in his organization. Should he purchase or rent? Should he make or buy? What is expected usage of the equipment? How much of his budget can he make available for equipment? The purchase of equipment is a long-term investment. It is more than filling out a requisition or listening to salesmen. The purchase of a piece of equipment by a production manager carries with it the implication that the production process will be built around that piece of equipment. If the process changes, and the equipment is no longer usable, the production manager is faced with a loss on his investment.

So, too, with the HRD administrator. When he purchases the equipment, he is committing his organization to a certain kind of learning. Some of the equipment is flexible and can be used for a variety of learning situations. Other equipment, notably the "teaching machine," has a very restricted application.

After procuring the equipment and materials, there is the need for storage. Too frequently, expenditures are carefully developed and screened for the purchase of equipment and materials. Less frequently is attention paid to the necessity for storing the equipment and materials. The HRD administrator is responsible for protecting these assets of his organization. He need not be a miser concerning the use of expendable materials but must guard against their wasteful consumption. Equipment must be stored where it is safe, for whatever that connotes in his organization, yet readily obtainable for use with a minimum of confusion and time.

Distribution is more complicated. There are times when somebody outside the HRD office but still within the organization may wish to borrow a projector, easel or other equipment. Making this equipment available to other parts of the organization is more than a service function—it also provides opportunities for the HRD administrator. It may provide him with a linkage point into other parts of the organization that are using equipment and materials for learning. These other organizational units may only see HRD as a supply source rather than a learning resource. The relationship may start with meeting an immediate need—supplying a projector. It can blossom into a full relationship if the HRD administrator has the techniques for working with other parts of the organization and having them see him as helpful in a variety of ways.

The distribution mechanism should be as convenient and flexible as possible without jeopardizing the safety of the equipment or the effective utilization of materials. Whether the materials are used by the HRD personnel directly or are made available to other members of the organization, there should be some record of use. This should not encourage more record keeping than is necessary, but at the same time the use of the equipment and materials can be indicators to the HRD administrator of some of the activity within his own unit.

For example, in reviewing he may find that a particular film was purchased with a high degree of enthusiasm, but reports show it has been very seldom used. This may not be because the film did not meet expectations but rather that those who could utilize the film do not know of its ready availability. At the same time, the use pattern may indicate that sometimes it is better to write off (in the accounting sense) some equipment or material because it is not used and will not be used. To maintain and store the equipment may be more costly than absorbing the loss.

Budget

The essential item is budget. Without provision for budget, development of human resources is a concept but not a reality. There are different ways to handle budget, and there is no one best way. This applies not only to the HRD budget but to budget in any part of the organization. Concepts and policies are merely statements of intent. They do not become reality until there is a commitment of the necessary financial resources.

Each organization has its own procedures and cycles for budget. Too few people realize, for example, that at the federal level the HRD administrator is usually working with a budget that was prepared almost two years earlier. Despite this time lag, some government agencies are still pointed out and admired because they seem to move so easily with the newer trends in HRD.

The budget is only a statement of intent to commit funds. The HRD administrator must also identify in his own organization how the funds are actually obtained. Where the organization has cash flow problems, the periods for purchasing may not coincide with HRD needs. If the HRD administrator does not coordinate his program plans with the budget/allocation cycles, he can have an excellent program but not be in a position to financially support it. In many organizations, the budget is only one step in the process of obtaining funds. There may be other specific steps which must be taken in order to make sure that the funds are available to his department when needed.

As part of the budget is the question of cost accounting. HRD has no secret formula on this and is plagued by the same problem as most parts of the organization—how to maintain adequate cost records. Cost accounting is a highly specialized area of operations. The HRD administrator will find that it is best to work with the financial people in his organization and have them set up a cost accounting system for him. This does not imply that costs will control the HRD operation. It does mean that the HRD administrator will be able to supply some answers relative to cost to those in management who need such data for their long-range financial planning.

Reliance on only cost data leads into the trap of quantification of data and cost-benefit ratios, which can reduce HRD to an accounting function. How often is polarization of an issue warned against? Here is a case in point right within this area of operations. The HRD administrator must not allow himself to be caught in the trap of providing essentially financial data—he must likewise not back into a position of rejecting all attempts to relate HRD to cost and expenditure factors.

Seeing HRD in its component parts (i.e., training, education and development) can be helpful in the financial aspects. Where training is the objective, there should be little question about asking for evidence on return of the expenditure in terms of improved job performance, reduced absenteeism, higher quality or any other job-related measure. With education and development, it is not that easy to find financial measures which can indicate how the expenditure has been beneficial to the individual and the organization. In any event, the HRD administrator must be prepared to respond to queries as to how he used the funds which his organization made available to him.

An exciting development in the use of assets and HRD is in the work just being started in human resource accounting. It is still too early to tell if this is a significant contribution or merely another abortive attempt at relating people and expenditures. It may have the same implications for HRD as the application of the systems engineering approach a decade earlier. The synthesis of seemingly opposite concepts can prove helpful or disastrous.

One essential contribution provided by those working with human resource accounting is the recognition of the difference between an expense item and an investment item. HRD is usually written off as an expense. In accounting terminology, this implies that it has only limited value beyond the fiscal year. Yet, if education and development are future oriented, they certainly go beyond the immediate fiscal year. They are truly an investment in the future of the individual and the organization. To write them off as expense items is to engage in improper accounting practices. Yet, at this time, it is not certain that the appropriate methods for handling the investment have been developed. The concept is there—hopefully the supporting methodology will be forthcoming.

Funding of HRD need not be restricted to only in-house sources. Westinghouse recognizes this when they state: "Wherever possible, veterans will use such public laws as appropriate for their continued education. Once eligibility expires, such employees will consult with their supervisors to continue their education under the company plan" (12). Funding may also come from private foundations and professional organizations. As with the G.I. Bill for veterans, there are no strings attached which would diminish the prerogatives of the organization. In the case of the "hard-core" and minority groups, few companies have had difficulty obtaining the funds made available by the Manpower Administration. From its inception the program has continually modified its procedures to make application easier and repayment more rapid. As of 1970, an organization can recover up to $3,000 per man for extra expenses incurred in such training. It is improper if the HRD administrator has not brought this to the attention of his organization. Of course, if a specific policy is developed which commits the organization to reject the use of federal funds, the HRD administrator must comply. But, the policy should be made with full knowledge of the experiences of other organizations.

Physical Facilities

In addition to the regular office space required for the HRD function, there is usually the need for additional sites for the learning to take place. This can range from one small conference room to elaborate out-of-plant learning environments. It can be a corner of the shop or a well-developed vestibule training arrangement. The HRD administrator may actually be operating a school such as that of IBM at Sands Point and General Electric at Crotonville.

The range of physical facilities is great. They should reflect the philosophy of the HRD administrator as well as his ability to obtain the necessary financial support within his organization. Where the physical facility is under the control of the HRD administrator, there are many factors to be considered.

If it is truly a learning center, it may require a great deal in the way of multimedia equipment to support the various kinds of learning which can take place. The furniture should be designed to support the flexibility which can make a variety of learning situations possible.

Once the HRD administrator has a physical facility, he may then find himself in the business of booking the facility. This may mean that it must be used at a certain rate in order to warrant the investment of funds. Or, he may find that the demand far exceeds the physical capacity, and then he must decide who has priorities.

The "make-buy" decision continually confronts the HRD administrator. In physical facilities, there is a possible alternative. If the HRD administrator needs an outside facility, he may find one that almost meets his needs. Then, through effective bargaining, he may encourage the owner of the physical facility to give his organization preference or to obtain certain kinds of equipment which relate to the particular program of the organization. This can provide the physical facility without the capital investment.

The effective use of physical facilities underscores, again, the need for the HRD administrator to be involved in organizational planning so that he can relate the facility to the developing needs of his organization.

As a Cost Center

There is a growing tendency in HRD functions to put it on a paying basis. It is not expected to make a profit, but it is expected to charge for its services and through this approach to meet its basic budget. This is accomplished by having the various parts of the organization charged for their use of HRD personnel, facilities, equipment and materials.

It is anticipated that through effective costing procedures, the HRD function can cover its overhead and operational costs. Some organizations have even gone so far as to establish the criterion that if the various parts of the organization that are involved in HRD wish to meet their needs by going to outside sources, they may. In this situation, the in-house HRD organization must compete with outside resources which are available on the open market. Of course, it presents a problem, for there is no easy way of measuring which instructor is better or which program is better. It presents the in-house HRD function with a competitive factor, which is congruent with the economic system.

The establishment of HRD as a cost center has another implication. It may at a later time evolve into a profit center. That is, the organization may find that the resources of the HRD function are so effective that they can be marketed outside the organization. This has been one of the changes in the emerging education-industry complex. Organizations have discovered, as they explored entry into the field of HRD, that the core for such an operation existed within their own organization. It is not suggested that this is a desirable direction, and it does raise some ethical questions, but it is a direction which will become more pronounced in the decade of the 70's.

Literature Citations

1. The model for administrators is developed and discussed in Daniel R. Davies and Robert T. Livingston, *You and Management.* (New York: Harper, 1958).
2. The experience is described in Leonard Nadler, "Developing Non-Professional Trainers," *Journal of the American Society of Training Directors,* September/October 1955, pp. 23-28.
3. Reported in the *Federal Trainer,* October 1969, No. 2, issued by the Office of Agency Consultation and Guidance, Bureau of Training, U.S. Civil Service Commission, Washington, D. C.
4. The National Association for Public and Continuing Adult Education suggests that Teacher Aides may soon outnumber the teachers in adult education. Suggestions for orienting and using Teacher Aides is contained in their publication, *Techniques,* December 1969, 4 pages (1201 Sixteenth Street, N. W., Washington, D. C., 20036).
5. By no means is the federal government the only group sponsoring research in HRD. The most likely single source for research and related documents is the Educational Resources Information Center (ERIC) Clearinghouse on Adult Education, 107 Roney Lane, Syracuse, New York, 13210.
6. For example, during 1968 they sponsored 482 seminars throughout most of the United States. See *Annual Report 1968,* Office of State Technical Services, U.S. Department of Commerce.
7. One study has suggested against placing all manpower programs in one agency. See *Employment and Training Lesiglation - 1968,* Background Information Supplement, prepared for the Subcommittee on Employment, Manpower and Poverty of the Committee on Labor and Public Welfare, U.S. Senate, June 1968.
8. Leonard Nadler, "The Trainer and the Legislative Hopper," *Training and Development Journal,* September 1969, pp. 4-8.
9. Samuel Burt, *Industry and Vocational-Technical Education.* New York: McGraw-Hill, 1967.
10. Ralph E. Boynton, "Budgeting and Controlling Training Costs," in *Training and Development Handbook,* ed., Robert L. Craig and Lester R. Bittel (New York: McGraw-Hill, 1967), pp. 593-604.

11. This is a word coming into common usage but with the wrong spelling. It is usually spelled "carre*l*," which according to the dictionary is "a fabric of the seventeenth century." The less frequent spelling of "carre*ll*" is defined as "a small enclosure of space. . .designed for study or reading by individual patrons" (from *Webster's New Twentieth Century Dictionary,* unabridged, 2nd ed. [New York: The World Publishing Co., 1960], p. 277).

12. *Continued Education for Westinghouse Professional Personnel,* Westinghouse Training and Development Department, 1968-1969, p. 5.

10

Consultant

The role of the HRD consultant is the most recently evolved. Actually, to use the past tense is not entirely accurate. This role is still emerging and changing.

The emerging conceptualization of this role can be seen by a comparison of the models over the past five years. In 1965, the author worked with others on developing this model in connection with an institute being conducted by the Training Officers Conference of Washington, D. C. The result of this model was included in the article on the "Emerging Roles of the Training Director" which appeared in 1967 (1).

At the ASTD Conference in 1968, this model was used as part of a full-day workshop on "The Changing Role of the Training Professional" (2). Once again, at the 1969 annual conference of ASTD, the model was the basis for a full-day workshop on "Role Concepts for Training: Implications for Individual Development."

In addition to these exposures, the model was constantly tested in the author's work with client systems and more particularly with his students. Almost all are experienced in HRD, as two years' experience is required for entry into this particular graduate program.

During the summer of 1968, the author worked with several companies in relation to the National Alliance of Businessmen program. He tested out the model of the HRD consultant and found that the developing model needed further revision. Rather than try to defend the model, he constantly applied it in his work and encouraged others to test it out in their own relationships, both in-house and out-of-house.

While developing this book, in teaching his classes at the university and in his outside consulting work, the author continued to test the model. The result is this chapter; it presents a revision of the model which has not previously been published. The conceptualization can be seen in Figure 10.1.

It is likely that the next few years will see further changes. Particularly, the emphasis on organization development may cause an emphasis of some of the subroles far out of proportion to the others. This may mean a new major role for HR developers, but it is still too early to tell. It is much like the experience of HRD with educational technology.

When educational technology gained momentum in the early 1960's, there were those who insisted that this was a major role. As the decade progressed, a better perspective evolved, and no difficulty was found in including educational technology as one aspect of methods and materials development. Of course, there are still those in educational technology who would insist on more of a major role.

The impact of educational technology was direct and a challenge to the role of the learning specialist. Today, the same experience is occurring through the impact of organization development on the role of the consultant. Yet, as will be discussed in this chapter, organization development is seen as only one of the subroles of the HRD consultant. Admittedly, today it is a significant role and has much to offer. It is believed that it will react with the same pendulum swing as educational technology and become one of the subroles of the human resource developer.

Consultant

The total role is that of a consultant, but the word needs further clarification if it is to be used meaningfully. The term is used to describe many different kinds of behavior and expectations. In the case of the consulting engineer, or the consulting medical specialist, he is the man expected to produce an opinion or an answer to a problem. This is much different from the consultant perceived as being in a helping relationship whose function is to release the potential of the client with whom he is working. The designation "consultant" is used to describe a range of behaviors.

The subroles, as seen in Figure 10.1, lend themselves to a division of the consultant role which does reflect the two aspects of the specialist and the helper. As an advocate or expert, the HRD consultant is a *resource person.* He is expected to bring in the answers and have specific and definite responses to an identified problem.

As a stimulator or change agent, the HRD consultant serves in the role of *facilitator.* He diagnoses, assists in identifying appropriate goals for change and assists in developing a plan or strategy for change.

When entering a situation as a consultant, it is important for the HRD person to understand his role and to help others understand it. Mutual expectations need to be explored so that role confusion does not abort the contribution the HRD consultant hopes to make.

In-House or Out-of-House

As with the learning specialist, the consultant may be either an in-house or out-of-house resource to his organization. It is

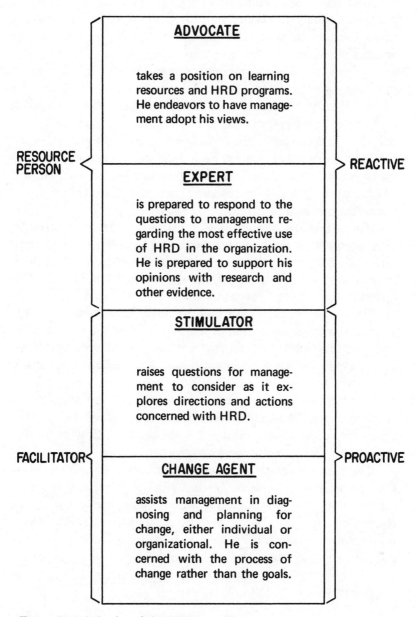

ADVOCATE

takes a position on learning resources and HRD programs. He endeavors to have management adopt his views.

RESOURCE PERSON

REACTIVE

EXPERT

is prepared to respond to the questions to management regarding the most effective use of HRD in the organization. He is prepared to support his opinions with research and other evidence.

STIMULATOR

raises questions for management to consider as it explores directions and actions concerned with HRD.

FACILITATOR

PROACTIVE

CHANGE AGENT

assists management in diagnosing and planning for change, either individual or organizational. He is concerned with the process of change rather than the goals.

Figure 10.1. Subroles of the HRD consultant.

more common to find the out-of-house consultant, as the skills required are unique and many organizations cannot afford to put a full-time HRD consultant on their payroll. This is sometimes handled by long-term contracts, but the more frequent practice is a short-time relationship.

There is nothing to preclude an organization from having its own in-house HRD consultant. However, such a person must be placed at a high enough level in the organization so that his skills may be effectively used. The consultant does not serve only top management—his skills are needed throughout the organization. However, unless he is placed close enough to top management, the value of his unique role may be lost. He will be able to function as the resource person, but less able to make a contribution as a facilitator.

Where the HRD function is subsumed under the personnel department, it is unlikely that there will be an HRD consultant. The skills and background he brings to the situation do not fit comfortably within the personnel department, and his identification is not with the personnel field.

The out-of-house consultant is quite familiar either in the person of a single individual or a group of individuals. The latter can take the form of a regular company with consultants on their payroll for use by client systems. A more common form is the network in which a variety of persons form a rather loose organization so their mutual skills can be made available to client systems. The clients sometimes become confused, for the temporary society is exemplified in the constant flow of outside consultants from one network to another.

The decision for an in-house consultant is also influenced by the tolerance the organization has for the kind of ambiguous services that can be expected of a consultant. Particularly in his facilitator subrole, it becomes quite difficult to assess the direct return to the organization. And, if he performs his roles appropriately, there are times when he can be expected to generate a certain amount of discontent as he encourages management to confront issues rather than bury them.

Reactive and Proactive

The tendency of HRD has been to be reactive—that is, to provide good and valuable service but only as a reaction to problems. These might be new personnel, changes in production, new plant start-ups, hiring the hard-core, new materials or any of the other kinds of problems which are a constant part of the life of any organization. No apology needs to be made for reactive behavior; it is appropriate and functional and needed by the organization.

Reactive behavior is concerned with endeavoring to reduce tensions and toward seeking new equilibriums. If an organization is to continue to live, there are times when reactive behavior is not only appropriate but necessary (3).

To remain only in a reactive posture, however, is to deprive the organization of the flexibility it needs in the rapidly changing world. It is also necessary for some aspects of HRD to move into the proactive stage, or anticipating the newer movements and developments. To be proactive is even more than that—it also implies the practice of creating change situations as appropriate.

In the course of many HRD learning activities, complaints and suggestions come forth as a result of the group learning experience. These are too often lost rather than being recognized by the consultant and utilized.

Role Movement

The HRD consultant must be flexible and mobile. In a given situation, he may start in one subrole and then find that by the very nature of the situation, he can be more effective in a different subrole. This is not too much different from the behavior of the HRD person as a learning specialist or administrator. There are times when the HRD instructor will move into the role of curriculum builder. Indeed, for some learning experiences, these two roles are supportive and performed by the

same individual. A programmer may rely on a curriculum builder for the in-puts from which he develops the program. Or, the
programmer may become involved in building the curriculum as
he develops the program.

An example of the mobility of the HRD person, within the
major roles and subroles, can be illustrated in work done by the
author in 1969 with the Miquon Plant, Paper Division,
Weyerhaeuser Co. (The client gave his permission to cite this
example). They had a problem of high turnover of entry-level
personnel to the point where they might have had to close
down the plant. An initial diagnosis, by the in-house HRD director, indicated that there was the need for training for the supervisors and managers. The author was called in as a learning
specialist to conduct a particular kind of program related to
minority group employment, as this constituted most of their
entry-level employees. Also, the supervisors had reached the
point where they were demanding that the company conduct a
training program for the entry-level employees before sending
them on the plant floor.

The in-house man and the author agreed that the latter's
role was that of instructor but also to help the supervisors in
beginning to build the curriculum for the training program for
the entry-level employees.

About two hours after the two-day program had started, it
became obvious that other factors were involved. With the permission of the in-house HRD director, the author moved to the
position of stimulator to encourage the group to explore more
dimensions of the problem than just an entry-level training program. In the course of that afternoon and the next morning,
they made many suggestions, including the following.

1. Entry-level employees were on probation for 30 days. During that
    time, they could be sent to as many as six different supervisors.
    Suggestion: entry-level employees should not have more than two
    supervisors during probation.

2. Entry-level employees were sometimes assigned to physical tasks above their capabilities. For example, a 150-pound man might be asked to lift a 240-pound shaft by himself and with no equipment. Suggestion: relate the assignment of personnel to the physical needs of that particular job.

3. Entry-level workers were so desperately needed that they were assigned much like "battlefield replacements" (the words used by the supervisors). Usually, the new employee did not know what he was being sent to do and could see no relation to a permanent position in the organization. Suggestion: specifically identify which jobs would be for entry-level employees, and train accordingly.

4. Entry-level employees could not see any possibility for advancement. They were told that such possibilities existed, but the whole picture was too vague and confusing for the entry-level employee. Role-playing among the supervisors (half being themselves and half role-playing entry-level employees) disclosed that equal opportunity was not a reality. Suggestion: specific goals for advancement must be developed by personnel and the supervisors.

The actual list was much longer. However, the group did not endeavor to bring about action, and in his subrole as stimulator, the author had helped bring the group into an area which was beyond the scope of his present assignment. Now, the in-house HRD director had to provide leadership. He was only too pleased, for the author had truly stimulated—he had opened up gates which an in-house man would have hesitated to unlock. The last half day was devoted to curriculum building, but with the understanding that a training program only would be insufficient to deal with the problem of the entry-level employee in that mill.

In the course of working with that client system, the author had moved through several roles. Starting as a learning specialist-instructor he then went to learning specialist-curriculum builder. After the first half day, he functioned as a consultant-stimulator, and then back to the learning specialist-curriculum builder role. Each time he shifted, it was with the acknowledgment of the in-house HRD director.

This is but one example, and any HRD person with some experience has probably seen himself equally as mobile. The caution is to avoid the subroles which are beyond one's area of competence—know when to bring in the outside resource. Knowing one's own developmental needs is the first step in developing the competencies to be effective in many of the subroles.

For the remainder of this chapter, the four subroles will be examined, though it will not be possible to keep them from interacting with each other. They are not discrete nor need they be.

Advocate

As an advocate, the HRD consultant takes a position regarding learning resources and HRD programs. He endeavors to have management adopt his views. This is a highly directive and almost rigid posture. But, it can be a necessary and helpful one. The HRD consultant will already have diagnosed the situation as one directly involved with HRD. He will have explored the various possibilities and decided on a specific course of action. In all fairness to his management, he is expected to suggest what he considers the most appropriate HRD response to that particular problem. If he is not prepared to take this stand, then he is not performing the subrole of the advocate but one of the other subroles of the HRD consultant.

As an advocate, he must know the available programs and resources for that particular aspect of HRD. This may be the general experience in the field or the particular experience his own organization has had with the learning approaches he is suggesting. It does not mean that he closes his eyes to other experiences and other resources but that he has carefully weighed them and has come to a decision which he now wishes management to accept.

He is recommending to management his specific approach as a person who is knowledgeable in the field, has explored the alternatives and now suggests this course of action. To do this, he will have collected data and be able to document the basis for his decision.

As an advocate, he will need to know not only the advantages of the particular course of action he is recommending but also its limitations. He may, for example, have made the decision to use programmed instruction. He must be able to substantiate this in its relationship to meeting the needs of the learners in the particular situation, the particular kind of learning desired and the contribution it will make to the organization. He cannot merely fall back on statements such as: "Well, everybody is using programmed instruction" or "So many people are using P. I. it must be good." He should have a specific reason and be able to indicate the basis for his choice.

Expert

As an expert, the HRD consultant is prepared to respond to the questions of management regarding the most effective use of HRD in the organization. He is prepared to support his opinions with research and other evidence.

To do this, the HRD consultant must have the expertise the situation requires in developing learning situations and in the use of media to support learning. As with the advocate, the expert will have determined that the problem or situation is indeed amenable to the HRD approach. However, he will not present a specific course of action but will bring to the attention of management some of the possibilities which could meet the need. He will be prepared to share with management various alternatives concerning the different methods and approaches which might be used in that particular situation.

As an expert, he may still have a specific recommendation but he is not so much concerned with selling this recommendation as he is to responding to the queries of management about the proper course of action. Indeed, he encourages them to question the various alternatives and therefore become more involved in the HRD process.

Involving Management

Of course, this assumes that management is interested. It may be that serving in the subrole of the expert, the HRD consultant must encourage management to be willing to explore the various possibilities. Management may take the position that if they are paying the HRD consultant to be the expert, then he should just tell them what to do. If the HRD consultant responds to this, he is then more of an advocate. Instead, he should encourage management to explore with him some of the possibilities of what HRD can do in that situation and share with them the research of others. Then he is performing his role as an expert. The ultimate decision may still be his, depending upon his role in the organization and the nature of the problem.

Communicating with Management

This is one of those situations where the ability to communicate is absolutely necessary. As an expert, the HRD consultant involves management in the decision making, rather than recommending a specific course of action as he would in his role of advocate. But, it is too easy to wave the flag of the expert by using terminology which others could not possibly be expected to understand. At times, this does stamp the expert as different from the layman. Almost as often, it creates a communication barrier which is difficult to penetrate. Review your own language over the past two weeks. What words or phrases have you used that somebody outside of HRD would have difficulty in understanding, unless you took time out to explain?

Research is important, and the HRD consultant must be familiar with the research in the field. He must share this research with management. But, the method of sharing will vary according to the audience and the objective of communicating with that audience. This is not new—any person with some experience in HRD knows this. But, it is more difficult to apply when one is trying to impress the higher-ups with his expertness in the field.

It is necessary for the HRD consultant, as an expert, to determine the level of understanding of the persons he is dealing with and the amount of data they are prepared to absorb in his field. He cannot make them experts in HRD but knowledgeable enough so that he can work with them effectively and so that they can be involved in the decision making.

Recognition by Management

One often hears HRD persons complaining because their organization does not give them sufficient status or recognize them for the experts they are. But, do they really mean "expert," or is something else intended? How do you want your management to see you? Is it as a first-rate teacher, conference leader, programmer or any of the other subroles? If the HRD person is not clear on this in his own mind, how can he expect his organization to know how to accept him?

The subrole of the HRD consultant as an expert requires that he first have some background and preparation in the field. The preparation may have come after he was placed on the job, but just the learnings from the job are insufficient to make one an expert. To function as an expert, the HRD consultant must become involved in those activities outside his organization which will indeed build up the fund of knowledge and experience one expects of the expert.

He must be able to identify those situations to which his expertness can make a contribution. Then, he will be seen by his organization as an expert and treated accordingly.

Stimulator

As a stimulator, the HRD consultant raises questions for management to consider as it explores directions and actions concerned with the development of human resources. In this subrole, the HRD consultant has moved into the proactive area. He no longer waits for issues to present themselves, but encourages the exploration of issues. He will probably encounter some which go far beyond the area of HRD, and he must be prepared for this. Not enough people are prepared to look at broader issues. There are still too many people who prefer single causations or polarity of thinking.

As a stimulator, he will not be giving answers nor even asking questions. Rather, he will be helping others to ask questions. He will assist them in thinking through the alternatives which are present in most situations.

Earlier, an example of this was given in work with the paper mill. There are many such examples that can be given by those who have functioned as consultant-stimulators. Sometimes, it seems almost too easy. The situation is there and is obvious. It is not always certain why it takes the presence of an outsider (i.e., who is not part of the problem situation) to assist in the problem-solving situation. But, if that is the case, then the HRD stimulator must recognize those situations to which he can contribute.

Identification of the situation is only the start. Equally important is having the skills and experience for appropriate interventions. Then, the consultant must likewise be able to disengage without impeding the on-going progress of those with whom he has been working.

Inter-disciplinary Competencies

The HRD person, in any role, has need of special competencies to perform effectively. The role of stimulator demands competencies in several different disciplines and fields. As a stimulator, the HRD consultant becomes a different kind of educator. He is no longer working in a classroom environment, though he will still be working with groups in growth situations. He will need to know much more of what is usually included in the behavioral sciences. There is no clear indication of where this is to be found. A search of college catalogs will show that such course work is available in a number of departments. Whether this is desirable or not is evading the point. That is how they exist, and the HRD stimulator who wishes to improve his skills must search out the appropriate academic opportunities.

Some nonacademic opportunities are also available, but here, too, a search is required. There is no accreditation of the nonacademic opportunities for developing the skills of the stimulator or of the change agent.

Change Agent

As a change agent, the HRD consultant assists management in diagnosing and planning for change. The changes may be either individual or organizational. The HRD change agent is more concerned with the process of change than with the goals of change.

In this subrole, the substance of the change may have little or nothing to do with HRD. Except, if people are involved, and people are expected to change, there is a legitimate and necessary place for the HRD change agent.

Once again, his skills are in the behavioral sciences, including education. He is now more of the nondirective consultant who must be sensitive to the needs of his client. Most of his work will be with groups, and his process skills in group situations must be of the highest order.

Organization Development

Today, Organization Development (O.D.) appears to be one of the more significant movements. It is important, and it can be helpful. However, it is a trap for those who look to it as the panacea for all the ills of the organization. It is misleading to consider it as *the* answer to the development of human resources. It is one aspect and today an important one. As society continues to change, the need for human resource development will still exist. It is not possible to make that same statement for O.D.

Given the present situation, O.D. is one of the highly visible activities and one of the more obvious activities of the HRD change agent. It is not possible to delineate this aspect of the subrole much further for the literature presents a wide scatter of opinion. Leslie This has contributed to the understanding when he asks, "Organization Development—Fantasy or Reality?" (4).

As a change agent, the HRD consultant is endeavoring to assist his organization to improve its capability for problem-solving and decision making. These are important activities in all aspects of human resource development and will continue to be important in the years to come.

The Future

The roles of the HRD consultant are truly emerging as awareness of the need for working with organizations, as well as with people, increases. As organizations become more complex—as they become more concerned with social responsibility—the contribution of the HRD consultant will significantly increase.

Just to change labels, to now be called an "organizational developer," is insufficient. Newer skills are required, yet the previous skills should not be ignored. There is still the need for all the other roles of the HRD specialist. No one role is consistently the most important, and no subrole can be left unfilled without a cost to the organization.

For the future, the HRD specialist will require more skills, more preparation before coming to the job and a greater recognition of the impact he has on individuals and organizations.

Literature Citations

1. For those interested in how a model is built, the following would be of interest. As seen through published articles, so the reader can follow this if he wishes, the first development of the model was contained in Leonard Nadler, "Professional Preparation of Training Directors," *Training and Development Journal,* April 1966, pp. 12-18. In this model, only the learning specialist and administrator were considered as the article was based on research conducted some six years earlier. In the intervening years, I had been working outside the United States and had missed the evolvement of the consultant role. I am indebted to Ross Pollack, then of the U.S. Civil Service Commission, for bringing this to my attention. The next article resulted from the further development of this model for a workshop of the Training Officers Conference in Washington, D. C. The revised model was described in Gordon Lippitt and Leonard Nadler, "Emerging Roles of the Training Director," *Training and Development Journal,* August 1967, pp. 2-10. Testing the consulting part of the model with a variety of organizations produced the modification contained in Leonard Nadler, "Multiple Consulting Approaches of the Trainer and the Hard-Core Unemployed," *Training and Development Journal,* February 1969, pp. 8-12. The entire model was further developed in Leonard Nadler, "The Variety of Training Roles," *Industrial and Commercial Training* (Great Britain), November 1969, pp. 33-37.

2. A short article describing the workshop can be found in "The Changing Role of the Training Professional," *Training and Development Journal,* March 1968, pp. 39-40. This workshop was developed by C. Hoyt Anderson (Ford Motor Company) and Leonard Nadler.

3. A brief discussion of reactive and proactive behavior can be found in James V. Clark, "A Healthy Organization" in *The Planning of Change,* Warren G. Bennis, Kenneth D. Benne and Robert Chin (New York: Holt, Rinehart and Winston, 1969), p. 283. The entire book is a stimulating book of readings which are vital to the HRD consultant.

4. Leslie This, *Organizational Development: Fantasy or Reality,* no. 7 (Washington: Society for Personnel Administration, 1969).

Additional Reading

The following is a listing of some of the published materials which should be of interest to those involved in HRD. It is annotated by the author of this book and is intended only as a general guide. The range of materials is vast, as is the field of HRD. As can be expected, practically none of these volumes utilize the terminology of HRD as used in this book, so the reader is cautioned about words in titles bearing the description of training, education or development. When used in the annotation, these words relate to the definition contained in this book.

Ackerman, Leonard. "A Study of Selected Employee Development Specialists in the Federal Government: Their Background and Perceptions of their Role and Organizational Location." Ed.D. diss., The George Washington University, 1967.
A follow-up of a study originally done by the Civil Service Commission but with additional and more specific data on the EDO as an educator rather than a personnel specialist.

Aker, George F. *Adult Education Procedures, Methods and Techniques.* Syracuse: Library of Continuing Education, Syracuse University, 1965.

248

section IV

Epilogue

Since *Developing Human Resources* was first published in 1970, this author has had the opportunity to apply and advance the concepts of HRD far beyond what had been done before. The articles for the chapters in this section were chosen to capture the essence of some of these applications and extensions from graduate classes, public workshops and work with individual organizations.

Chapter 11 reviews the conceptualization of HRD and explores five implications for organizations applying this concept: responsibility, mutual expectations, learning theory, human resource accounting, and evaluation. Chapter 12 reports the results of a study of managers' perceptions and expectations of the role of the human resource developer. Chapter 13 views training, education, and development from the standpoint of economic classification, evaluation, and risk level as a way to permit organizations to re-examine their HRD goals and practices.

249

11

Implications of the HRD Concept

Broadening the scope of training and development

All organizations are faced with the necessity of using certain kinds of resources to meet their goals and purposes. Over the years, the words have changed, but the three categories still remain:

- Physical Resources
- Financial Resources
- Human Resources

This article is primarily concerned with *human resources.* This does not mean that we are unaware of the other two categories or that they are less important. However, the effective use of each category requires a core of specialists. The majority of the readers of this paper will likely be specialists in the human resource area.

Within that area, as in the other two, there are specialties. The two most apparent are:

- Human Resource Utilization (HRU), which includes recruitment, selection, placement, appraisal and compensation

Article by Leonard Nadler reproduced by special permission from the May/1974 TRAINING AND DEVELOPMENT JOURNAL. Copyright 1974 by the American Society for Training and Development Inc.

- Human Resource Development (HRD), which includes the various kinds of learning experiences which contribute to individual and organizational effectiveness

Obviously, we are most concerned with HRD but by no means does this deprecate the necessity for the HRU function. Each of these specialties requires staffing by persons with a particular kind of preparation and experience.

Within the HRD function we find that there are essentially three different kinds of learning experiences provided:

Job: those learning experiences designed to enable the employee to function more effectively on the job he or she now has.

Individual: those learning experiences designed to prepare the individual for a future but fairly well-defined job. There is also the expectation that the individual will move to the new job within a reasonable period of time.

Organization: those learning experiences designed to open the individual to new jobs and performance patterns based on the possible future directions of the organization.

One way of categorizing the learning experience is in terms of the focus of the experience. Using a time frame we find:

JOB   NOW
INDIVIDUAL   SOON
ORGANIZATION   SOMETIME

The categorization of the learning experience cannot be made until another factor is determined—namely the target group. Or, who are the learners? Let us say that your organization offers a program entitled "Supervisory Performance." Into which category of learning experience will it fall? To decide, you must ask: who are the target groups; who will the learners be? Let us take this through several possibilities.

If the program is for those who are currently supervising, then this program is *job* related. If the target group are those individuals who are being prepared to become supervisors then this program is *individual* related. The program might be made available to any employee who thinks that someday he might become a supervisor, though he is not currently perceived that way by the organization, and in that case would be *organization* related.

Hopefully, the reader can see these distinctions among the three areas of learning. For some readers it may be difficult for we have not been in the habit of making such distinctions. Rather, our tendency has been to conduct learning experiences without reference to the *job, individual* and *organization*. This has been the usual pattern from our earliest schooling experiences right into the learning experiences provided by employers. At times, there have been those who have tried to make these distinctions but they soon felt isolated in their attempts and succumbed to the more general practice of providing the experience and let the learner select out for him or herself the three elements.

In workshops I have conducted and consulting I have done, it usually takes several hours to work through the concepts stated briefly above. Examples are given by me and then we endeavor to find practical examples in the organizations represented. When we all feel comfortable with the concept, it is time to move on to assigning some kind of label to facilitate communication.

Labels and Semantics

It has been said that meaning is not in words — meaning is in people. This becomes evident when we try to put labels on the concepts.

McGregor[1] faced this problem and used "Theory X and Theory Y." Reich[2] faced a similar problem and therefore wrote of "Consciousness I," "Consciousness II," and "Consciousness III." Some persons, when faced with labelling concepts, have tried to coin new words or some other device for enabling others to focus on the concepts rather than the semantics. After trying several approaches over the years, I have finally succumbed to using words more familiar to us, being fully aware of the risk of using words already in use.

Therefore, in conceptualizing HRD, the following familiar terms are used but with the more distinct and specific meanings:

- *Training* = *job*-related learning experiences
- *Education* = *individual*-related learning experiences
- *Development* = *organizational*-related learning experiences

At this point we could have a healthy discussion on the use of these terms. The reader is asked to forego this digression and accept the terms as defined above. If it proves too difficult, merely substitute whatever is easier in order to avoid confusing the concept. Some readers might want to use labels like: concept T, concept E and concept D or concept 1, concept 2, concept 3. The reader will find it more helpful, however, for at least the purposes of this article, to accept the labels offered but not lose sight of the concepts involved.

Implications

Once we have the concepts firmly in mind, the implications are many. From the numerous individuals who have been involved in this concept over the past years, we have been able to identify five implications which result from applying this HRD concept. The implications discussed further are:

- Responsibility
- Mutual Expectations
- Learning Theory
- Human Resource Accounting
- Evaluation

Within the framework of this article, the implications can only be discussed in general terms. When they are applied to a particular organization, the resulting data are much more significant and can have a greater impact on HRD activities.

Responsibility

Within an organization, where is the actual responsibility for HRD and where should it be? This is an often posed question and frequently it is responded to in terms of the ability of the HRD person to relate to a particular part of the power structure of the organization. Yet, there is another way of looking at responsibility for HRD.

First, we must gather data about the current responsibility for HRD. In this context, *responsibility* refers to: who has the budget, who assigns employees to the learning experience, who expects to see results, who can integrate the learning experience into the on-going organizational behavior?

In gathering the data, first it is necessary to list various HRD programs as to:

Activity	Target Group
Training	
Education	
Development	

The list should be as comprehensive as possible, reflecting all of the HRD activities which can be located. It then rapidly becomes obvious that the title of the activity alone does not enable us to categorize that activity. Earlier we gave the example of the supervisory learning activity. Another example might be: The impact of multi-national companies (MNC). For an employee who is preparing to move into a job where knowledge of the MNC is important, it would be education. Where a company has no direct contact with the MNC but feels that there might be an impact, the learning experience for the employee would be in the development area. Therefore, the target group data are extremely important.

The data gathering exercise can sometimes be traumatic. Up to this point, there may be the nodding of heads which indicates agreement with the HRD concepts. Now, a confrontation occurs when the activities currently being conducted must be categorized. If there is evidence of blocking on this aspect of the data gathering, it would be significant to determine the cause. Sometimes the blocking may occur because this form of data gathering is new to the organization and the HRD personnel.

As we would expect, it must be filtered through previous experiences as well as current behavior patterns. For most persons in the field of HRD this is one of the first times they have been challenged by such a conceptualization. I have found it non-threatening when done in a public workshop and most of the participants have been able to produce the data with adequate time and careful thought. In an in-house workshop or consultation, the process has been a bit more difficult though not impossible. It requires that HRD persons engage in an activity which surfaces their own philosophy and practices for all to see.

When these programs have been categorized, it is possible to move on to responsibility. Using the same activities listed previously in the left hand column, the right hand column is now changed as follows:

Activity	Responsibility
Training	
Education	
Development	

Now list the place/person in the organization where one will find the responsibility for each of these activities. When the data has been gathered, some generalization immediately becomes apparent.

Training will be found to be the responsibility of the first line supervisor. This is not surprising and should be obvious. The organization rewards the first line supervisor for getting work done. Therefore, anything which contributes to this objective will be of prime concern to the first line supervisor. As defined earlier, training is directly related to the present job of the learner, which is where we find the interface with the supervisor.

Responsibility for education is more likely to be found in the middle levels of management. Where in the organization are we most likely to find responsibility for promotions and manpower planning? Probably in the middle levels of the organization.

Therefore, these are the levels which utilize education activities to meet future, but identifiable, manpower needs. The organization looks to this level for such responsibility and rewards accordingly.

Responsibility for development is more likely to be found at the higher levels of the organization. That is where the people are located who are concerned with long-range planning and possible changes in organization goals and purposes. They are the people who can make the professional estimates as to organization activities and products which generate the need for the kinds of development programs most meaningful to the organization.

Sometimes, when reaching this understanding, it is possible for the HRD person to observe how these conceptual differences are reflected in organization behavior. There should be no surprise that first line supervisors are not particularly concerned with education. Why should they be? Education prepares individuals to move out of their present job, and the organization seldom rewards a supervisor for turnover, even if it is for promotion. Supervisors are not likely to use their physical and financial resources to lose their better employees, those who are likely to be promoted. So, the first line supervisor can see the benefits of training, but will usually not provide education and certainly not development.

Of course, once this implication is understood, it is possible to bring about changes in organizational behavior to facilitate a different approach, if the organization so desires. In one organization, at this stage, management proposed a quota system. Each supervisor had to provide sufficient education so that 10 percent of his or her employees were promotable each year. At the end of the year, if the supervisor had not met his or her quota, it had to be explored by the HRD Advisory Committee. There could be good reasons and this would indicate other areas of organizational behavior which needed to be examined.

In one organization, the data gathered reinforced an unwritten company policy. That is, they promoted first and trained afterwards. The higher echelons of the company knew this and

assumed that everybody else did. When this practice was highlighted as a result of the instruments and experience indicated
above, it explained some of the dissatisfaction which was expressed during exit interviews. Employees could see little that
they could do to prepare for promotions which seemed to be
merely the whim of somebody "upstairs." In these days when
employees are seeking more voice in how they work, and how
they prepare for promotion, the company practice was counter-
productive. It would be rewarding to be able to report that as a
result of this experience the company changed. In this case, it is
not possible. The HRD practitioner supported the company and
said that this was exactly the way they wanted it. At least, it was
now possible for this to be generally known and for the company
policy to be appropriately clarified.

Mutual Expectations

In any learning situation, a variety of individuals are involved.
Primary, of course, is the learner. There is also the person guiding
the learning experience (e.g. instructor, group leader), the person
who selected or arranged for the learner to attend (e.g. supervisor)
and the non-person in the form of the organization which includes the peer workers as well as many levels of management. It
might even be extended to include the stockholders in the case of
private sector organizations, and the average citizen in the case
of government.

The learner should know what is expected of him or her, in
terms of what will be learned and how his or her behavior might
change. The learner has to know the expectations of those who
sent him or her. Do they expect the learner to behave differently
on the job he or she now has and to which he or she will return?
Or, is the learning to be used on a future assignment which will
be given at some near-future date? Or, is it part of the continuing,
changing organizational pattern and is there no intent that the
learning be used immediately or in the near future? If the learner
does not have these expectations clearly understood, he or she

has no framework into which new learning can be placed. This becomes one of the main differences in adult learning (androgogy) as contrasted with children learning (pedagogy).[3] The adult learning experience is usually problem-centered and the adult must be able to relate the learning to the problem to be solved. Is it on his or her present job, or for the future?

The same questions of application and expectations arise among all the various individuals indicated in the opening paragraph of this section. Take supervisors—do they expect learners to behave differently on the job (i.e., training) or are the learners to use new knowledge when they are transferred or promoted out of the unit (i.e., education)? Unless there is some clear understanding as to the nature and relationship of the learning and the expectation of application, there is bound to be confusion and mutual distrust. It is much healthier for the individuals and the organization to concentrate on defining the mutual expectations and avoid the negative results due or ambiguity.

In training situations, where all agree it is training, it is possible to build a support system so that the learning can be readily integrated into the job context.[4] With education it is much more difficult and with development it is even questionable if it is necessary.

Public seminars present an outstanding example of how this lack of clarification of mutual expectations contributes to general dissatisfaction. I, as many others, have been involved in conducting public seminars for many years. I now use the approach, whenever possible, of having the participants identify why they have come to this public seminar. It is:

- *Training* - I and my organization expect me to use this material when I return.
- *Education* - I have come to this seminar to prepare for a different job.
- *Development* - my organization felt that somebody should attend so that there would be somebody in the organization who had some idea of the topic.

This depicts an outstanding example of the unnecessary confusion in the multitude of public seminars which were conducted towards the end of the 1960's on the "disadvantaged worker." Some organizations sent participants because they were cooperating in the National Alliance of Businessmen and, therefore, they came to the public seminars for training. Other organizations sent a participant because the organization planned to hire the disadvantaged or, in some other way, become involved in the programs of this nature. The organization wanted somebody who could move into this job (e.g. counseling) within the near future, so the participant attends for education. There were other organizations who were merely on a legitimate "fishing expedition." The organizations felt they should have somebody in their ranks who had some understanding of the problems and the opportunities just in case the organization decided to become involved. Participants from such organizations were there for development.

Within these public seminars, I often found individuals who could not clearly state why they had attended. In some cases, they said that their company president wanted to cooperate with the NAB people so they agreed to send somebody to the seminar. This was really for development, as previously defined, but the lack of clear understanding of the mutual expectations was confusing to the participant and the organization.

The confusion does not stop there. How about those responsible for designing and conducting the learning experience? How do you create a meaningful experience for the participants when you have all three expectations present in the learning group? The desirable approach is to design the public seminar to provide for the individual differences and expectations.

But, this is usually too costly for a public seminar, which is a high risk economic activity. So, the person conducting the experience tries to make it as broad as possible to encourage the largest number to attend the experience and must, therefore, try to meet the needs of a group with widely varying expectations. Is it any surprise that there is such a general disenchantment with the public seminar? It is extremely difficult for most of them to meet the needs of the participants when they cover the whole spectrum. The more homogeneous the group is as to expectations (i.e., training, education *or* development), the more likely it is that there will be success for the learner and for those who have designed and conducted the learning experience.

Learning Theory

There are many learning theories[5] but there are general areas of agreement which relate to the HRD concept. Among the most important generally agreed upon concepts is that of *reinforcement.* Stated simply, and hopefully including most of the theories, that learning which is reinforced is more likely to result in behavioral change. Where the new learning and the situation in which it will be used are in conflict, it is highly likely that the situation will determine the behavior.

How often have we seen or heard of the employee who attends a learning situation and acquires new understanding or skills which can enhance performance on the job. But, on returning he or she is greeted by, "O.K. you've had your vacation, now let's get back to work and get some things done around here." Or, "What you learn from those fuzzy-headed instructors out there is of no use in here." Part of the approach to this problem has been discussed earlier under mutual expectations. Applying the HRD concept gives us another way of looking at this prblem. If we are examining a training experience, then the reinforcement must come from the immediate work situation and the peers and supervisors in that situation. Why? Simply because, by definition, training applies to the job the person now has and that is where the learning is to be applied.

When considering education, it becomes a bit more difficult. The new learning is to be used in a situation which is not the job the individual now has. By definition, it is for a future job. Therefore, the new skills, attitudes and knowledge have been acquired for some future situation. The learner and the organization must realize that is is highly unlikely that there will be any reinforcement on the present job. That was not the focus of the learning situation. Therefore, other kinds of reinforcement must be provided if the learning is not to be a wasted experience. In the interim between the learning experience and placement on the new job, the learner must have the new learning reinforced. Once again, this can prove costly, and, therefore, the planning of an education experience must be consistent with the manpower planning and assignment within the organization. If the learning experience is for development, then reinforcement is not required. That is, unless the learning experience is intended to keep the learner in a constant learning posture. But, more on this later in this section.

Fade-Out

Another side of the issue is that of *fade-out*. This means that there is a tendency for the learning which is not utilized to fade out and even disappear. This is a restatement of reinforcement, but stated in this fashion it can help us develop the previous statements a bit further. If there has been training, there is less likelihood of fade-out, for the simple reason that the new learning *can* immediately be used on the job. However, if the learner is not provided with the opportunities for using the new learning, then fade-out can wipe out the advantages of the learning.

If a worker has acquired a new skill related to the job, such as using an electric typewriter rather than a manual, provision should be made for applying that new skill. This may require shifting assignments so the learner can have some time on an electric machine. In some cases, such machines are assigned to individuals who have seniority, status or some similar criteria. But, if a new employee has now been trained for the electric machine, fade-out will certainly take its toll unless time is allotted for the new employee to retain the skill acquired on the electric machine.

Where the experience has been for education, the employee is not expected to use the new learning until placed on the new job.

If there is a considerable time lag, fade-out will once again take its toll. If is necessary to provide on-going opportunities to apply the learning if it is not to fade-out.

A distinction also occurs in the area of learning theory known as *frame of reference*. This says that learning is more likely to be successful when the learner has a setting into which the learning can be placed. For example, a worker who is learning a task which relates to his or her job, can learn it in relation to the environmental factors with which he or she is familiar. When applying the learning, the learner does not have to take it into a strange environment. While learning, he or she can place it in the real work site, in his or her mind, until he or she returns. Of course, when the learning takes place at the work site, learning is even more readily facilitated. The frame of reference goes beyond only the physical environment including the social and emotional environment in which the learning is taking place, and where it will be used.

When the learning focuses on training, the frame of reference is readily available: It is the job. Where the goal is education, the learning becomes more difficult, for the learner will back a realistic frame of reference. He or she may create one, but it might be different from that envisioned by those who designed the program or those who are conducting it. When development is the goal, the learner must have a high tolerance for ambiguity. The learner must deal with a frame of reference which may be quite indistinct. Therefore, in all three cases, a different system of learning is required.

Another aspect of learning theory is association. That is, new material is learned in terms of what the learner has previously learned and experienced. Particularly with adults, the filter of previous learning and experiences strongly affects the learning possibilities. The learner may have difficulty accepting some material because he or she has no earlier base on which to build. He or she has difficulty in finding the associative base. Or, the learner experiences the new material but knows that earlier experiences are in conflict with the new learning.

When the goal is training, there is a strong associative base available. The new material should link in directly to what the learner is already doing. Although there may be new materials, or new processes, these can easily be related to existing behaviors. For education, the problem becomes critical. Many persons responsible for pre-supervisory programs have experienced the difficulty. A worker who has never been a supervisor views that position as being powerful and having much control over the lives of others. If learners have never been supervisors, their associative base is only vicarious. They may have to be provided with role models, case studies, film and other media to provide an associative base on which they can build the supervisory learning experience.

Continuous Learning Posture

There is still another aspect of learning theory which becomes clearer when we make the conceptual difference in the three kinds of HRD. Research has shown that those who remain in a learning posture tend to learn more easily. This research suggests that keeping individuals in a learning posture may have benefits for any organization even though not directly related to the job. That is, it may sometimes be advisable to violate that basic of all cliches in our field—"Never train for the sake of training." By providing training we may help individuals stay in the learning posture so that they will be ready to learn when the need arises. This may facilitate moving persons into education programs to prepare them for promotion. It may even be helpful for an organization to provide development learning activities for larger portions of its work force than it is now doing. My own observations (research is lacking) indicate that development is usually found at the higher levels of the organization. But, are these the only levels of the organization where learning may suddenly be required to cope with change? If change is to be experienced throughout the organization, and if learning is to bring about that change, an organization can find that it enhances the possibility for rapid adaptability when they provide development throughout the organization.

Today there is a great deal of discussion, and some activity, concerning Organization Development (OD). Generally, those who practice OD speak of themselves as change agents, and of the objective of change as the organization. But, this also means changing people. Is it not possible that we can facilitate change by providing continuous learning experiences so that people are ready to change? If so, organizations that are serious about OD should be providing much in the way of development (as previously defined) learning experiences to enable their employees to be in a constant state of learning readiness.

From my own experience, I cite an interesting example of the use of development to facilitate change. The following example, it should be understood, is based on my own experience and was not extensively researched. From 1959-1962 I worked in Japan and observed HRD efforts in Japanese industry.[6] One activity looked very strange to a westerner. Many companies provided instruction in the tea ceremony, flower arranging, and other non-job related topics. My tendency, like so many HRD people from industrialized countries, was to scoff at this as merely a manifestation of the paternalism that was ritual in Japanese industry.

Maybe it was. But I think I can now see that by providing these development programs, Japanese industry was keeping its workers in a constant state of readiness for new learning. When transistors, quality control and other industrial improvements were introduced, the Japanese worker was ready to accept the new learning required. He had been constantly learning, and it became merely a matter of changing the subject matter.

Human Resource Accounting

There are currently attempts being made to put a dollar figure on the financial resources allocated to human resources. It goes beyond HRD, but has implications which relate directly to the concepts we are discussing.

Human resource accounting (HRA) has the potential for making a contribution to HRD similar to that made by systems engineering to learning design.[7] The breakthrough and general acceptance hoped for have not yet occurred, but should not be ignored, as the potential still exists.

One element of HRA which is particularly pertinent relates to expense and investment. An expense represents money paid out for identifiable items which are expected to be consumed by the organization within the fiscal year. For example, when the organization pays rent, it expects to have a certain amount of square feet available. If the organization pays for typing paper, likewise, it expects to have typing paper which it can use within the fiscal year.

An investment represents money paid out, or any other allocation of financial resources, with intent to insure the organization in the future. Some investments are clearly defined, such as Treasury Bonds, and the rate of return can almost certainly be calculated. But, by the very nature of the investment, there is no guarantee as to the actual rate of return or even if the principal will be recovered. Of course, in the case of the Treasury Bond, there is less risk and therefore less return. The higher the risk involved in an investment, the higher the rate of return.

Training is an expense. When there is a pay-out, the organization has a right to expect some kind of direct and observable return. Education is an investment, with all the risks involved in any investment. Development is also an investment, but of a much higher risk nature.

It can be seen, then, that the concepts of HRA and HRD are mutually supportive. Hopefully, HRD will proceed to the point where it is possible to support the concepts of investment in human resources which are now emerging.

Meanwhile, the use of terms like *expense* and *investment* also enables the HRD person to relate to the language of general management. One of the difficulties in using learning experiences in the market place is that business has specific terminology relating to cost factors. In the past decade we have tried to link learning to cost-benefit and other economic factors with less than adequate results. At this time, we have some common terms which enable the HRD person and the management people to improve their communications relating to HRD and financial resources.

Evaluation

The evaluation of learning experiences has been one of the most controversial areas of HRD particularly in the era when we had vast sums of money made available by the Federal government. From the first programs in the early 1960's until today, the cry has been for more evaluation. Within the private sector, particularly in times of recession or retrenchment, the demand for evaluation has sometimes taken on the aspects of an old-fashioned witch hunt. Some persons will raise the hue and try to find the culprit, as if evaluation is easy but some are refusing to do it.

Evaluation is probably one of the most difficult areas of HRD. This does not mean we should not pursue it, and constant attempts are being made to find ways of improving our concepts as well as our tools.[8] There have been some successful efforts, but we need a continuing search for ways to improve evaluation.

Applying the concept of HRD can facilitate evaluation, though by no means is it a full answer. However, as we need all the help we can get, let us see how applying the HRD concept enhances the possibilities for evaluation.

Where the learning experience has been for training, the evaluation can take place on the job. Education is for the future job, and therefore a real evaluation cannot take place until the learner gets on the new job. Of course, it is possible to evaluate the education-learning experience, but this only tells us if the learner has learned. It does not tell us if he or she will be able to apply it on the job. Such data can only be gathered when the learner is placed on the new job.

Development, as was noted earlier, is a high risk learning endeavor. One element of that risk is the difficulty in evaluating. As with education, it is possible to evaluate if the learner has reached the objectives of the development-learning experience. But, by definition, there is no intent to apply it on the present job, or on a future defined job. Therefore, the evaluation of the application of a development experience is almost impossible, at present. As more research is done on development-learning experiences, it is likely that we will be evolving some sophisticated ways of obtaining evaluation data.

Therefore, it can be seen that by applying the HRD concept, we can at least differentiate among the kinds of evaluation which are most appropriate. For each kind of learning within the concept, different techniques are more meaningful. It is the responsibility of the HRD person to be able to adequately apply the concept so as to communicate the evaluation possibilities to all of those concerned.

Three-Step Application

There are many ways in which the above material can be utilized within any organization. The following is one example of how the HRD concept can be used to diagnose the HRD posture of the organization. The basis for this is the form in Figure 1.

There are three steps involved. First, identify the key target groups in the organization. Each member of the organization belongs to some identifiable group. In some cases, it may be necessary to make some artificial categories. Others in categories may be only temporary. But, agreement should be reached so that each person falls into one, and only one, category. The data for this will come from working with other parts of the organization. It may require intensive work with the HRU people, or with various levels of management.

Experience has shown that just identifying the target groups becomes a growth experience, and various philosophies may be found in conflict. Some managers may feel that there are certain categories of workers for whom HRD should not be provided. Before deciding if the analysis would be helpful to the organization, we must first put such workers in a listing of the key groups. Later, the data can be analyzed, but to start with, gathering it is the most important feature.

The second step is to list all the HRD programs. Once again, the data gathering may surface some real differences. Just what

Figure 1

ORGANIZATIONAL DIAGNOSIS FOR HRD

Groups

1.   5.

2.   6.

3.   7.

4.   8.

Programs	Training	Education	Development

is an HRD program? Is there some kind of reporting system in
the organization? What about the ubiquitous on-the-job training
activities? How does on-the-job coaching get included? In one
case, just seeking such data surfaced the inadequacy of the
reporting system within the organization. At present, we can
anticipate that some OD programs might not be listed. The
criteria might be, does it have a learning component? If so, then
how does it differ from any other HRD program?

The third step is to place the number of the key group in the
appropriate column for each program. This should reflect only
programs actually conducted, not planned programs. At this
time, we would not be interested in quantity or quality, but just
whether or not the experience has been conducted.

Very soon, a pattern will emerge. The significant questions
which are surfaced are:
- Which groups never appear on the profile sheet?
- Which groups appear more often than most of the others?
- For which groups is there more training? education?
  development?
- Can we identify any development?

As the data are discussed with various parts of the organization, other pertinent questions will arise. It is important to
remember that this is just a diagnostic instrument, and therefore
indicates possible areas for further exploration. The directions
to be taken will be the result of the interests of the HRD persons
and the organization. It is a starting point, which can lead in
many fruitful directions.

Conclusion

The field which started as "training," moved to "training and
development," has emerged into something much broader and
much more important to organizations and society. Given this

movement, it is incumbent upon us to spend more of our efforts in conceptualizing what we are doing and to transmit our concepts to others through professional preparation programs and to communicate with those whom we ask to provide the financial and physical resources.

References

1. McGregor, Douglas, *The Human Side of Enterprise*. McGraw Hill, 1960.
2. Reich, Charles. *The Greening Of America*. Random House, 1970.
3. Knowles, Malcolm. *The Modern Practice Of Adult Education*. Associated Press, 1970.
4. Nadler, Leonard. "Support Systems for Training." *Training and Development Journal*. October, 1971.
5. Knowles, Malcolm. *The Adult Learner: A Neglected Species*. Gulf Publishing, 1973.
6. Nadler, Leonard. *Employee Training In Japan*. Education and Training Consultants, Los Angeles, 1965.
7. Silvern, Leonard, *Systems Engineering Applied To Training*. Gulf Publishing, 1972.
8. Nixon, George. *People, Evaluation, and Achievement*. Gulf Publishing, 1973.

12

Managers' Views of Employee Development Specialists' Role in an R & D Organization

Human Resource Development[1] as an inherent part of a manager's personnel management responsibilities blossomed forth after World War II and grew in leaps and bounds since that time. During the past twenty-five years we have seen an increase in the complexity of organizations, rapid growth in knowledge of management, and ever-increasing basic and applied research in the behavioral sciences. Many of the resulting theories and research findings directly relate to the responsibilities of line managers and staff personnel with respect to developing human resources. Further, since Sputnik was orbited in 1957, research and development (R & D) organizations and the scientists and engineers in them have been scrutinized and examined from many perspectives. Some of these reviews have centered around the need for personnel management and administration concepts for R & D organizations unlike those which existed in the more traditional organizations. The prime mission work force in R & D organizations—the scientists and engineers—was in short supply during the two decades 1950–1970.

Article by Jack Epstein and Leonard Nadler reprinted from *European Training*, Winter, 1972, by permission of the authors.

In 1970 the picture began to change with the layoffs in the American aerospace industry. Nevertheless, R & D organizations did pay special attention to the type and style of personnel management, in order to make the scientists and engineers more creative and productive.

Within this context, there is a need for Human Resource Development personnel in R & D organizations to understand more clearly the perceptions and expectations of their operational functions as held by civilian line managers. This better understanding can lead to improved relationships between line and staff groups responsible for Human Resource Development and a sharper delineation of the functions of each with respect to training, educating and developing the work force.

In this connection, there has been a considerable amount of discussion among people in the field about the operational functions (role) of a human resource developer in organizations. Opinions range from performing as an instructor in courses, or similar experiences for employees; to behaving as an administrator by coordinating all Human Resource Development efforts and programs, processing paperwork and developing procedures for getting people into programs; to assisting, guiding and working with management in developing a comprehensive Human Resource Development program to meet specific needs of individuals or those of the entire organization. Further, it has been stated that the human resource developer should perform all these roles, but with different emphasis.

Purpose of Study

Within the framework described above, it was considered worthwhile to conduct research[2] which would add to the knowledge of the role of the human resource developer in organizations. As will be indicated later in this article, other research in this area examined the operational functions of and knowledge and skills needed by such a person as perceived by him or his boss. This study aimed at exploring both the perceptions and expectations of line managers with respect to the operational functions of a Human Resource Development person. (In the U.S. Federal Government he or she is identified as an Employee Development Specialist.) The results would shed additional light on this matter as reflected from the "other side of the coin"—the management side, since both management and Human Resource Development staffs share responsibilities for Human Resource Development.

Briefly stated, the purpose of the study was to examine perceptions and expectations of civilian line managers—first, middle and executive levels—with respect to (1) what the Employee Development Specialist was doing and (2) should be doing in his day-to-day operations.

Hypotheses

It was hypothesized that the perceptions and expectations of the operational functions of the Employee Development Specialist will differ among the three levels of civilian line managers as follows:

1. First level managers will focus on the learning specialist function which includes instructing and designing in-house programs.
2. Middle managers will focus on the administrator function which includes budgeting for, developing procedures for, and coordinating Human Resources Development.
3. Civilian executives will focus on the internal consultant function which includes guiding, assisting, and working with management in solving problems through learning experience.

Definition of Terms

To help assure common understanding of terms, the following definitions apply:

Line Manager: Those persons in an organization who have the authority and responsibility for accomplishing an objective or mission through the efforts of others. These people are typically responsible for organizing, communicating, coordinating, evaluating and, within the context of personnel management, placing, developing and appraising the performance of subordinates. In organizations these managers normally form a hierarchy consisting of first, middle, executive or top levels.

First Line Manager: Someone, with the authority and responsibilities described above, who is immediately above the worker or non-supervisory level and is accountable and reports to a higher level manager.

Middle Manager: Anyone who has other managers reporting to him and who, in turn, reports to a higher level manager.

Top Level Manager: Anyone who is or reports directly to the director or commander of a laboratory. Examples of top level managers are directors, chief scientists and division chiefs.

Perception: The active process of integrating and interpreting sensory data based on past experience and current needs of the individual in relation to the situation in which he finds himself.

Expectation: With perception as an underpinning, the looking forward to an action or a predominant manner or functioning on the part of someone else. This is based on some reasons or concepts which make that which is awaited as probable. Expectation differs from perception in that the latter is concerned with "what is," i.e., the here and now or the current state of affairs. An expectation is related to what "should be" as the future situation.

Operational Functions: The typical or characteristic pattern of an individual's actions or behavior, interactions and sentiments along with his rank and the degree to which he conforms to the norms as perceived and expected by those with whom he works or is associated.

Employee Development Specialists: Individuals in Federal Government agencies assigned to staff support organizations and who are concerned with and involved in the process of "developing a well trained work force... assisting employees toward achieving and stimulating a sense of participation."[3]

The Organization in Which the Study was Conducted

The U.S. Air Force Systems Command (hereafter referred to as Systems Command) is controlled, directed and managed primarily by military personnel in key positions throughout the organizational hierarchy. The Commander is a four star general; the Chief Scientist is a civilian. The Command's mission is militarily oriented and related to the overall Department of the Air Force's mission which, in turn, is related to that of the Department of the Defense. The Systems Command's mission briefly stated, is to accomplish the rapid advancement of aerospace technology and its adaptation into qualitatively superior operational aerospace systems.

The civilian work force of the Systems Command fluctuates around 32,000 people. Of this number, approximately 6,000 are scientists and engineers. Of the 6,000, about 1,300 civilian scientists and engineers work in the six laboratories included in this study. The 6,000 scientists and engineers compose the prime mission work force. They are responsible for the basic and applied research, development, and test of the superior operational aerospace systems indicated in the above description of the Command mission. It is their knowledge, skills, talents, and capabilities which receive first emphasis with respect to Human Resources Development.

Earlier Studies

There have been several studies of the functions and competencies of Human Resource Development personnel. The populations for these studies were primarily Human Resource Development directors and their superiors. Guyon,[4] by sending questionnaires to these directors in private enterprise concluded that the highest level of management must show confidence in and support the director if he is to function effectively.

Reeve[5] mailed questionnaires to selected individuals listed in the 1952 ASTD Directory. Based on a 54.6% return, he found the following duties of Human Resource Development directors to be most common (listed in rank order):

Advisory to management

Administration

Conducting conferences

Training instructors

Training management

Training subordinates in training department

Employing subordinates

This list points in the direction of the concept that the Human Resource Development director considered himself to be a kind of in-house consultant who is concerned with helping managers become more effective as trainers, educators, and developers of subordinates.

Nadler's[6] study was aimed at determining needs of Human Resource Development directors which could be met in order to improve their professional competence and then identifying those needs which could be met by educational institutions. He included coverage of what these directors in Pennsylvania do and should do. His data were gathered by a series of in-depth interviews with nine directors and six of their subordinates. Nadler's data reflected the following as examples of what Human Resource Development directors actually do:

Account for and control facilities and finance

Develop subordinates

Determine training needs

Plan curricula

Conduct training

Evaluate training

Maintain effective relationships

With respect to what the directors should do, Nadler examined the above-listed tasks in relation to the specific local situation and concluded that it was fruitless to talk of a universal, ideal Human Resource Development director.

It is noted, as in other studies, that Nadler's data were gathered from the Human Resource Development directors, their superiors, and subordinates; not from the line managers with whom these staff people worked.

Roberts[7] studied the competencies needed by people in the Human Resource Development function in business, industry, and government. He analyzed data received as responses to a questionnaire sent to 557 ASTD members. Among fourteen knowledges and nineteen abilities identified, the following were included:

Knowledges: Role of line managers and supervisors in the training program; principles of human relations; objectives of the total training program and how a learner acquires skills and knowledges.

Abilities: Communications; administraton of the training program; stimulations of interest in instructions; and development of training programs and curricula.

These competencies were found to be needed by Human Resource Development officials in large or small organizations, either government or non-government.

Roberts' study provides the competencies which, when translated to tasks, can become the operational functions of an Employee Development Specialist.

One of the purposes of Leonard Ackerman's[8] study was to analyze the perceptions of the Employee Development Specialists in the Federal Government with respect to their present role and what they thought it should be.

Ackerman used a questionnaire which was sent to 212 of these Federal Government specialists. Based on a 60 per cent response, it was determined that:

> The largest category of responses (34%) dealt with advice and assistance to management on employee training and development.... .
>
> The majority (58%) felt there were no major differences between the role they felt they should be filling and the one they were actually performing... .[9]

In summary, research studies were concerned with the various aspects of a Human Resource Development person's role as viewed by him and his supervisors. The study described in this article attempted to build upon those findings by exploring line managers' perceptions and expectatons of the operational functions of an Employee Development Specialist.

Perceptions

Perceptions are a highly complex phenomenon, differing among people and subject to modification and change. Perception, more than a reaction to a stimulus, is a transaction between the perceiver and the environment which includes the perceived.

Perceptions are both subjective and objective at the same time. What a person sees, touches, tastes, or feels about an event or another person is his subjective experience. How he describes what he saw, touched, tasted, or felt about another person is objective. Further, perceptions are modifiable and can vary from circumstance to circumstance. The point to be made is that the study was based on perception for the managers rather than observed behavior by an independent researcher.

Among the several tools of research considered, the questionnaire was selected as the most practical for gathering data for this study.

Building a Questionnaire

The questionnaire was built on a model-foundation based on four sources addressing themselves to the operational functions or role of an Employee Development Specialist.

First, Paul Buchanan mentioned perceptions and expectations of operational functions of Human Resource Development people. He stated:

> A role may be thought of as a pattern of behavior which is appropriate to a person in a given position. One of these is his role as the person thinks he is performing it. A second is the actual role the person is performing..., as indicated by factual information or the judgement of others.[10]

Second, the core concept of the model-foundation was based on Nadler, who stated:

> ...Human Resource Development specialist has three major roles: learning specialist, administrator and consultant.[11]

Third, a pamphlet by Leonard Nadler on a systematic process of training provided substantive support to the core of the model-foundation. Nadler points out that the training person has different operational functions to perform depending on the phase of the process.

> Training...can be analyzed and developed through a deductive approach...an orderly process which involves the following steps:
> 1. Develop job standards.
> 2. Identify needs.
> 3. Determine objectives.
> 4. Develop curriculum.

5. Select methods and materials.
6. Obtain instructional resources.
7. Conduct training.
8. Evaluate feedback.

These are not discrete steps and cannot be followed in rigid order, but require a great degree of interaction and recycling.[12]

Any one or combination of these steps pertains to the previously mentioned three general functions or roles of the Human Resource Development person—learning specialist, administrator, and internal consultant (contributor to organizational problem solving). For example, steps 4 and 7 impact on the learning specialist role.

The fourth component of the model-foundation also provided substantive backing to its core. This substance is the Employee Development Specialists' competencies composed of education, knowledge, and ability or skill. Root and Roberts delineate these competencies:

Relation of training program to overall aims of management

Objectives of the total training program

Working with line management

Obtaining organization support for the training function

Defining the objectives of the training program

Planning, organizing and coordinating training operations

Principles of human relations[13]

Tabulating and Analyzing Completed Questionnaires

The resulting data were translated into punch cards for computer use with the biomedical chi square library program. This statistical test was considered to be the most appropriate for comparing the anticipated differences of perceptions and expectations among the three levels of civilian managers. The criterion level of significance was established at .05. Through the application of chi square, it was determined that statistical significance at the .05 level was not achieved among the three levels of managers.

Within this brief article, no attempt will be made to provide an in-depth analysis of the data. Such an analysis is available in the study for those who desire to work from the original data. At this time, the hypotheses will be discussed, as well as some general implications which emerged. However, the tables from the study are reproduced.

Hypothesis 1 focused on the first level manager and the role of the Employee Development Specialist as a learning specialist. As the data show (See Table 1), the perceptions of the first line manager did not differ greatly from those of other levels. This can be seen by comparing the perceptions of the first line managers with all managers. Likewise, the expectations of the first line managers were not significantly different from all managers in seeing the Employee Development Specialist as a learning specialist.

Hypothesis 2 focused on the middle level manager and the role of the Employee Development Specialist as an administrator. Only one item shows a difference of +10% and that is "plan for on-the-job training." This difference exists in both the perception and expectation data.

Hypothesis 3 focused on the executive level manager and the role of the Employee Development Specialist as an internal consultant. Among the perceptions there were no items in which the executive level was more than ±10%. However, on expectations we do find some differences. On the item "assisting management examine problems," the executive level is −12% from all managers. In "assist management in exploring how training can solve problems," the executive level is −10% from all managers. However, the expectation on the former item is almost three times the perception while for the latter item the expectation is twice the perception. This finding provided an indication of another trend which will be discussed later.

Table 1
Managers' Responses to the Learning Specialist Function

		Management level by %								
		Perception (does)				Expectation (should do)				
		N	All Managers	First	Middle	Executive	N	All Managers	First	Middle	Executive
Instruct in on-the-job training	Yes		13	12	14	19		25	25	25	19
	No		87	88	86	81		75	75	75	81
	Total	183	100%	100%	100%	100%	183	100%	100%	100%	100%
Instruct in off-the-job training	Yes		26	28	24	27		45	47	42	38
	No		74	72	76	73		55	53	58	63
	Total	175	100%	100%	100%	100%	181	100%	100%	100%	101%
Instruct others to be instructors	Yes		17	12	27	13		41	40	44	44
	No		84	89	74	87		59	60	56	56
	Total	164	101%	101%	101%	100%	179	100%	100%	100%	100%
Design in-house training programs	Yes		35	39	23	44		66	65	67	69
	No		65	61	77	56		34	36	33	31
	Total	176	100%	100%	100%	100%	184	100%	101%	100%	100%

Table 2
Managers' Responses to the Administrative Function

		Management level by %								
		Perception (does)				Expectation (should do)				
		N	All Managers	First	Middle	Executive	N	All Managers	First	Middle	Executive
Plan for on job training	Yes		33	39	22	31		64	69	53	64
	No		67	62	78	69		36	31	48	35
	Total	183	100%	101%	100%	100%	184	100%	100%	101%	100%
Process paper work	Yes		89	88	88	94		96	95	97	100
	No		11	12	12	6		4	6	3	0
	Total	184	100%	100%	100%	100%	185	100%	101%	100%	100%
Develop and implement procedures	Yes		81	82	83	63		96	96	97	94
	No		19	18	17	38		4	4	3	6
	Total	183	100%	100%	100%	101%	185	100%	100%	100%	100%
Approve training	Yes		54	57	48	60		36	38	34	25
	No		46	43	53	40		64	61	66	75
	Total	183	100%	100%	101%	100%	185	100%	99%	100%	100%
Budget for training	Yes		41	47	35	31		60	62	60	44
	No		59	53	66	69		40	38	40	56
	Total	177	100%	100%	101%	100%	181	100%	100%	100%	100%
Coordinate training	Yes		71	69	73	73		92	93	93	88
	No		29	31	27	27		8	8	7	13
	Total	178	100%	100%	100%	100%	181	100%	101%	100%	101%
Establish training priorities	Yes		31	35	27	19		26	26	32	13
	No		69	65	73	81		74	75	68	88
	Total	178	100%	100%	100%	100%	183	100%	101%	100%	101%

Table 3
Managers' Responses to the Internal Consultant Function

		Management level by %								
		Perception (does)					**Expectation (should do)**			
		N	**All Man-agers**	**First**	**Middle**	**Executive**	**N**	**All Man-agers**	**First**	**Middle**	**Executive**
Assisting management	Yes		26	32	16	19		62	69	53	50
examine problems	No		74	68	84	81		38	31	48	50
	Total	176	100%	100%	100%	100%	185	100%	100%	101%	100%
Assist management in	Yes		31	35	23	38		85	88	81	75
exploring how training	No		69	65	77	63		15	12	19	25
can solve problems	Total	176	100%	100%	100%	101%	185	100%	100%	100%	100%
Work with management	Yes		47	47	45	56		93	96	86	94
in developing overall	No		53	53	55	44		7	4	14	6
training plans,	Total	179	100%	100%	100%	100%	186	100%	100%	100%	100%
programs											
Explore and recommend	Yes		46	46	45	44		92	95	86	94
resources to accomplish	No		55	54	55	56		8	5	14	6
training plan	Total	176	101%	100%	100%	100%	186	100%	100%	100%	100%

*Managers' Listing of Employee Development
Specialist Functions*

Subjective responses were elicited by an item in the questionnaire where the respondent was referred to the earlier listed
items and asked to indicate by referring to specific questions:

1. Your *perceptions* of the two most significant operational functions of the Employee Development
   Specialist. *Please explain.*

2. Your *expectation* of the *two* most significant operational functions of the Employee Development
   Specialist. *Please explain.*

The purpose of this question was to provide respondents with
freedom to express their perceptions and expectations. Figure 1
is based on the items listed by the respondents.

Figure 1

Managers' Listings of Employee Development Specialist Functions

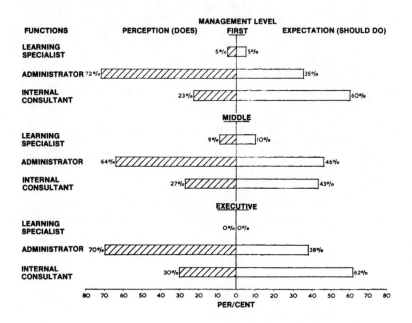

Figure 1, on the *perception* side, shows that all levels of managers perceived the Employee Development Specialist:

As doing very little as a learning specialist (e.g., instruct courses; instruct others to be instructors; design in-house courses)

As concentrating his efforts on the administrative function (e.g., coordinating training; budgeting for training; processing paperwork for training)

As not performing to a great extent as an internal consultant (e.g., working with and assisting managers in preventing, alleviating or solving problems through training).

Figure 1, on the *expectation* side, shows that all managers expected the Employee Development Specialist to:

Continue to spend a very small amount of effort in the learning specialist function

Reduce his functioning in the administrator role, but that this area should continue to be emphasized

Considerably increase his activity as an internal consultant.

Managers' Usable Statements on Employee Development Specialist Functions

First level managers' comments on the learning specialist function indicated that they perceived and expected the Employee Development Specialist to do practically nothing in this role. The same pattern was followed by middle and top level managers.

Middle managers' comments concerning the administrative function reflected their very strong belief that he was performing in this role. The percentage of middle managers' expectation comments showed that they believed the Employee Development Specialist should considerably reduce his activity in the administrative area. First and top level managers followed the same pattern.

Executives' narrative remarks indicated that they perceived the Employee Development Specialist as doing nothing as an internal consultant but expected him to greatly increase his role in this respect. It is noted that the other two managerial groups' percentages followed the same pattern (See Figure 2).

Figure 2

Managers' Usable Statements on Employee Development Specialist Functions

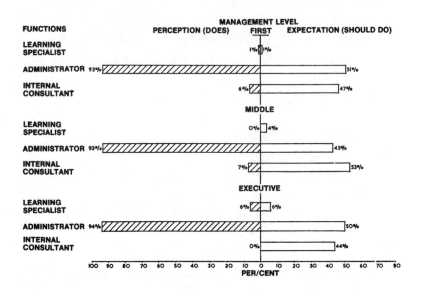

Summary

The data presented above supported the following findings:
The three previously specified hypotheses were not supported.

Each level of management perceived and expected the Employee Development Specialist to limit his activity as a learning specialist.

Each level of management both perceived and expected him to function as an administrator of Human Resource Development. In this connection, the managers' listings of Employee Development Specialist functions and narrative statements on these functions (Figures 1 and 2) were not consistent with managers' responses to the administrative function (Table 2).

Each managerial level perceived the Employee Development Specialist as performing the internal consultant function in a very limited manner, but expected him to greatly increase his efforts in this role.

Recommendations

1. It has been recommended that the Systems Command, as the employer, provide the climate, stimulation and opportunities for the Employee Development Specialist to continually update and increase his knowledge and skill as an internal consultant. Then he should apply what he learned to his day-to-day practices on the job by experimenting with new behavior and solidifying those behavior patterns which prove to be effective in his typical mode of operation.

   As the findings in this study seem to indicate, the Employee Development Specialist has to add the internal consultant dimension to his behavior and still keep certain learning specialist and administrative skills continuously updated and honed.

   An applied research approach, aimed at refining the Employee Development Specialists' operational functions, would be useful to both managers and Employee Development Specialists. The delineation of their respective functions, responsibilities, and authority with respect to Human Resources Development should lead to improved relationships between the two, closer integration of Human Resources Development with organization plans and programs, and a more mission-oriented and impactful Human Resource Development program.

   Such applied research could use this study as a foundation for a series of planned team building meetings of managers and Employee Development Specialists. These meetings could consider the more specific definition, meaning, and extent of action perceived and expected by managers with respect to specific job behaviors. More specifically, these sessions should concentrate particularly on delineating the activities included in the administrative function which, according to a finding in this study, seemed to need clarification.[14]

2. Reference is made to the previously cited conclusions on the Employee Development Specialist increasing his activity as an internal consultant and sharpening his talents in this respect. Benefits would accrue to the Department of the Air Force if it investigated the subject of the most effective organizational location for the Human Resource Development function.

Assuming that military and civilian managers, in all kinds of organizations in the Air Force, expect the Employee Development Specialists' internal consultant role to be a significant one, then can he perform effectively in this capacity best as a member of the civilian personnel office?

In examining this question consideration could be given to the roles of other civilian personnel functions. Are these roles congruent to the role of the Human Resource Development function? If it is decided that this function does not belong in personnel, where should it be placed for it to be most effective in meeting organizational goals? For example, as now constituted in many Air Force commands and bases, it is subordinated within another civilian personnel function such as placement or classification and wage. Bases with separate Human Resource Development functions and full time Employee Development Specialists are the minority. In either case, the function is normally given a secondary or lower priority within the civilian personnel office in comparison to other functions.

With managers desiring the Employee Development Specialist to assist them in problem solving through Human Resource Development, the present organizational structure seems to provide an inefficient means for such specialists to function with the freedom and flexibility necessary to be an effective consultant to management.

An exploration of the place of the Human Resource Development function within the total organization would prove to be useful to Employee Development Specialists, managers, and civilian personnel specialists.

The availability of purposeful and orderly Human Resource Development opportunities in organizations and participation in them is a significant approach for assuring that employees are continually renewed. Life-long learning by the work force will prove useful to organizations. Collaboration among people will develop coping processes necessary for them to be proactive in the face of change, enabling them to impact on its control rather than vice versa.

The Employee Development Specialist functioning in this kind of "natural" instability needs to be continually aware of, understand, and develop his ability to impact on the forces of change through constant interaction with managers at all levels. The three functions of learning specialist, administrator, and internal consultant with respect to Human Resource Development are seen as essential roles for the Employee Development Specialist in the next decade and beyond. However, the increasing requirement for the early identification of problems and possible problems confronting managers suggests that greater emphasis needs to be placed on the specialist applying consultative skills to assure the developing of an integrated and systematic Human Resource Development continuum aimed at meeting both the immediate and future needs of an organization and the employees who give it life.

Note

This article was based on Dr. Epstein's dissertation for his Ed.D. in Human Resource Development, earned from the George Washington University under the direction of Dr. Nadler. Dr. Epstein currently heads J.H.E. Associates, consulting in the areas of HRD and management. Some of his recent efforts cover career planning/counseling, supervisor/manager development, EEO/affirmative action, and organizational effectiveness. His extensive and varied professional experience includes serving as Chief, Civilian Training and Career Programs, Air Force Systems Command; Chief, Civilian Training and Development, Fort Belvoir, Virginia; Executive Career Counselor and Consultant, Executive Development, Department of Labor; Civilian Management Development Program Manager, Department of the Army; and personnel director in the private sector. He has also published numerous articles in professional journals.

References

1. Throughout this paper the term Human Resource Development is used to encompass those activities usually labelled as training, education and development.
2. Epstein, J. H., "Line Managers' Perceptions and Expectations of the Operational Functions of an Employee Development Specialist in a Federal Government Research and Development Organization," (Unpublished doctoral dissertation, George Washington University, Washington, D.C., 1971).
3. U.S. Civil Service Commission, *Federal Personnel Manual* (Washington, D. C., U.S. Civil Service Commission, March 30, 1966). Chapter 250, para 3–6a.
4. Guyon, R., "Survey of the Training Director," *Journal of Industrial Training, 4,* 1 (January-February, 1950), Part I, 14–23; see also, 2 (March-April, 1950), Part II, 8–12, 14–15.
5. Reeve, D. F., "A Survey of Duties and Responsibilities of Training Persons in Business and Industry," *Journal of Industrial Training, 7,* 5 (September-October, 1953), 4–35.
6. Nadler, L., "A Study of the Needs of Selected Training Directors in Pennsylvania Which might be Met by Professional Education Institutions" (unpublished doctoral dissertation, Teachers College, Columbia University, New York, 1962).
7. Roberts, R. R., "A Study and Analysis of the Competencies Needed by Personnel with Major Responsibilities for the In-Service Training of Employees" (unpublished doctoral dissertation, George Washington University, Washington, D. C., 1964), p. 1.

8. Ackerman, L., "A Study of Selected Employee Development Specialists in the Federal Government, Their Background, Role and Organizational Location" (unpublished doctoral dissertation, George Washington University, Washington, D. C., 1967).

9. Ibid., pp. 95–6.

10. Buchanan, P. C., "The Function of Training in an Organization," *Journal of the American Society of Training and Development,* XIV, No. 4 (April, 1960), 56.

11. Nadler, op. cit. p. 149.

12. Nadler, L., *A Process of Training,* Washington, D. C.: Leadership Resources, Inc., 1968, pp. 2–3. (A later version of this model can be found in "Using Critical Events to Develop Training Programmes." *Industrial Training International,* April 1971, pp. 53–6; May 1971, pp. 57–60.)

13. Root, B. S., and Roberts, R. R., "Competencies Needed by Training Directors," *Journal of the American Society for Training and Development,* 20, 6 (June, 1966), 13.

14. In December 1971, the Air Force Systems Command initiated a year long program to implement this recommendation.

13

Learning From the Effect Of Economic Decline On Human Resource Development

Planning for the future by looking at the past

In this fast-moving world of our, it is not always possible to separate the present from the past, and even the present from the future. Right now, we are in a possible transition period. We are in (or passing out of — depending on your point of view) the worst economic situation we have had in more than 40 years! Unemployment is at its highest level, inflation is still hovering around the double-digit figure and other indices of economic catastrophe are still with us.

In the hopeful assumption that, by the time this article is being read, there will have been an upturn in the usual economic indicators, this article will be written in the past tense. That is, what can we learn from this past experience which will help us plan for the future?

Article by Leonard Nadler reproduced by special permission from the January/1976 TRAINING AND DEVELOPMENT JOURNAL. Copyright 1976 by the American Society for Training and Development Inc.

The basic premise is that, during the depressed economic situation, human resource development (HRD) tended to be *re-active* rather than *pro-active*. Indeed, it is likely that too many HRD directors weren't even reactive, but continued doing business in the same old way. So, let us take a look at the "past" and then explore its implications for the future.

To the Future

What has gone before, even in this article, is prologue. For some organizations, it is now too late to do much about the reactive responses to the economic decline. More important now, what about the future? The next crisis may not be an economic one, although this could very well happen again. But there are other challenges just beyond the next page of the calendar. To list just a few:

- Foreign companies taking over American companies.
- Foreign managers coming to work in the U.S.
- Minority groups entered the work force in appreciable numbers during the 1960s. During the latter part of the 1970s, we can expect to find more minority members at higher levels of the organization.
- The Third World is becoming economically powerful.
- Energy resources may be very tight for the next five years.
- President Ford announced the need for 14 million new jobs by 1980.
- The end of the postwar "baby boom" means fewer young people entering the work force and more older people trying to stay on in the work force.

And to all of this, each reader can probably add some more items. We are not dealing with some of the predictions of the Futurists, but just with what is already beginning to be seen on the organizational horizon.

What are some of the proactive responses we should be

exploring to cope with these possibilities? In what ways can and should HRD be preparing to respond? I can give no answers at this time, but can only propose that what we need are continuing dialogues and explorations so we will be prepared to meet the next crisis, the next challenge.

All organizations and occupational groups have their myths. Usually, these are based on experiences within the groups and even sound research is often overwhelmed by the myths.

In the field of what is commonly called "training" (which emerged as a clear area of organizational behavior during WWII), one of the pervasive myths has been that: *When the economic going gets rough, training is the first thing cut!* Although we have no hard evidence, it is likely that this may have been the case in the recessions since WWII.

As a result of our recent economic crisis, organizations are taking a closer look at their use of economic resources and what they are prepared to pay for. Training, as any other field of organizational behavior, is being closely scrutinized. However, I have discovered that during the period of 1974–1975, in many organizations, training was not cut! In some cases, even more of the organization's limited financial resources went into the training activity than during the previous periods of relative prosperity.

In looking at training, we find what is obvious in any area of organizational activity. When there is a declining economy, any part of the organization which persists in "business as usual" is going to be left behind. "Training as usual" is definitely being cut. However, training, education and development, where they react to the changed economic situation, are given a fair share of the organization's financial and physical resources.

Two major trends will be discussed in detail. First: it has become more evident than ever before that training must be close to where management decisions are made. These decisions need training for effective implementation. For example, if management decides to encourage early retirement, then the appropriate educational experience can encourage employees to seek early retirement. Just such a program will be described later in this article.

The second trend is for the training part of the organization to use this opportunity to re-examine goals and practices. Out of this have come some encouraging insights and new activities.

Training, Educating or Developing?

In the field of "training," there is a tendency to use words very loosely. There are sound reasons for this which are beyond the scope of this article. (A book for managers and others on this topic is needed at this time.) But, it is important to grasp the conceptual differences if managers are to make sound decisions related to this area of organizational activity, particularly in a slack economy.

The differences in terms are conceptual, not semantic. In Figure 1 there is a comparison. All three are labeled human resource development (HRD) and for the remainder of this article the words will be used as set forth in the figure.

There is a growing tendency to use HRD to mean many things. However, its most common usage is limited to *learning* experiences provided for employees and non-employees related to the organization's goals. In a declining economy, the emphasis is on training. It is a low-risk position for the organization, but a necessary one! As training relates to jobs now being done, good training programs can increase productivity and that is the key to survival during a recession or depression.

The usual education programs are not as necessary as previously. For example, with expansion slowed down and movement in the work force not so active, there is less need for education programs. As will be seen below, however, education can now have increased importance, but not for the usual reasons that existed under a growth economy.

Development will suffer most, being a high-risk learning activity and almost impossible to evaluate. When resources are limited, an organization is likely to support development.

Once an organization accepts the distinctions set forth in Figure 1, it is possible to look more closely at what is happening within the organization. It is possible to diagnose the HRD functions within the organization and to put the physical and financial resources behind those activities which are more congruent with management decisions.

The reader is cautioned once again, for the remainder of this article, *training, education,* and *development* will have the meanings described in Figure 1. This is crucial to understanding what is happening in HRD within organizations.

Figure 1

THE CONCEPT OF
HUMAN RESOURCE DEVELOPMENT

Activity Label	Focus	Economic Classification	Evaluation	Risk Level
Training	*Present job* held by individual	expense	on the job	low
Education	*Future job* for which individual is being prepared	investment (short range)	on future job	middle
Development	Future organizational activities	investment (long range)	almost impossible	high

Early Retirement

One management decision which some organizations made to cope with the economic situation was to encourage employees to retire early. This allows for shrinkage in the work force, within the organization, without the necessity for layoffs being the only response. However, management decisions do not always result in changed behavior. Some organizations, including the Federal government, have tried to encourage retirement by sweetening the "financial pie" for retirees. Organizations have increased some of the benefits, within the parameters of their retirement plans. It is working, but such an approach also assumes that the financial aspect is the only element related to retirement.

We know that many persons fear retirement, for they have no idea what they will do with themselves when they no longer have a regular schedule. We also know that, in our society, we have dealt very poorly with this problem. We have the research which shows that being retired carries the implication that the individual now has a reduced worth in a producing society. Therefore, financial enticements alone will not suffice to encourage early retirement.

Organizations have sought to meet this situation with expanded preretirement education programs. These are on-the-clock programs, emphasizing the involvement of the organization in helping employees to make early retirement decisions. As needed, the learning program is supplemented by a preretirement counseling program.

On the learning side, employees can learn how to readjust their own lifestyles, where there are opportunities to use what they have learned during work years, where there are vast opportunities for volunteer work using the experience gained in a lifetime of working, and how to work out what is the most appropriate lifestyle after retirement. Once the management decision is made to urge early retirement, it becomes necessary to establish the age group or work group which should be involved in such education. There must be congruent managerial styles which support early retirement as an organizational practice. One organization changed the words and called their programs "Planning Your Next Career." Everybody knew the focus and nobody was fooled. The HRD people were not trying to fool anybody. But, it did take some of the sting out of the words "early retirement."

If your organization has an HRD program for early retirement, this may be the time to re-examine it. When the program was developed, it was for a different audience and purpose than now exist. Many important facets may be overlooked if the decision is only to increase the size of the group which should attend, without carefully re-examining the content.

Early retirement has other implications. Another employee must be prepared (i.e., educated) to move into the position being vacated. Or, through job enlargement, the job being vacated must be absorbed into an existing job and then the incumbent will need training for the new duties. Without appropriate training or education, the organization will find that it has shrunk its work force through early retirement, as management had planned, but now does not have the appropriate work force to continue organizational operations at a sound economic level.

Planned Layoffs

Layoffs are not new, but the scope of them is now staggering imaginations in executive suites. In prior years, layoffs were not usually planned, but came about as a result of declining sales (temporarily), strikes in subcontractor plants, temporarily large inventories, etc. Usually, when the layoffs took place everybody sympathized with the predicament of the particular organization. In the recent past we were faced with planned and nationwide layoffs. These are simetimes planned months in advance and appear in the newspapers and trade journals far in advance of the actual event. As layoffs must be planned, so must an organization plan for the HRD activities which are related to the layoff situation.

A generalized myth is that on-the-job counseling is done by supervisors. Most job descriptions for supervisors contain statements to that effect. Yet, the supervisor may not see this as a regular part of the job. I have been in organizations where the training program for supervisors did not include anything on counseling. In one nationwide organization, the term "counseling by supervisor" appears in their union contracts, but only as a part of the grievance procedure! Otherwise, counseling is not done.

Yet where layoffs are to occur, the supervisor has a great deal to do as a counselor. This is vital to the organizational image and to the well-being of the employees. When layoffs are a regular part of managerial decisions, as they have been recently, supervisors need additional training in their role as counselors. Of course, this must be within the limits of what the organization expects the supervisor to do. By no means is it suggested that the supervisor should take over the functions of counseling as performed by the personnel or industrial relations staff. But, on-the-job counseling is a must when layoffs are so pervasive.

A layoff suggests the possibility of recall. One organization has instituted a "pre-layoff education program," which contains several elements. They help the employee explore how the layoff time could be used most effectively. Of course, it is much easier to plan for this when unemployment and supplementary benefits are adequate. Some auto workers have benefited from the layoff period by taking courses sponsored by Wayne State University in Detroit in conjunction with the United Auto Workers. However, this occurred *after* the worker had been laid off. What can be done before?

One service-type organization recognized that when the economy is once again on the upswing, the organization and its employees may want to be doing things differently. Accordingly, they used some of the pre-layoff time to provide education programs. This way, when their workers are recalled they will come back to the organization prepared to do additional and different jobs. This also makes it more likely that the workers will be recalled, for they can now qualify for more jobs than when they were laid off.

Some organizations see this pre-layoff education program as a contribution to their image in the communities in which they function. As with most public relations, there is no way to assess the effectiveness of this approach.

HRD Facilities and Staff Underutilized

Some organizations find they have classrooms, equipment, materials and staff in the HRD part of the organization which are not being fully utilized. One response, of course, is to lay off the HRD staff or at least to reassign them. The equipment can be "moth-balled" and the classrooms turned into storage rooms or offices.

More positive approaches can be taken. But, these require some significant management decisions. They have far-reaching implications, beyond the present economic crisis.

On an immediate basis, there is the Comprehensive Employment and Training Act (CETA). For some organizations, the concept of this Act was not new. Such organizations were part of the Plans for Progress, the Manpower Development and Training Act, and may even currently be actively participating in the National Alliance of Businessmen activities. CETA combined most of the previous manpower legislation into one package. But, it went further—it introduced revenue sharing. For most managers, this may have been overlooked, as it appears to have no relation to regular business activity. It was just political re-alignment—or so it seemed.

However, this political realignment means that programs no longer come out of Washington. They now originate at the local level. Obviously, the entire process is too complicated for this article, but some significant points need to be introduced. Under new legislation, which still exists, Federal monies for educating parts of the work force can only be utilized at the state, city or county level. These political units are called "primes" and only they can contract for the funds Congress has made available.

However, the primes can subcontract where they lack the resources.

So, there are primes who want to provide education for jobs and there are organizations with HRD facilities being under-utilized. The law does not require that the organization hire those who successfully complete the educational program. Under Title I of the Act, there are three different kinds of activities which are relevant to the private sector. There is (1) the provision of work experience, (2) classroom training, and (3) on-the-job training. Of course, classroom training is the area which is the most relevant to the purpose of this article.

Of all the grants given up to September, 1974, 31.8 per cent were for classroom training and more could have been done if organizations had made their less utilized HRD facilities available to primes. Contracts could have been worked out which would have utilized the personnel on the HRD staff who had the competence, but who had less call on their services than previously. Of course, the cost of equipment, space, etc., could also have been recovered, in part.

To get additional information about this activity, contact your local manpower administrator. Most large cities have one. If you can't locate the individual at that level, contact the governor's office for the correct person in manpower at the state level. If all else fails, contact your regional Department of Labor, Manpower Administration office and find out who the prime would be for the geographical area with which you are concerned.

Another approach is to turn the HRD operation from a budgeted item or a cost center into a profit center. Many organizations have done this in the past. Essentially, it means that the HRD part of the organization will make programs available to outsiders, for a fee. This can be done by selling a program originally designed for in-house use, such as the General Electric course on economics for recent college graduates. Or, it can actually involve using the HRD facility and setting up a form of proprietary school. Here, the organization will have to check on whether state and local regulations are rather easy to live with.

It is possible to couple marketing with HRD resources. For

example, 3M Visual Products Division conducted short seminars on how to run meetings. The focus was on communicating effectively in meetings, of course, using 3M products. Many organizations which deal in consumer products could look to their HRD people for help in designing programs to reach nonemployees. There is money to be made in conducting workshops and money to be made in selling the products. It is not a new use of the HRD staff, but it is certainly beyond where most companies use their HRD people today.

Increase Purchasing Power

How would you like to be able to say to your employees: "We want to help you in this time of economic difficulty . . . so, although we cannot give you more than the usual wage increments, we can help you learn how to spend your money better. In effect, this can increase your present purchasing power." This is not fantasy. It is reality. Some companies are doing it by very direct methods.

A major bank in New York City has opened a company-operated department store in the basement of its building. Employees can purchase from limited stocks and variety, but what they do purchase is at much lower prices than on the open market.

A less direct and possibly more effective approach is to provide training programs in consumer affairs. Materials are available from the office of the President's Advisor on Consumer Affairs. On the state level, many of the state governments also have consumer affairs offices. Some are regulatory, but there are those which have the kinds of information that can serve as the basis for an in-house consumer affairs training program.

In larger organizations, there is an available in-house resource. Where there are skilled purchasing departments, there are people who know some of the elements of what to look for. The person who makes fleet-car purchases could certainly advise others on what to look for when purchasing an individual auto. Additional resources may be present in other departments of the organization. The maintenance people could probably be a resource on how to be successful as a "do-it-yourselfer" on home repairs. The financial people may be able to help on how to budget and spend wisely. Just look around any large organization and there is much talent that could be used within this program.

Of course, these people may not themselves facilitate the learning—this is a more complicated matter requiring managerial examination and decision-making. If internal people are to be used, the HRD staff could certainly help in organizing the learning activity. After all, that is why an organization has an HRD staff!

As these HRD activities would not be related to the employees' economic role in the organization, some of the usual measurements of program success will not be suitable. HRD staff, working closely with management, will have to determine how the program would be evaluated and the terms of accountability.

What Do You Do With Down Time?

During normal operations, some organizations found that down time (when machines are out for repair or there is a low service load) could be used effectively for training programs. When there is a slump in the economy there is more down time because production or service is not required at the usual level. For a variety of reasons, the organization may not be able to, or want to, lay off employees. However, there may not be sufficient work to keep them totally employed. Some managements have gone to the four-day week, with fewer than 40 hours. One management was surprised when the older workers chose to accept a four-day week rather than keep their five-day week since the option would have been to lay off the younger, newly hired workers. The older workers indicated their concern for their fellow employees as well as for the organization by taking the four-day week.

It would be wonderful if I could then cite this as an example of the "down time" principle. Unfortunately, I have no idea of what the workers did with their day off (without pay). But, their management could have taken a cue from the workers and set up training and education programs for the fifth day, with the agreement that it would be off-the-clock, for no pay. It would not have been mandatory, but any worker who chose could have used that fifth day to obtain training and/or education related to company operations at the company facility.

One company described its process a bit differently. They told me that they used the slack period to introduce more extensive job rotation. The purpose was not to get more work done, but was for training and education. It enabled workers to really discover what other jobs were about and to obtain additional skills if they needed them. The company felt it was helpful for them as they had a situation where they could not really have a layoff except on a day-by-day basis. That could lose them many of their employees who would prefer a permanent layoff so they could qualify for unemployment benefits. Despite what some would believe, the employees opted for less work, less pay rather than unemployment. The offer of job rotation by the organization signified good faith and they felt better about the organization.

Usually, HRD programs are conducted either on-the-clock (company time) or off-the-clock (employee's time). In some rare cases, programs are offered on a split basis—part on and part off the clock. This may be the time to offer more combination arrangements. However, management should be cautioned against using this as the basis for a new and permanent policy. It is still much more desirable to have all training on company time. Education may have elements of both time arrangements. Development will usually be on company time. The temporary economic situation may call for temporary new time arrangements. These would be arrangements which should definitely be only temporary and not carried on into an improved economic period.

Training for Managers

The recent period of declining economy was preceded by unusual growth. During the 1960s and into the early 1970s most of our larger organizations were in a constant growth pattern. During this period, for some companies, the training of managers had low priority. It was not that managers did not need training, but that they were under pressures to produce and expand rather than to increase their own effectiveness.

Now, expansion and growth have slowed. For example, American Telephone and Telegraph Company reports that the number of new phones added was down 14 per cent when comparing 1974 with 1973. In two of the local operating companies I spoke to last year, this has brought about an expression of need by managers. They are saying now is the time for us to get additional training, when we are not pressed by growth.

More In-House Programs

It has been customary for many organizations to make use of out-of-house programs. These have usually been what are termed "public seminars" and are conducted by a variety of organizations. Many universities offer these programs, as do private organizations. The facility may be a local motel or an elaborate conference setting.

With a declining economy came the reduction of travel funds and a closer look at the public seminar activity. The results have been most uneven, but many of those offering public seminars have been forced to cancel well-advertised programs featuring national figures. Hotels are also reflecting this cutback. The Jack Tar Hotel in San Francisco had one conference booking 300 rooms for five nights. When the meeting was actually held, only 16 rooms were used. The International Association of Sales Personnel had anticipated 13,000 visitors at its big convention in Las Vegas. Just hours before that opening they had to cancel, due to lack of attendance. These are just two of the numerous stories that can be told.

This does not mean that there is less HRD—just that there is less where travel is involved. As a result, organizations are turning inward and looking for ways they can sponsor programs within their own organizaton. The internal HRD unit of one nationwide insurance company is virtually swamped. Previously, the units of the organization (with decentralized HRD operations) would send personnel to out-of-house programs. Now, they are asking their own internal HRD staff to meet their needs. The result is that this particular staff has been promised at least a 10 per cent increase in budget and staff next year to meet the increased demand.

It would be unfortunate if there was too strong a trend toward eliminating out-of-house programs. There are many ways in which external programs can contribute to growth which cannot be matched by internal programs. However, this is certainly the time to more carefully scrutinize the use of external programs, recognizing that the alternative is not to eliminate these kinds of HRD programs, but to increase the in-house capability.

One of the frequent problems with public seminars, no matter what the topic, relates back to the conceptualization of HRD. As public seminars survive by sufficient attendance, they tend to encourage all who can to attend. The result is that in the same seminar there will be persons who are there for training, for education and for development. Obviously, their needs are much different and the seminar usually cannot meet all the needs reflected by the participants.

It is important for management to assess each external HRD experience, as related to each individual and as to its specific target within HRD. Where there is a lack of congruency among management, the learner and the seminar leader as to whether the experience is training, education or development, it is highly likely that somebody will be disappointed. In a strong economy, such disappointments may be tolerated. In a time of tight economy, the lack of congruency is too costly.

More In-House Resources

As noted above, the reaction to reduced travel funds, etc., should not be a reduction in HRD activity, but rather, should be a shift to meet the need. When more programs are being done internally, more internal resources must be provided.

One organization began to develop its capability to design its own HRD programs. This meant adding people who could design and this was not always easy. The organization tried to meet this need by continuing to use external resource persons, but not to conduct programs. These external resource persons helped to design programs which the internal people conducted. More significantly, the external resource persons were required to assist the internal HRD staff to improve its competency in course design and evaluation. Therefore, external persons were used less as presenters and more as resources to help improve the internal staff. The initial cost was higher, but it means less dependency on external resources.

There are many reports of various organizations going back to an old technique which had fallen into partial disuse...once again relying on supervisors and other line personnel to conduct HRD programs. Non-HRD persons can be very effective, particularly where experience or technical know-how are crucial to the learning program. However, when an organization decides to utilize this approach (sometimes called "training the nonprofessional trainer") they are actually buying into a complex system. It is more than just assigning line personnel to conduct sessions.

My own experience in using this approach and in helping others use it, over the past 25 years, suggests that the following basic elements must be implemented following such a policy decision:

1. Provision of special training or education for those who will be expected to conduct the learning programs.

2. Development of specialized materials. Nonprofessional HRD personnel cannot be expected to utilize material, equipment, exercises, etc. which have been designed for use by professional HRD persons.

3. A feedback system must be obvious—so the HRD unit knows what is happening and provision whereby the nonprofessional can automatically call for and receive assistance in conducting the program.

Where organizations move to increased use of line people, that is nonprofessional HRD staff, without careful attention to these three elements the results can be disastrous! Sometimes, the high-risk position of mounting a program without first providing for these elements can be tolerated in an organization. In a time of declining economy, each program must contribute to the organizational goals with a minimum loss of time and resources.

There are no easily stated criteria for selecting line personnel to conduct HRD programs. It is easier to indicate what to avoid. Do not:

- Select an individual merely because he is the one available or the most easily spared
- Isolate the employee from his regular job by prolonged HRD assignments
- Assign a person to HRD tasks as punishment or part of an intimidation ritual
- Make it a "sink or swim" experience

For Potential Employees

At this stage of our economic crisis, it would seem that little can or should be done for persons who are only potential employees. Prior to the recent situation, Chrysler Corporation had an exciting program where they provided potential employees with a one-week program. At the conclusion, the potential employee was in a much better position to decide whether to accept the employment offer or not. Chrysler was in a better position to assess where the employee might be most productive in the organization. Of course, with the change in the economy and the subsequent layoffs, this program is no longer needed.

I was surprised to find the same kind of program operating successfully at this time, though not in the auto industry. There is an insurance company doing the same kind of thing despite the economic picture. They found that it is even more important now to screen incoming employees. With high unemployment and a surplus labor market, there are more people applying for jobs. The organization found that, if they provide a one-week program on insurance company operations, they have the basis for some mutual understandings about their industry and the kinds of people who can be successful in it.

This is not an assessment center approach, though it might superficially look like one. There are no tests or exercises to determine who should be in or out. Rather, it is an orientation to the organization and the insurance industry, recognizing that the average person has many misconceptions about the nature of the work involved. The general feeling in the company is that it has paid off by reducing the paper load which is required to process persons who express an interest, but then turn down offers of employment. Although they could not share their statistics with me, they did report that they had been able to reduce turnover among new personnel and attributed this, in part, to their potential employee program. Cynics might say that this could be expected...that during a time of high unemployment individuals are less likely to leave their jobs, once they have one. However, before introducing the program the company experienced a high level of turnover among new employees who appeared to take their insurance company jobs on a temporary basis, while looking for another job. With the new program, this tendency has apparently been reduced.

There has been a change which is only indirectly related to management decision-making. HRD persons within organizations are moving in two directions: increased use of media and increased use of modules. They are discussed in this article, addressed to managers, for a specific reason. Managers need to be more aware of what is happening to HRD both inside and outside their own organizations, because managers are constantly being asked to make decisions which are directly related to HRD.

The increased use of media will require management decisions regarding the availability of financial resources...media costs money! It is expected that the movement in this direction can ultimately produce savings, but it is not always possible to produce a cost-benefit ratio. The increased use of modules means different kinds of programs and scheduling than previously. The scheduling of employees to participate in programs is usually a reflection of management policy regarding HRD. It may be necessary to rethink the existing policies.

Note that the previous paragraphs emphasize the "increased use of." These methodologies are by no means new! However, with the shift in the economy, I am finding a shift in the thinking of HRD persons about the efficacy of these methodologies.

A brief description may be in order, as managers cannot be expected to be familiar with the HRD methodologies. Media is the general term used to encompass the presentation of learning by a machine or device to supplement or replace a live instructor. The media can be as simple as a programmed book and as complex as computer-assisted instruction. There are a variety of "teaching machines" and one should not overlook the ever-present tape recorder.

The use of modules is simply a matter of taking a program and clearly identifying its component parts or lessons. Each lesson can then be a module. However, programs can be developed which allow for variations in taking the modules. One person may start with Module A and go through to Module F (if that is the end of the program). Another person might start with Module D and proceed through to Module F. Modules can also be created where there is not a straight line from beginning to end, with interdependency. Instead, each module stands by itself. So, there can be a module for salespeople on closing the sale, another module on reporting to the home office, another module related to product information, etc. The salesperson would take that module needed at a particular time.

With the restrictions on travel funds in many organizations, the media/module approach becomes more attractive. It is possible to provide HRD programs for personnel scattered in many different places without sending an HRD person on the road. Of course, the development of the media and the modules can be expensive and should not be used unless there is sufficient utilization to produce a low unit cost. Also, the contents of the modules may have to be changed frequently to reflect new product information and new organizational policies and procedures.

At the present time, I cannot report any specifics on organizations which have actually moved strongly into the media/module direction. Rather, I am being told that they plan to do this. There is some hesitancy, because it does take time to develop the modules and to identify the appropriate media.

It can become too easy to rely on the media and the modules for elements of the program where such methodologies are not appropriate. That is, once the investment has been made in equipment, it becomes incumbent upon the HRD staff to see that the equipment is used. It can result in the equipment controlling the program rather than the HRD staff being in control.

To This Point

The economy has been declining, but HRD programs are on the upswing! This is a good and healthy sign. We are not retreating into a depressed state, and there are organizations which are using this time to re-examine their HRD activities. The results appear to be increased rather than decreased activity.

Managers and HRD personnel are urged to refer to Figure 2, "Questions for Managers and HRD Personnel." Take it into your organization and use it. It is by no means complete, but merely indicates some starter questions. There is no absolute measure whereby we can indicate the appropriate response. Rather, it is another case of where organizations must constantly re-examine their operations to cope effectively with a changing economic picture. This process can help managers identify some decisions to be made about HRD during a time of declining economy.

Figure 2

QUESTIONNAIRE FOR MANAGERS & HRD PERSONNEL

Question	If "No"	If "Yes"
Do we differentiate among training, education, and development?	Should we differentiate? What is to be gained? How do we know how HRD is organized?	What is our balance among the three elements? How should the balance shift in reflecting the state of the economy?
Have we made a management decision to encourage early retirement?	Would such a policy be helpful to us? What would be the effect on our operations?	What kind of HRD are we providing to support the decision?
Do we have planned layoffs?	Why have we been able to avoid this to now? What provisions have we made for future possibilities?	What HRD programs do we have to cope with planned layoffs? How do we know our supervisors are adequately prepared to counsel in layoff situations? Which kinds of HRD are preparing our laid-off employees for recall?
Have we provided for adequate utilization of HRD facilities and staff during the changed economic picture?	What could we be doing? How can CETA be helpful to us and the community? How can our HRD operation become a profit center?	How do the new HRD operations relate to long range organizational goals? How have we been able to couple HRD with other parts of the organization (e.g., marketing)?
Have we considered programs designed to increase employee purchasing power?	How would such a program be viewed by our employees and the union? What internal and external resources would we need?	How is the program evaluated? What other internal resources could we use to improve the program? In what ways could other external resources be helpful?

Question	If "No"	If "Yes"
Have we provided for HRD during down time?	How much down time do we have? If significant down time exists, how is it now being used?	How do down time HRD activities relate to organizational planning? What is the reaction of employees, at all levels, to this use of time?
Has our training for managers changed during the changed economic picture?	How has the work load of our managers changed?	Are we providing traditional manager HRD programs or is there the need for redesign of content?
Are we doing more HRD programs in-house?	How do external programs relate to need and current budget? How has reduced travel effected HRD programs?	Given the increased work load, how has the HRD staff and budget changed? How do we know we have the internal capability to reflect the increased need for in-house programs?
Are we using more in-house resources?	Why are we not using more in-house resources? What in-house resources do we have for HRD which could be used more effectively?	How have we provided for the training and/ or education needed when using in-house resources? What selection criteria do we have for involving in-house personnel in HRD?
Do we have educational programs for potential employees?	How could such a program be helpful to us? What formal or informal systems exist for educating potential employees (e.g., union, relatives, schools)?	What basis do we have for assessing the program?
Has HRD methodology changed since the economic slump began?	How do we know if HRD staff have re-examined their methodologies?	What are some of the changes? How do the changes relate to long-range HRD plans?

Additional
Reading

The following is a listing of some of the published materials which should be of interest to those involved in HRD. It is annotated by the author of this book and is intended only as a general guide. The range of materials is vast, as is the field of HRD. As can be expected, practically none of these volumes utilize the terminology of HRD as used in this book, so the reader is cautioned about words in titles bearing the description of training, education or development. When used in the annotation, these words relate to the definition contained in this book.

Ackerman, Leonard. "A Study of Selected Employee Development Specialists in the Federal Government: Their Background and Perceptions of their Role and Organizational Location." Ed.D. diss., The George Washington University, 1967.
A follow-up of a study originally done by the Civil Service Commission but with additional and more specific data on the EDO as an educator rather than a personnel specialist.

Aker, George F. *Adult Education Procedures, Methods and Techniques.* Syracuse: Library of Continuing Education, Syracuse University, 1965.

316

An annotated bibliography on some of the more common methods and techniques used with adults in a variety of settings.

Anderson, Richard, et al. *Current Research on Instruction.* Englewood Cliffs: Prentice-Hall, 1969.
Collection of readings on research related to instruction. Does not differentiate between adult and child, but some studies do indicate the level of the learner. Heavy emphasis on programmed instruction.

Assessing and Reporting Training Needs and Progress. U.S. Civil Service Commission. Personnel Series No. 3. Washington: Government Printing Office, 1961.
A pamphlet which provides some valuable material in concise form to help in identifying needs. Although many years old, still valuable for much of HRD today.

Axford, Roger W. *Adult Education: The Open Door.* Scranton: International Textbook Co., 1969.
Provides a general overview of adult education. Good material on university extension and how it can relate as a resource for others in providing HRD.

Barlow, Melvin L. *Vocational Education.* 64th Yearbook of the National Society for the Study of Education. Chicago: University of Chicago Press, 1965.
Includes material on post-secondary vocational education.

Bass, Bernard M., and Vaughn, James A. *Training in Industry: the Management of Learning.* Belmont, California: Wadsworth Publishing, 1966.
Helpful material on the learning processes in HRD programs.

Beal, George M., Bohlen, Joe M., and Raudabaugh, J. Neil. *Leadership and Dynamic Group Action.* Ames, Iowa: Iowa State University Press, 1962.
Mostly concerned with agricultural settings, but provides basic materials on group process.

Bell, Gerald D., ed. *Organizations and Human Behavior.* Englewood Cliffs:
   Prentice-Hall, 1967.
   Book of readings on various aspects of individual behavior in organiza-
   tional environments.

Bennis, Warren G., Benne, Kenneth D., and Chin, Robert. *The Planning of
   Change.* 2nd ed. New York: Holt, Rhinehart, and Winston, 1969.
   Excellent book of readings on various aspects of planning change,
   roles of the consultant and organizational change.

Berelson, Bernard and Steiner, Gary A. *Human Behavior: An Inventory of
   Scientific Findings.* New York: Harcourt, Brace, and World, 1964.
   Provides definitions and sources as to original studies or conceptual
   developments.

Bergevin, Paul. *A Philosophy for Adult Education.* New York: The Seabury Press, 1967.
   Discusses the philosophical concepts of adults in learning situations
   and in society.

Bergevin, Paul and McKinley, John. *Participation Training for Adult Education.* St. Louis: The Bethany Press, 1965.
   A laboratory approach to involving adults in their own learning.

Bergevin, Paul, Morris, Dwight, and Smith, Robert M. *Adult Education
   Procedures.* New York: The Seabury Press, 1963.
   Basic Treatment of some of the variety of techniques available to the
   learning specialists in HRD.

Bienvenu, Bernard J. *New Priorities in Training.* New York: American
   Management Association, 1969.
   Provides a broader view of training coming close to the HRD concept.
   Explores new roles for the HRD specialist.

Bradford, Leland P., Gibb, Jack R., and Benne, Kenneth D. *T-Group Theory and Laboratory Method.* New York: John Wiley and Sons, 1964.
Provides historical and conceptual base for the laboratory method. Also provides history and examples.

Brickman, William W., and Lehrer, Stanle. *Automation, Education, and Human Values.* New York: School and Society Books, 1966.
Collected papers of conferences held at Pennsylvania State University. Raises ethical as well as practical issues in various aspects of HRD.

Broadwell, Martin M. *The Supervisor as an Instructor: A Guide for Classroom Training.* Reading, Massachusetts: Addison-Wesley, 1968.
Designed for the supervisor who wants to become familiar with some of the usual techniques used in classroom training by HRD specialists. Helpful for the supervisor who is expected to be involved in training.

Burt, Samuel W. *Industry and Vocational-Technical Education.* New York: McGraw Hill, 1967.
Reports cooperation between education and industry.

Cenci, Louis, and Weaver, Gilbert D. *Teaching Occupational Skills.* New York: Pitman Publishing, 1968.
Directed toward teaching vocational education at the secondary level, but useful to HRD staff responsible for in-house company schools concerned with manual skill training and education.

Clark, Harold F., and Sloan, Harold S. *Classrooms on Main Street.* New York: Teachers College Press, 1966.
A brief study of specialty, or proprietary, schools in the U.S.

———. *Classrooms in the Military.* New York: Teachers College Press, 1964.

Brief study of some of the HRD activities sponsored by the military. Limited by having been done in the early 1960's and therefore does not reflect some of the current directions.

————. *Classrooms in the Stores.* New York: Teachers College Press, 1962.
Describes retail training programs.

Community Programs on Employment and Manpower. Washington: National Association for Community Development, 1966.
Describes community-oriented HRD programs.

Craig, Robert L., and Bittel, Lester R., ed. *Training and Development Handbook.* New York: McGraw Hill, 1967.
Collection of articles by leaders in the field on various aspects of HRD.

David, Henry. *Manpower Policies for a Democratic Society.* New York: Columbia University Press, 1965.
Final report of the National Manpower Council. Presents concise statement of the issues facing us in the 60's, many of which are still unresolved.

DeCarlos, Charles R., and Robinson, Ormsbee W. *Education in Business and Industry.* New York: Center for Applied Research in Education, 1966.
Explores some of the practices and issues in HRD.

DeCrow, Roger, and Grabowski, Stanley, ed. *A Register of Research and Investigation in Adult Education, 1968.* Washington: Adult Education Association, 1968.
Collection of some of the recent research, presented in abstract form with information as to original sources.

Dees, Norman, ed. *Approaches to Adult Teaching.* New York: Pergamon Press, 1965.
Description of techniques and methods used in extension programs in England in particular academic subject matter areas.

DePhillips, F.A., Berliner, William, and Cribbin, J.J. *Management of Training Programs.* New York: Richard D. Irwin, 1960.
Describes HRD programs from the viewpoint of management with some attention to the HRD specialist.

Devine, Donald W. *The Critical Requirements for Training Directors.* Philadelphia: University of Pennsylvania, Graduate School of Education, 1962.
Doctoral dissertation using the critical incident approach to identify the activities of HRD specialists in private industry.

Glaser, Robert. *Training Research and Education.* New York: John Wiley and Sons, 1965.
Report of activities of various researchers and practitioners in HRD with emphasis on programmed instruction.

Glaser, Barney G., ed. *Organization Careers.* Chicago: Aldine Publishing, 1968.
Sourcebook for theory and practice in how people develop careers in organizations.

Glaser, William A., and Sills, David L. *The Government of Association: Selections from the Behavioral Sciences.* Ottawa: The Bedminster Press, 1967.
Collection of readings about behavior in groups, organizations and associations. Includes examples from business and industry though emphasis is on voluntary associations.

Gordon, William J.J. *Synectics.* New York: Harper and Row, 1961.
An explanation by the developer of an approach to using creative potential for problem solving.

A Government Commitment to Occupational Training in Industry. Report of the Task Force on Occupational Training in Industry. Washington: Government Printing Office, 1968.
Volume I is concerned with general work and findings of the Task Force as well as its recommendations. Volume II contains specially prepared papers by various persons concerned with HRD.

Griffiths, Daniel E., ed. *Behavioral Science and Educational Administration.* 63rd Yearbook of the National Society for the Study of Education, Part II. Chicago: University of Chicago Press, 1964.
Applications of behavioral sciences to administration, with emphasis on administration of activities in educational institutions, including the adult level.

Halsey, George D. *Training Employees.* New York: Harper and Row, 1949.
One of the early books in the field. The content is, of course, less appropriate to the world of today.

Harris, Ben M., and Bessent, Wailand. *In-Service Education.* Englewood Cliffs: Prentice-Hall, 1969.
Theory and practice exercises for in-service programs for teachers and administrators in public school systems. Also has application for HRD administrators with large instructional staffs.

Hill, Winfred F. *Learning: A Survey of Psychological Interpretations.* San Francisco: Chandler Publishing, 1963.
Overview of various schools of educational psychology.

Holding, D. H. *Principles of Training.* New York: Pergamon Press, 1965.
Reports research in various aspects of psychology as related to HRD activities in Great Britain.

Houle, Cyril O. *Continuing your Education.* New York: McGraw Hill, 1964.
An helpful book for adults who are returning to formal learning situations.

House, Robert J. *Management Development: Design, Evaluation, and Implementation.* Ann Arbor: Bureau of Industrial Relations, The University of Michigan, 1967.
Explores aspects of HRD as applied to managers.

Investment for Tomorrow. U.S. Civil Service Commission. Washington: Government Printing Office, 1967.
Report of the Presidential Task Force on HRD in the federal government.

Jakubauskas, Edward B., and Baumel, C. Phillip, ed. *Human Resources Development*. Ames: Iowa State University Press, 1967.
Papers from a conference held in 1966. Uses the term HRD in a broad sense, as well as exploring manpower needs.

Jennings, Eugene Emerson. *The Mobile Manager*. Ann Arbor: University of Michigan, 1967.
Reports on a study and methodology for identifying job movement among managers.

Kidd, J. R. *How Adults Learn*. New York: Association Press, 1959.
Though more than a decade old, contains essential material on the adult as a learner which is still valuable today.

King, David. *Training Within the Organization*. New York: Barnes and Noble, 1964.
Report of the work of a British consultant in working with the Norwegian garment industry, basically in the training aspects of HRD.

Levitan, Sar A., and Mangum, Garth L. *Federal Training and Work Programs in the Sixties*. Ann Arbor: Institute of Industrial and Labor Relations, 1969.
Discussion of the history of some of the specific programs such as Job Corps and MDTA.

Lippitt, Gordon L. *Organization Renewal*. New York: Appleton-Century-Crofts, 1969.
Application of behavioral and management sciences in maintaining viable organizations. Discusses the role of the HRD specialist as a renewal stimulator.

Lynton, Rolf P., and Pareek, Udai. *Training for Development*. Homewood: Richard P. Irwin, 1967.
HRD in community development, based on experiences in India.

Mager, Robert F. *Preparing Instructional Objectives*. Palo Alto: Fearon Publishers, 1962.
Using the scrambled book technique, explores the writing of specific behavioral objectives.

_____. *Developing Attitude Toward Learning*. Palo Alto: Fearon Publishers, 1968.
Explores student attitudes toward learning and the role of the learning specialist.

Mesics, Emil A. *Education and Training for Effective Manpower Utilization*. Ithaca: NYS School of Industrial and Labor Relations, 1969.
Annotated bibliography in the field of HRD.

Miller, Harry L. *Teaching and Learning in Adult Education*. New York: Macmillan, 1964.
Explores the process of adult education with emphasis on involvement of the learner.

Morgan, Barton, Holmes, Glenn E., and Bundy, Clarence E. *Methods in Adult Education*. Danville: Interstate Printers and Publishers, 1963.
Basic book on some of the variety of techniques available to the HRD learning specialist.

Nadler, Leonard. *Employee Training in Japan*. Los Angeles: Education and Training Consultants, 1965.
Practices in HRD in larger Japanese industrial companies. Also discusses personnel practices as related to HRD.

Nylen, Donald J., Mitchell, Robert, and Stout, Anthony. *Handbook of Staff Development and Human Relations Training*. Washington: National Training Laboratories, 1967.
Designs, exercises and experiences with laboratory training in Africa.

Ofiesh, Gabriel. *Programmed Instruction.* New York: American Management Association, 1965.
Reports of the use of P.I. during the early 60's.

Parnes, Sidney J. *Creative Behavior Guidebook.* New York: Charles Scribner's Sons, 1967.
Concepts and workbook for the development of creative thinking.

Planty, Earl G., and Freeston, J.T. *Developing Management Ability,* 1954.
One of the early books in the field. Helpful as a reference point.

Proctor, John H., and Thornton, W.M. *Training, a Handbook for Line Managers.* New York: American Management Association, 1961.
As indicated, is designed for the line manager who must have some responsibility for training.

Rindt, Kenneth E. *Handbook for Coordinators of Management and Other Adult Education Programs.* Madison: University of Wisconsin, 1968.
Helpful for the administrator of an HRD facility, particularly one providing a service for out-of-company experiences.

Rummler, Geary A., Yaney, Joseph P., and Schrader, Albert W. *Managing the Instructional Programming Effort.* Ann Arbor: University of Michigan, 1967.
For the administrator in presenting programmed instruction to management and developing and purchasing programs.

Rose, Homer. *The Development and Supervision of Training Programs.* Chicago: American Technical Society, 1964.
Covers many aspects of the administrator and learning specialist roles of the HRD specialist.

Serbein, Oscar J. *Educational Activities of Business.* Washington: American Council on Education, 1961.
Describes relations between business and colleges and universities. Written from the viewpoint of the American university.

Shaw, Nate C., ed. *Administration of Continuing Education.* Washington: National Association for Public and Continuing Adult Education, 1969.
Book of readings addressed to the administrator of public supported adult education.

Stout, Ronald, ed. *Local Government In-Service Training.* Albany: Graduate School of Public Affairs, State University of New York, 1968.
Annotated bibliography covering many aspects of HRD in the public sector.

Tracey, William R. *Evaluation Training and Development Systems.* New York: American Management Association, 1968.
Basic book which includes suggested forms for evaluating training programs.

Training Methodology. Public Health Service Publication 1862. Washington: Government Printing Office, 1969.
Series of annotated bibliographies:
Part I: Background Theory and Research
Part II: Planning and Administration
Part III: Instructional Methods and Techniques
Part IV: Audio-visual Theory, Aids and Equipment.

Venn, Grant. *Man, Education, and Work.* Washington: American Council on Education, 1964.
Based on some of the work of the Task Force which resulted in the Vocation Education Act of 1963. Good background on post-secondary vocational and technical education.

Warren, Hugh Alan. *Vocation and Technical Education.* New York: UNESCO Publications, 1967.
Review of vocational and technical education in a variety of countries. Describes practices, curriculum and requirements.

Warren, Malcolm. *Training for Results.* Reading: Addison-Wesley, 1969.
A modified systems approach which deals essentially with the training part of HRD.

Wolfbein, Seymour. *Education and Training for Full Employment.* New York: Columbia University Press, 1967.
Explores changing concepts of work and manpower. Basic material on the early days of MDTA by the author who was its administrator.

Index

About the Author

Professor of Adult Education and Human Resource Development at The George Washington University, Dr. Leonard Nadler has had extensive experience – in the U.S. and abroad – in these fields. He has provided assistance in organizational, managerial, and individual development to hundreds of public and private organizations. An active member of many major professional associations, he currently serves on the National Board of Directors of the American Society for Training and Development and was the recipient of ASTD's *1977 Gordon M. Bliss Award* for his significant contributions to the field. Dr. Nadler's professional contributions also include the development of an outstanding graduate degree-granting program in HRD at The George Washington University. Widely published in a variety of professional journals and author of several major books, Dr. Nadler's work in conceptualizing the field identifies him as the "Architect" of HRD.